GIDE and
the Hound of Heaven

GIDE AT SEVENTY-EIGHT

GIDE and the Hound of Heaven

by HAROLD MARCH

UNIVERSITY OF PENNSYLVANIA PRESS

Philadelphia

1952

Foreword

THE LITERARY CONTINUITY OF ANDRÉ GIDE LAYS BARE HIS underlying moral discontinuity. He recognized, accepted, even flaunted his inconsistencies, and though he was continually trying to explain the significance of his career he never succeeded in doing so to his own satisfaction. "We each of us have a reason for living," he wrote, "superior, secret—secret even for ourselves—and assuredly quite different from the external objective which most of us assign to our lives."

The purpose of this book is to attempt to discover this secret reason for Gide's life and work. It is not concerned with autonomous art, the closed domain of literature, and it does not pretend to complete coverage of his writings, although by far the greater part of them have a bearing on our problem. Nor does the book try to give a full account of Gide's life, but only of such parts of it as illuminate the inner drama.

For quotations from Gide's works I have made my own translations; not because I think I can improve on the versions of such skilled translators as Justin O'Brien and

v

Dorothy Bussy, but simply (and it seems to me obviously) because it is necessary where possible to work from originals and to render their thought with the greatest possible fidelity; the actual words which implement this fidelity will naturally differ somewhat from one translator to another. References to the Journal are given by dates, so that they may be looked up with equal facility in the original or in Mr. O'Brien's translation. The passage of Dostoevsky quoted on pp. 260-61 is translated from the Russian by my son Andrew March, to whom I express my thanks.

H. M.

Swarthmore, Pennsylvania
December 1951

Contents

Illustrations

Portrait of a Haunted Man

"I SUFFER ABSURDLY," WROTE GIDE AT THE AGE OF TWENTY, "that everybody does not already know what later I hope to be, shall be; that from my look they do not have a fore-knowledge of the work to come." And in his mind's eye he saw the empty shelf before him filled with his Complete Works.

These shadowy volumes now substantially exist, the shelf is full, the record complete. Even *Et nunc manet in te*, the material about his wife which, omitted from the Journal, was published in a private edition in 1947, has now joined the public record. A year before he died he impressively read over the radio the closing words of his *Thésée*: "I have built my city. . . . For the good of humanity to come I have accomplished my work. I have lived." In the serene cadence of these words there is an echo of the biblical language in which he was steeped; one thinks of Saint Paul's farewell to life: "I have fought a good fight, I have finished my course, I have kept the faith."

But could it be said of Gide that he kept the faith? He

had not one faith but many; one is tempted to say that because they contradicted each other it was impossible for him to be faithful to any one of them. There is Gide the prophet of Dionysus, the exponent of the gratuitous act, of primitive spontaneity, of the joys of the senses, of the rightness of unrestrainedly following desire. Then, antithetically, there is Gide the Christian, now penitent and now exalted, and capable in either mood of passages that might have been lifted from a manual of religious devotion. Again there is Gide the classicist and humanist, the believer in art as selection and restraint, the proponent of discipline, of dynamic equilibrium, of harmony, and the defender of culture against barbarism. And accompanying and interpreting these facets of his personality is Gide the self-revealer, the autobiographer and diarist—the exhibitionist some have called him, for he seemed to suffer from a compulsion to publicize acts and habits of a sort that most men would nervously try to conceal. To readers who found inspiration in one of his books he would forthwith present another of opposite tendency; what he gave with one hand he took away with the other. Ostentatiously he refused to collaborate in the formation of his legend, but only because he did not like the one that critics and gossipers made for him; he preferred his own version which all the time he was assiduously and secretly constructing—or in the long run not so secretly, for with a candor that matched his acute self-awareness he wrote in 1938 of "that detestable comedy which we all play more or less, which I should like to consent to less than so many others. . . . Our concern with our figure, our public character, keeps reappearing. We are on the stage and often more concerned with parading than living."

Seldom in the history of literature has there appeared so controversial a figure as Gide's. For some he is Antichrist, the immoralist, the enemy of religion and social stability, the perverter of youth; for others, particularly for the young whom he is asserted to have led astray, he is at once a religious seer and the defender of the virtues of the Enlightenment: reason, tolerance, freedom of thought and of speech. Still others, like the early Claudel, admit that he is a great artist in style and construction, but complain that he has nothing to say. Yet this same Claudel in 1947, resentful at Gide's refusal to be converted to Catholicism, would not grant him so much as art, though he was forced to concede his influence: "From the artistic and intellectual point of view Gide is nothing. His influence is one of the mysteries that surround me." Even Gide's loyal and lifelong friend Paul Valéry, brilliant but opinionated and intolerant of "values not listed on his exchange," had small use for his work, and showed it by a courteous refusal to comment.

The opposing camps of detraction and defense have not remained stable and equally matched, for Gide's reputation and literary fortunes have known extreme vicissitudes. At first his work was ignored, smothered by a conspiracy of silence. *Les Nourritures terrestres*, published in 1897 and now considered one of his most influential works, sold only five hundred copies in the ten years following its appearance. To judge by sales and the opinions of the critics all of his books were failures until *La Porte étroite* in 1909; but the success of this book, and even more that of the *Nouvelle Revue Française*, which was dominated by Gide and in whose opening numbers *La Porte étroite* was serialized, made him for the first time worthy of attack by those whose ideas he challenged. It was then, properly speaking, that the controversy about him began. Yet these early criticisms were amenity itself compared to the furious onslaughts begun a few years later by a group of converts to Catholicism. Their zeal, however, proved self-defeating, for Gide's reputation was magnified by attack; as he said himself, the uproar created by Béraud and Massis made him more famous in three months than his books had succeeded in doing through the preceding thirty years.

Detraction became most virulent and defense most ardent in the period of the nineteen-twenties; thereafter excitement ebbed, and the great rebel became an accomplished fact. People began to see in this aging champion of unpopular causes certain stable virtues that have always, given time, been admired: integrity, sincerity, courage. The apotheosis came in 1947 with the award of the Nobel Prize for literature; his enemies, still numerous, still unreconciled, were reduced to impotence, and for the augmented band of his admirers he became an object of veneration whose lightest word was piously preserved like the nail paring of a saint.

More than once Gide expressed the desire to be judged primarily as an artist. The wish is natural enough for a man who had been attacked in the name of religion but with a singular lack of charity; and yet it is inconsistent. He himself admitted to an ineradicable urge to instruct, to influence, to disturb, and it is evident to any reader that moral convictions, explorations of the possibilities of behavior, the search for a philosophy of life are the very stuff of which nearly all his books are made; such materials cannot be understood as merely esthetic considerations.

Many people believe that the really enduring part of Gide's work will prove to be the Journals and *Si le grain ne meurt* (the memoirs of the first twenty-six years of his life), rather than his strictly literary books. Yet one cannot make a separation between literature and self-revelation because all his work is really self-revelation. The problems successively explored in his tales, parables, novels, and plays are his problems; the life in them, no matter how transposed and with however great a regard for the niceties of form, is his life. "One must dare to be oneself," he stated at the beginning of his career, and many years later he made his spokesman Œdipus say, "I felt myself to be the answer to a yet unknown question."

In the early days when he was frequenting artistic salons, a literary man of extreme self-assurance cornered him, seizing him by a button of his coat and pressing close: "If you had to sum up your future work in a sentence," he insisted, "in a word, what would that word be? Come, out with it!" And Gide, who disliked having people lay hands on him, furious at his predicament, blurted out in a strangled voice, "We must all represent." The other, astonished, released his hold. "Well, my boy," he said, "go ahead. Represent."

Gide's rage was not at saying something he did not mean but at being forced to reveal to a man he did not esteem the secret aspiration of his life; for nothing less to him then was the belief that it was his central duty faithfully to represent the Idea he was born into the world to make manifest. What that Idea was he could not know at the outset, nor was he wholly clear about it at the end; yet not only his literary works but his life, and his telling of his life, went into the effort of manifestation. It is here, rather than in exhibitionism, that we must look for the explanation of his compulsion to self-revelation.

Underneath the legend, back of the self-detected posturing, Gide remained sincerely anxious that his career, life and work together, should have enduring significance: "To create an enduring work: that is my ambition. And for the rest—success, honors, acclamation—I care less than for the least particle of true glory: to bring comfort and joy to the young men of tomorrow." He hoped too that his readers might succeed in detecting a total meaning where he himself had, comparatively speaking, failed: "Is it not natural that the deeper meaning of the work, for any artist conscientious about his trade and *sincere*, should at first escape its author? For his personality, whatever he may do, breaks through his works, and what takes on meaning is not so much the work as himself."

It is for us, then, to search for the deeper meaning, and the first of our discoveries is an obvious one: that the controversies which have raged about this man are but the external reflection of conflicts within him. Some of these conflicts seem to break through in his photographs, particularly if we look at a chronological series of them such as appears in the collected edition of his works up to 1929.

We see him at the period of his first book in a deliberately artistic pose, with hair worn long, a lavallière tie, self-consciously tilted head, and hand held expressively high on the breast. His eyes are heavy lidded and slumberous, his nose, though straight, looks fleshy, and the straggling beginnings of a moustache appear above a de-

cidedly loose and sensual mouth. His prose style at this
time is loose, vague, ejaculatory, heavily larded with
scriptural quotations; his ideas are now mystical, now
skeptical, now sensual; he is still torn between sensuality
and asceticism, a virgin with a depraved imagination,
yearning for God amid the fires of hell.

Next we see him at the time of his first North African
adventure. The now abundant moustache overflows at the
ends and curls down to join a chin beard, and the two
encircle a still thick and prominent lower lip. The nose
and indeed the whole face has thinned, and the eyes have
sharpened remarkably. He is wearing a broad-brimmed
black felt hat—a *chapeau américain,* the kind Americans
do not wear; a stiff collar and tie, black coat and double-
breasted vest incongruously surmount loose wrinked gray
trousers. Over his shoulders is thrown the cape that is to
become his trademark. At this period he is trying to learn
the life of the senses, to stifle his puritan conscience; uneasily and experimentally he exposes himself to sun and
wind, but on his ventures into the open he is accompanied
by an Arab boy laden with shawls, just to be on the safe
side, and in his pocket is a book, in case the beauties of
nature should fail him.

A pose at the turn of the century shows the gentleman-
scholar delicately inspecting a book in a comfortable
library. The hair line has retreated to reveal an imposing
brow; at the back the hair is less bushy than in the early
picture, about midway in its progress toward the close clip
of later years. The beard has disappeared, the moustache
is long and slightly curling. He is fully dressed in the
baggy tweeds he has come to like. This is the man who,
in the *Nourritures terrestres,* has stirringly called on youth

to burn their books and go out into the sun, who writes beautifully turned travel sketches and has lectured in Belgium on the question of influences in literature.

Then at last the moustache disappears and the Gide of mid-career stands fully revealed. It is a striking if somewhat enigmatic face: someone has suggested that it looks like a Japanese mask. The top of the head is now frankly bald, and the hair at the sides and back close cut. The long stretch from nose to mouth surmounts lips so thin and straight and firm that one can scarcely believe that they are the same ones we saw thirty years earlier. The set of the mouth and the sharpness of the eyes make the face severe, almost cruel; he looks like a self-disciplined disciplinarian. Puritanism, driven out of his life, has settled like a mask over his features and has rigorously chastened his once lush style.

Gide of the later years flashes by in a succession of odd hats and elaborately simple clothes. His face is almost grim now, with deep vertical lines framing the still severe mouth. He wears glasses, and between his fingers there is often a cigarette—a habit against which he has long and vainly struggled. His erotic curiosity is failing, and he nostalgically recalls the days when his mind seethed with voluptuous images and his soul despaired and his senses were not yet dulled by tobacco.

A final picture shows us an old man in a motion picture theatre with a kerchief knotted over his head, dimly and questioningly peering through his bifocals at the flickering images on the screen. It is Gide in the "somewhat tedious last act" of his career; he has said his say, and is waiting for the end.

And then the lights go out.

Many of Gide's conflicting traits show that he belonged to a familiar temperamental type: the artistic and intellectual introvert. His intense eroticism centered in the imagination; sexual acts, though they afforded a temporary physiological relief, found their chief significance in the support they gave to the imagination in memory, and through memory in anticipation. And his strong imaginative sexuality was closely associated, as is so often the case, with an equally strong religious bent.

In society he could on occasion, especially when he was on his own ground, be completely charming—gay, playful, witty, considerate, and affectionate by turns. At other times he was a specter at the feast, glacial in manner, stalking uneasily and clumsily about and spreading consternation in his wake. The austerity of his appearance made men watch their language, and silenced the breezy anecdote which the unhappy specter would have liked to hear. He loved music and was a capable pianist, but if he had an audience his fingers froze. Yet he liked appreciation; perhaps he played his best when he suspected, without being sure, that someone could overhear him.

He felt a somewhat theoretical attraction for the common people: peasant farmers, manual laborers, and even—but here the attraction had a sexual aspect—disreputable toughs. Yet he could never feel quite at ease with them; their worlds were too different, their languages not the same. With them he would find himself suddenly in a situation that paralyzed him; only later, and regretfully, would he think of how he should have dealt with it.

One day in a subway station he noticed a decently clad young woman walking very slowly, wholly absorbed in reading a large book which was evidently not popular literature. His curiosity aroused, he approached to see if by a discreet glance over her shoulder he could catch the title. But just then a big laborer lurched up and slapped the book out of the girl's hands. Gide was furious. Ideally, the man should be knocked down at once, but the practical difficulty was that he was a head taller than Gide, powerfully built, and accompanied by another proletarian of equally ferocious appearance. The man of letters decided to use his tongue instead of his fists, but all he could find to say was, "That was a witty (*spirituel*) thing you just did." He realized at once that the word was ill chosen; he should have said "smart" (*malin*). *Spirituel* was greeted with a shout of laughter and a mincing repetition evidently intended as a caricature. Then the big man said, "I find it as much fun to do that as to read." To this Gide had no answer ready; belatedly he thought he could help the girl pick up the scattered leaves of her book, but she had already disappeared.

It does not take a great deal of experience with Gide's *Journal* and other writings to teach one to be cautious about the author's statements concerning himself, particularly if they are emphatic and often repeated. Not that he is deliberately trying to create a false impression; there is always some truth in the statement, though it may be exaggerated. But overinsistence is the sign, not so much that the statement is true already but that he would very much like it to become so. A prime example is his declaration, repeated at intervals throughout his life, that he has preëminently the faculty of "sympathy"—and the word is usually used not in the sense of "compassion" but with the more literal meaning of a facility at sharing the feelings, adopting the viewpoint, seeing with the eyes of another. For instance, we read in the *Journal des Faux-Monnayeurs:* "In life it is the thought, the emotion of others that inhabits me; my heart beats only by sympathy. That is what makes all discussion so hard for me. I immediately abandon *my* point of view. I leave myself, and so be it. This is the key to my character and my work. The critic who does not understand this will do a bad job."

It is quite true that with his detached critical intelligence Gide readily understood the position of an opponent in debate and often made a show of adopting it and arguing against himself. It is true also that he disliked argument and preferred harmony to dissension. But to infer from these facts that his heart "beat only by sympathy" is unwarranted, as there is a host of evidence to testify.

In reality Gide was naturally solitary and a deeply lonely man. He had a profound craving for the society of his fellows but found it quickly exhausting, especially when the conversation was general. Moreover he was peculiarly subject to perversity of behavior: saying or doing in spite of himself the obviously wrong thing, or finding himself suddenly paralyzed, incapable of saying or doing the evidently right thing. An instance of this perversity in its negative aspect occurred in his youth. He had just published his *Traité du Narcisse,* and Maurice Barrès, his senior both in years and in reputation, invited the young author to dinner. On the table was a large centerpiece of narcissus. Gide immediately grasped the intended complimentary allusion and saw the necessity of making an appropriate acknowledgment; but throughout the dinner and the evening he found himself incapable of producing a single word of appreciation. At his next call Gide asked the servant if Barrès was at home, and from upstairs came the voice of the master himself saying, "I have just left five minutes ago." Gide did not call again.

But his errors of commission in conversation were as distressing as those of omission: "When I hear myself in a conversation," he once wrote, "I feel like becoming a Trappist. And all the disgust, the exasperation it gives me corrects me not at all." Here self-criticism is almost dissociative, and it is still more so in a passage like the following, where he is describing his conduct in the presence of a woman he knew but slightly:

What happens then? It is as if a trap door to the abyss opened up in me, as if all hell overflowed. What is this vapor that rises from the depths of one's being, that clouds the vision, that intoxicates? The self swells, inflates, spreads out, reveals all its horrors. With the aid of fatigue you lose all control of yourself; your voice rises, gets out of pitch, you hear yourself complacently uttering ill-considered words you would like at once to retract; helplessly you watch this wretched parody of an odious creature whom you would like to disavow, but cannot—for he is yourself.

To label such experience "dissociation" and dismiss it as pathological obscures rather than enlightens understanding, for in varying degrees all who are to some extent self-aware have known it. We decline to identify ourselves wholly with our experience of the moment; some part is held back, to view and to judge the reacting organism, and those in whom this schism of the self is acutely, even painfully, evident are apt to be the superior ones, those who have left their mark.

Gide's observer, his detached intelligence looking at himself without indulgence, is the source of many gloomy but illuminating passages throughout the Journal. Re-

peatedly he insisted that these unhappy entries were not
representative of his life as a whole, that he had periods
of happy productivity that left little or no mark in the
Journal, whereas in hours of demoralization he found support in the recording of his woes. He was convinced that
in health, vigor, and optimism lay his normal state, and
even when he was depressed he would remind himself
that his gloom probably had a physiological cause and
that he would feel ashamed of it as soon as he felt better.
For example, one morning in January 1912, at Neuchâtel,
he wrote a long, discouraged but penetrating passage
where, among other things, he said, "How difficult it is to
be at the same time, for oneself, both the one who commands and the one who obeys! But what director of conscience would have a subtle enough comprehension of
this wavering, this passionate indecision of my whole
being, this equal aptitude for contraries?" The same evening, at Zurich, he wrote, "Everything I wrote this morning will seem to me absurd in a short time. Already I am
feeling better; this keen air has put me on my feet again;
I am becoming conscious once more of my strength."

To cultivate a happy frame of mind and discount the
thoughts of depression is unquestionably a more practical
way of running one's life than to wallow luxuriously in
gloom; but how much real wisdom there is in the optimism
of mere health is dubious. It is worth noting that when
Gide's body prospered, his clear-sighted observer suffered; good spirits permitted him to lose his self-awareness in physical and mental activity, to approve of himself
by abstaining from self-judgment.

Moreover Gide's warnings about the unrepresentative
character of his discouragement are largely offset by such

an entry as this, written in 1932: "If my Journal is not more mournful it is because I find pleasure in writing only when I am in a state of felicity; the resolution made in my youth to let my work reflect only joy (or rather an encouragement to living) can lead to the mistaken belief that to it alone I am accessible."

In order to escape from the self-loathing and despair into which the lucidity of his observer plunged him he could either come to terms with his ego, accept himself as he was and stop worrying about it, or else he could lose himself in something higher, something beyond the limits of his individual personality. To say that he "could" follow one of these two courses is merely a way of saying that he had an apparent choice of alternatives; as it worked out he proved unable to follow either of them. To accept himself as he was, live simply from day to day as some men apparently can, was an impossibility both because of his temperament and because of the, to him, manifest superiority of the other alternative, losing himself. Neither in solitude nor in society, neither in intellectual nor in physical activity, neither at home nor in travel, could he quite shake off the observer and judge he carried about with him.

His preference for the way of self-loss was lifelong, and explains the frequency with which the Gosepl paradox of life, "He that loseth his life shall save it," or some such variant as "Except a corn of wheat fall into the ground and die . . . ," appears throughout the sixty-year length of the Journal and in many of his other writings. Not only did he want (and yet not want!) to lose himself in something higher, but he believed, most of the time and in some way or other, that it was possible. "For what I would, that I

do not; but what I hate, that do I," said Saint Paul, and
Gide could echo him. "O wretched man that I am! who
shall deliver me from the body of this death?"

He could not, however, continue with the Apostle's
triumphant "I thank God through Jesus Christ our Lord."
He tried that way, and failed. There must be some other
way, and through life the remembrance of the possibility
pursued him; in 1940, for example, while he was in the
course of reading *The Trial*, by Kafka, he wrote: "The
anguish breathing in this book is at times almost unbearable, for how can one help saying to oneself constantly:
This hunted man is myself."

One of the symptoms of his hunted feeling is his notori-
ous physical restlessness. La Rocque-Baignard, the Norman
property near Lisieux that came to him from his mother,
never gave him satisfaction and he sold it. Cuverville, his
wife's estate in the Department of the Seine-Inférieure,
served as a sort of base, but whenever he came back, expecting to get much work done, he was dissatisfied. Was
the air too relaxing? Was there too much comfort and consideration? Or was the example of his wife—so serene, so
steady, so full of Christian faith—a reproach to him? He
could not be sure, but he knew that he must set out again.
Paris, unlike Cuverville, was always stimulating, and he
built himself a large and complicated house in the Auteuil
quarter, with the intention of having like-minded friends
live there with him and work. But before it was finished he
lost interest, and it became "the villa without a master";
Paris was *too* stimulating, too hostile to the quiet medita-
tive atmosphere necessary to his writing. "I should like it
well enough in Paris," he wrote, "if it weren't for other
people, but I am good for nothing except in solitude. . . . If

I often rush off to Biskra or Rome, it is not so much in order to be in Italy or Africa as not to be in Paris." But in Biskra and Rome too he was restless; anywhere was apt to seem better than where he was. Marveling, he recorded his small daughter's reply to the question of where she preferred to be: "Why, in the place I'm in," as if no other reply were possible. For himself he said, "Never have I been able to settle myself in life. Always seated askew, as if on the arm of a chair; ready to get up, to set out."

Writers are apt to be restless if their circumstances permit, but Gide's case, from what he has told us about it, seems to be in a somewhat different category. He would tell himself that he was tired and needed a change, or that he could work better in the dry air of Florence, or something of the sort, but eventually, with the aid of experience and his observer, he realized that these were just excuses, as his *Renoncement au voyage* ("a farewell to travel") testifies. It was true that he was seeking for better conditions but in a deeper sense than he realized at the time: what he really wanted was to establish a firm contact between his lonely and rather frightened self and a solid reality outside. But just as people eluded his grasp so the physical world refused to become quite real.

We are scarcely more than infants before the idea of a separation between our own parcel of consciousness and the "out there" dawns on our minds, and from then on it is the problem of every man somehow to come to terms with his setting, with the world of nature and of other men in which he finds himself. But for some, Gide among them, the confrontation between the self and the not-self never quite loses its strangeness. His interest in each individual, he said, was of the keenest, and yet he always had great difficulty in recognizing people: "I think it comes from the lack of a certain *sense of reality*. I can be very sensitive to the outside world, but I never succeed completely in believing in it. . . . The real world is always a little fantastic to me."

With this dream-like way of seeing the outer world, what was more natural than that he should come to feel that in addition to the accepted realities of everyday living, in addition also to the spurious experience of dreams or storytelling fantasy, there was another reality all around him, invisible yet almost perceptible; it seemed sometimes as if he might catch it if he turned around suddenly. It was a feeling that came to him often in childhood, but he never quite got rid of it; we find him writing at the age of fifty-nine: "I have never succeeded in taking this life quite seriously, not that I have ever been able to believe (so far as I recall) in eternal life (I mean in survival), but rather in another face of this life, which escapes our senses and of which we can obtain only a very imperfect knowledge."

The physical world reported by his senses did not seem real and the invisible world, of which he had an obscure but stubborn intuition reinforced by the religious training of his youth, remained unattainable, but preferable. "I doubt," he wrote late in life, "whether any of the precepts of the Gospel has so deeply marked me, and from my early youth, as the 'My kingdom is not of this world.'" And in 1931 he stated, "Even today I retain a sort of nostalgia for that burning mystic climate in which my being then found exaltation; I have never recovered the fervor of my adolescence; and the sensual ardor in which I later took pleasure is but its ridiculous counterfeit."

Haunted by the observer he could not long forget himself in the life of the senses; sooner or later the voice would come back, "What are you doing here?"

Emmanuèle and God

GIDE HAS SPECULATED WHETHER THE WARRING ELEMENTS IN his nature, which he has striven to harmonize in art, were not due to the diversity of stock represented by his parents. In opposition to the thesis of Maurice Barrès in *Les Déracinés* that "uprooting" was the source of national calamities and that one should be faithful to one's native province and stock, Gide maintained that on the contrary uprooting, dangerous perhaps for the weak, was stimulating and productive for the strong, and necessary for evolution and the general good. As for himself, "born in Paris of a father from Uzès and a Norman mother, where, M. Barrès, would you have me take root?"

Uzès is a small town in the Department of the Gard, in the south of France, about twenty-five kilometers north of Nîmes. When in his childhood Gide went there with his parents, they would leave the train at Remoulins, to the southeast, or at Nîmes, and accomplish the rest of the journey in an old carriage. The route from Nîmes, although longer, was preferred for scenic reasons. It took them across the Garrigues, rolling foothills of the Cévennes

19

Mountains, where rocky arid stretches were interspersed with stunted oaks and thorny shrubs, and where the sun blazed with desert force and the sharp dry air was fragrant with thyme and rosemary. Here in the days of religious persecution the stubborn Huguenots of Uzès repaired for their clandestine services. Gide's paternal grandfather Tancrède Gide was one of this breed; he died before André's birth, but others still survived, austere monuments of a turbulent past, who kept their hats on in church in memory of the days on the Garrigue, when to be uncovered was to court sunstroke, and removed them only to recite the Lord's Prayer. After the old men dropped off, some of the widows were still to be seen, among them André's grandmother, whom he remembered. Deaf and half-blind they trooped to church on the Sabbath, recognized each other only after they got to their seats, and thereupon drowned the words of the pastor in their loud cackle of compliments and reminiscences, to the scandal of some and the amusement of others.

Gide found in the Protestant country folk around Uzès a noble simplicity and independence of mind that were lacking in the Catholic farmers, dull but grasping, of his mother's Normandy. One day, returning to Uzès from a visit to a minister cousin and absorbed, as usual, in reading, Gide missed a train connection and found himself stranded for the night with only a few sous in his pocket. He asked hospitality at a farm, where it turned out that the old father of the woman of the house had known Tancrède Gide and knew André's cousin the minister. At once he was taken into the family; two of the sons were made to sleep together so that André could have a room to himself; he shared the family meal, and at the close of a short evening attended family prayers. The old man read a Psalm and a chapter of the Gospels, then stood, the others kneeling, and addressed the Almighty with a familiar respect, giving particular thanks for guiding the youth to his door. After a short silence they rose from their knees and the children advanced in turn to receive a kiss on the forehead from their grandfather, and Gide, deeply moved, joined them. Like this old man, he felt, his grandfather must have been—robust, with a voice not gentle but vibrant, a glance in which there was no caress, but a straightforward honesty.

In contrast to the unmixed Protestant history of the Gide side, the Rondeaux family of André's mother had oscillated between the Catholic and Protestant faiths. Gide's great-grandfather Rondeaux de Montbray, a man of substance and at one time mayor of the great Norman city of Rouen, was a Catholic like all his forebears, but took as his second wife a Protestant. The children of this marriage were raised as Catholics, but one of them, Edouard, the grandfather of Gide, like his father married a Protestant and this time the five children were raised as Protestants. But one day the mother, going into the room of her son Henri, opened a wardrobe and collapsed in a faint: within it was an altar to the Virgin. At the age of eighteen Henri Rondeaux had become a devout Catholic and later married an equally devout wife of old Catholic stock. Juliette Rondeaux, the youngest of the children and André's mother, remained all her life a firm Protestant, perhaps all the firmer because of the zeal generated by the shifting allegiances in the family.

Piety and economic complacency travel well enough together up to a point, but neither can be pushed to an extreme except at the expense of the other. The hereditary wealth and prominence of the Rondeaux family gave Juliette's mother, and even more her oldest sister Claire, a strong sense of social prerogative, but Juliette herself from her childhood was deeply religious, self-effacing, and possessed of a strong sense of duty. Years later, when Juliette, after the death of her husband, was preparing to move to a smaller apartment in Paris, Claire, who had reassumed the authority of elder sister, showed herself uncompromising about the necessity of a porte-cochère. A walk-up was conceivable, though not desirable, but whether one owned a carriage or not, one "owed it to oneself" to have a porte-cochère, and she offered to draw up a list of those who would not come to call if it was missing. "And you, Claire," asked Juliette sadly, "would you refuse to come?"

As a girl she had for governess Miss Anna Shackleton, a Scotchwoman not much older than herself, very pretty and well bred, but without fortune or social position. When Juliette became of marriageable age it seemed to her revoltingly unjust that she should be put forward ahead of her governess. "Am I any prettier, or more intelligent, or kind-hearted?" she said. And she tried to efface herself behind Miss Shackleton, refusing one after another the most eligible suitors of Rouen society, and finally accepting Paul Gide, a penniless young law professor from the south of France who would never have presumed to ask for her hand had not Juliette's pastor, who understood her nature, urged him to the step. Claire did not take a favorable view of Juliette's devotion to Miss Shackleton, who, she felt, should not be allowed to forget that she was a governess. Nor did she forget; she followed Juliette into the new home, but neither her intelligence, nor her good breeding, nor her beauty were enough to efface her subordinate position, and the only home life she was to know was that of her charge.

Juliette's modesty was the expression of a lack of self-confidence which led her to seek support in something or someone outside herself. She became a competent pianist, but disliked playing alone, preferring four-hand arrangements; in the presence of successful and important people she was ill at ease, like her son later. To be herself—intelligent, attractive, wealthy—was for her obviously not enough; her good fortune was not deserved, and must be justified. And so she increasingly loaded her existence with obligations and little acts of service. With the passage of time their importance to her in themselves grew, and it became a matter less of giving or receiving happiness than of accomplishing a duty, performing a rite. She became constantly busy, eternally anxious and troubled about many things. Did an epidemic of typhoid break out on her estate at La Rocque? She must at once go down from Paris and care for the sick; it was the right thing to do, for they were her farmers; and neither the danger to her own health nor the consideration that her services might not be very useful and would probably be neither understood nor desired by the sufferers could deter her.

On her only son, born after six years of marriage, she lavished her high-principled attentions to the point of endangering his affection for her. "I think it might have been said of my mother," he wrote, "that the qualities she loved were not those possessed in fact by the people on whom her affection fell, but those she would have liked them to acquire. At least that is how I try to explain the continuous ferment in which she was about others, about me particularly. . . . She had a way of loving me that sometimes almost made me hate her." Even after his majority her solicitous guidance of his decisions, his acts, his thoughts continued. Concerts and plays, in his boyhood, were not to be considered as pleasures but as opportunities for improvement, almost for the acquirement of merit. Chopin was disapproved; he was "unhealthy," too sensuous, perhaps too easy to appreciate. A children's costume party became the occasion for picking the cheapest outfit, so as not to seem to take advantage of those who had less money to spend, and André went as a pastry cook, joining an army of children in like predicament and deeply envying a cavorting youngster attired as a devil, unique of his kind.

On the whole Juliette trod the delicate line of godly thrift with success, avoiding parsimony on the one hand and indifference to worldly goods on the other. Her nature was generous, but her class was the canny bourgeoisie, and her religion taught her that her money was the Lord's and that she was merely a steward, who had no right to waste it on selfish satisfactions. Only rarely did she overstep the line and appear stingy. One such occasion was when she told André that she planned to give Littré's dictionary to Anna Shackleton. The boy, who was devoted to Miss Shackleton, was delighted; but then his mother went on to say that the copy she had given his father was bound in morocco, but that for Miss Shackleton shagreen would be good enough. "She won't notice the difference," she added. All his life her son remembered the incident, when countless examples of his mother's generosity had

been forgotten—perhaps because he himself had to combat
a certain closeness about money.

For all her wealth, her approval of the arts, and her
conscientious application to music, Juliette remained a
puritan. It was in her husband—curiously enough, considering the much greater austerity of his background—
that graciousness and humor appeared; it was as if the
small stock of amenity available in Tancrède Gide's family
had all been concentrated in the eldest son Paul. He was
full bearded, courteous, a little ceremonious, a little awe
inspiring at first, of unimpeachable integrity: "vir probus,"
his colleagues of the law faculty called him. Busy with his
studies he found little time for his son, but occasionally
he would turn to him politely and say, "Would my little
friend like to take a walk with me?" And off they would
set, the mother urging them not to be gone too long, and
proceed sedately up the rue de Tournon to the Luxembourg Gardens, playing guessing games the while; and
on toward the Observatory, where they could watch some
rider perched high on the "siege perilous" of the grandfather of bicycles. Or on occasion the father would invite
André into the sacred precincts of his library and gravely
show him where a worm had bored into an ancient law
folio. This library was his sanctuary, filled with beautifully bound editions of the poets and of the Greek and
Latin classics. One of the rare occasions that disturbed his
gentle manners occurred when, on his birthday, he found
a screen, elaborately embroidered by his wife with a
vaguely Chinese scene, installed in his library. "No,
Juliette," he exploded, "this is my room, let me arrange it
to suit myself." Then, remembering the work she had done

to give him a pleasant surprise, he tried to convince her that the screen gave him much pleasure, although he preferred it in the parlor.

Beneath his imposing exterior Paul Gide was a kindly, dreamy man, fond of poetry and the arts, tolerant of others, and with a strong sense of the ludicrous. He and Miss Shackleton were amused by the same things, and at some absurdity would go off into gales of laughter, in which Juliette did not join. And his son remembered an occasion when they were all taking a walk across the Garrigue near Uzès, Paul Gide and Anna Shackleton strolling in full and childlike enjoyment of flowers, grasshoppers, and everything they came across, while Juliette, anxious about the importance of some destination or other, urged them to hurry. And when he began to recite poetry his wife said, "No, Paul, you can recite that later, this is not the time."

Paul Gide tended to have more faith in the immediate potentialities of a child than his wife had, and in matters of discipline his first impulse was to explain, hers to reprimand. "Like the Children of Israel," she reasoned, "a child should first live under the law, so as to be prepared for the regime of Grace." However this might be, she somewhat dubiously agreed to her husband's experiment in substituting readings in Molière, or the *Odyssey,* or the *Arabian Nights* for the insipid moralizing which then passed for juvenile literature. The success of the experiment was such that the father ventured on to the Book of Job, and although André could scarcely have appreciated its beauties to the full, he was deeply impressed by the sonority of his father's voice reading the magnificent language, and by the air of devotional recollection on his mother's face—her eyes closed, and opening only occasionally to bend a glance of tender hope on her son.

Paul Gide died of intestinal tuberculosis before his son was quite twelve years old. The last time André saw the "vir probus" was a few days before the end; he was lying in bed with a large volume of Plato bound in sheepskin face down on his chest, where his weakened hands had just laid it.

With his characteristic passion for honesty, and it may be also in deliberate opposition to the "Heaven lies about us in our infancy" school, Gide has given us a somber picture of his childhood, describing himself as stupid, silly, sly, living in a state of "half-sleep and imbecility," within him and around him nothing but darkness. In Uzès, he tells us (and one is reminded of a similar instance in the life of Stendhal), when he was four or five years old and a considerably older cousin, a beautiful girl wearing a low-cut dress, advanced to kiss him, he ignored the proffered cheek and bit savagely into the dazzling whiteness of her shoulder, then spat with disgust. He dwells at length on his nervous disorders, his malingering, the dangerous use of narcotics which his parents permitted under the guidance of an ignorant doctor, and which kept him in a state of brutish apathy. Above all he stresses the vice of self-abuse, which extended as far back into his childhood as he could remember, and which, practiced in class, caused his suspension from the École Alsacienne at the age of eight, to the intense mortification of his parents.

The relieving touches to this gloomy recital are furnished by outdoor adventures in Normandy and Uzès, to which his parents repaired alternately; there were games and fishing with his cousins in Normandy, and both there and at Uzès he enjoyed flower- and insect-collecting expeditions, with the enthusiastic encouragement and participation of Miss Shackleton. Music, too, early became a passion, and here his encouragement came less from a succession of uniformly ineffectual teachers (except for the last and the best, M. de la Nux) than from Albert Demarest, a cousin twenty or more years his senior and the son of Gide's Aunt Claire.

But the crucial incident of his youth, the one which gave a new direction and a new meaning to his life, came in connection with his cousin Madeleine Rondeaux, who appears in the Journal as Em., in the Congo journal as M., and in the autobiography, as well as in the semi-autobiographic *Cahiers d'André Walter,* as Emmanuèle; in *Et nunc manet in te,* however, he restores to her the name of Madeleine. "I did not much like the name of Emmanuèle," he wrote, "which I gave her in my writings out of respect for her modesty. Her true name perhaps only pleased me because from my childhood on it suggested all the grace, the gentleness, the intelligence, and the kindness that she represented for me. It seemed usurped when borne by someone else; she alone, it seemed to me, had the right to it."

That the appearance and personality of Alissa in Gide's *La Porte étroite* were those of Madeleine was categorically asserted by Francis Jammes in a review of the book; he also referred to Madeleine in a letter by the name of Alissa. Gide himself admitted that his cousin (later his wife) served as a point of departure for the fictional creation, though he warned against identification of Alissa's later development with that of the original. Here then is his portrait of Alissa-Madeleine:

That Alissa Bucolin was lovely was something I had not yet learned to observe; she held me by a charm other than that of mere beauty. Undoubtedly she greatly resembled her mother, but her expression was so different that I did not notice this resemblance until later. I cannot describe a face; the features and even the color of the eyes escape me; I can only recall her already almost sad smile and the line of her eyebrows, so extraordinarily high above the eyes and standing away from them in a wide curve. I have seen their like nowhere else—on second thought I have: in a Florentine Beatrice of the time of Dante; and I readily imagine that the child Beatrice had high-arched eyebrows like those. They gave to her look, to her whole person, an expression of questioning that was at once anxious and trustful—yes, an expression of passionate questioning.

At Rouen, after the death of Gide's grandmother Rondeaux, his uncle Henri occupied the old family house on the rue de Crosne. Nearby, on the dismal rue Lecat, lived his uncle Émile; the country property of Cuverville had fallen to him, and that of La Rocque to Gide's mother. Émile Rondeaux had five children: Madeleine (called Emmanuèle in the memoirs, two years older than André), Jeanne (called Suzanne, about his age), Valentine (called Louise, younger), followed by Edouard and Georges, grouped together by the older children as "the boys," and considered negligible when it came to recruiting personnel for games. Contacts between these cousins and André were frequent from his earliest years, at Rouen in the rue Lecat or preferably in the pleasanter and more commodious house in the rue de Crosne, in the country at Cuverville or La Rocque, and occasionally in Paris. Of the three girls André played the most readily with Jeanne, chiefly because she was active, uncomplicated, and disposed to play with him; perhaps too because she was *not* the one he preferred. His favorite was the gentle self-effacing Madeleine, whom he regarded with all the more veneration in that her maturity seemed to put her beyond his reach.

Madeleine was fourteen years old and André twelve when, at Rouen one day after play at the rue Lecat, he returned to the rue de Crosne expecting to find his mother at home. But the house was empty and he decided to return to the rue Lecat; it would be like turning around suddenly, just in time to catch a glimpse of a hidden reality. And that, as it turned out, was just what happened. Contrary to custom the outer door of his uncle's house was open, and André slipped in, hoping to come upon his cousins unobserved. But the maid was on the watch; evidently someone was expected and it was not himself, for she tried to stop him. He pushed on, however, past the little office of his uncle who used to shut himself in there for long hours and come out looking old and tired. On this day he was away from Rouen. André went on upstairs, intending to pass the rooms of his uncle and aunt and continue on to those of the children on the top floor. But his aunt's door was open, and within he could see her lying on a chaise longue while the two younger girls fanned her. Some instinct told him that Madeleine was not, could not, be there. He went on up to her room, knocked, and receiving no response he pushed and the door yielded. Madeleine was there, on her knees. Without rising she said, "Why did you come back? You shouldn't have." He went over to her, kissed her, and felt tears upon her cheek.

Her mother had a lover, and she knew, though the

other children did not. "I think today," said Gide in his memoirs, "that nothing could have been more cruel for a child who was all purity, love, and tenderness, than to have to judge her mother and to disapprove of her conduct; and what increased the pain was that she had to keep for herself alone, and hide from her father whom she venerated, a secret that she had somehow surprised . . . and that was the gossip of the town, the laughing stock of the maids who made fun of the heedless innocence of her two sisters."

The shock and the pain of this situation marked her, Gide believed, for life. "All her life," he added in *Et nunc manet in te,* "she remained like a child who has been frightened. . . . The now dim little photograph which represents her at that age shows on her face and in the strange arch of her eyebrows a sort of questioning, of apprehension, of timid astonishment on the threshold of life."

André's eyes were opened: Madeleine was not serene and unapproachable, but a suffering and frightened child who needed him. He felt that the devotion of a lifetime was not too much to offer in response; he was brought out of himself, lifted above himself, and though there was not immediately any great outward change in him, he knew that within he was different. He now knew that someone needed him; he had a purpose, and an ideal.

From his sixteenth year Gide's turbulent adolescent emotions were straining in four directions: God, Madeleine, literature, and sex.

God he first sought through the channels of the faith in which he had been reared. But preparation for confirmation through the uninspired theological indoctrination of the family pastor was incredibly dull, inadequate nourishment for the new ardors of his aspiration. Perhaps, he thought, he had been mistaken; it might be that Catholicism, the ancient faith with the richer symbolism and ritual, was the answer to his need, as it had proved to be with some in his mother's family. Naïvely he consulted his Protestant pastor, and the good man obliged with a pamphlet that was not openly either for or against the Roman Church, but contented itself with a straightforward exposition of its doctrines. Formal theology, however, was not what Gide wanted, and, disappointed again, he turned to the Bible, first devouring it all in greedy gulps, and then taking it up again more slowly and methodically. He became convinced that he had a religious vocation, and did not hesitate to say so on occasion. When an escaped canary fluttered down in the street and lighted on his head, he felt that it was a sign of election; his heart had been so overflowing with joy and peace that this creature of the air had been drawn to him. Morning and evening he prayed and studied, and during the day carried a Testament in his pocket, reading it in public conveyances and in school recess and accepting as salutary mortification the curiosity or ridicule his piety excited. In the evening he laid out his subjects of meditation for the next day, filled a tub with water, committed his soul to God for the night, and went to bed on a plank. At the first streaks of dawn he arose, plunged into the cold tub, and gave himself over to prayer and meditation. He dreamed of the life of a Carthusian monk, reveled in disciplines and austerities, and drove himself into seraphic exaltations, the recollection of which, thirty years later, dominated all other joys he had known: "Ah, I wish I could exhaust the ardor of that radiant memory! . . . O heart charged with light!"

After the revelation of the rue Lecat his intimacy with Madeleine increased rapidly. Everything took on a new life, a new light, because he could share it with her; when he read a book he kept putting her initial in the margin opposite a thought which seemed worthy of their common attention; no joy was complete unless she could at once be brought to share it with him. In the summers at La Rocque they would get up while the others still slept and set out through the cool dew, walking hand in hand, or single file if the path was too narrow, stepping delicately and in silence so as not to disturb the wild creatures, or some other presence, felt but unseen, some woodland god perhaps. Like this, he dreamed, she would accompany him everywhere and always. "Pure radiance," he wrote of these days many years later, "may your memory in the hour of death vanquish the dark!"

Together they discovered the Greeks, so important for Gide's later thought, in the sonorous translations of Leconte de Lisle, André sometimes reading aloud in the deep voice, vibrant with emotion, which has always captured his auditors; and to neither did their pagan fervor seem inconsistent with their common Christian devotion. Together they studied German, reading Goethe in particular, and André pushed on to philosophy, to which his introduction was Schopenhauer. Here Madeleine followed with difficulty, and though eager to follow, she listened to his explanations with distress at her incomprehension; but she had not far to go, for Gide himself could never develop much enthusiasm for philosophy any more abstract than that of Schopenhauer.

Always it was he who led and she who followed, although her mind was, as he said, "gifted with the most exquisite and the rarest qualities, suited for the most delicate occupations. Her natural humility would not admit that she could be superior in anything and thus she condemned herself to the most ordinary occupations, in which nevertheless her superiority was evident. . . . Had I complained of this she would have said that all these superiorities I saw her relinquishing existed only in my loving imagination."

Yet she had the stubbornness so often found in the very gentle, and in matters of faith and conduct she was unshakable. Whether from a natural disposition or because the warning her mother's behavior constituted for her was more efficacious than the example of André's virtuous mother was for him, it was she of the two who was the more severely self-governed, the more resolutely devoted to principle. Madeleine exacted from herself and from her young lover (if one may call him that) a continual growth in grace, an unremitting pursuit of perfection; André too wanted to enter in by the strait gate, but he recognized that a part of its attraction was Madeleine. Her guiding principle was to strive always for the best, at whatever cost to personal happiness; for him, Heaven itself was not enough without her. There were areas of his thoughts and desires in which Heaven had no part, and on this ground they could not meet; she was his Beatrice, his Emmanuèle —"God with us." And so it was that when these two young creatures, moved to the depths by each other's proximity, spoke of love, it was in the language of religious aspiration.

In his memoirs Gide speaks of a "fundamental inaptitude for mingling the spirit and the senses which I think is

rather peculiar to me and which was to become one of the
cardinal repugnances of my life." Yet surely it is far from
unusual for a first love to have a character of religious
exaltation, so that explicit physical desire seems like a
profanation. It is considered normal in such a case that
sexual desire, at first apparently independent of the adoration, should gradually blend with it, and that physical
union, rather than a poetic and intangible communion of
spirit, should become the foremost preoccupation of the
lovers. Then romantic love, which is the yearning for the
unattainable, becomes passion; possession, satiety, disil-
lusion, readjustment on a new basis follow almost as a
matter of course. But there is apt to linger in the minds of
the lovers the ghost of that first overwhelming emotion,
that intimation of a something else which somehow they
contrived to miss. Were they simply naïve children and
have they now learned to face the realities of life? Or was
there really some invitation in the early experience which
they misunderstood and rejected?

The peculiarity of the case of André and Madeleine is
that the early experience endured; it is the ghost of the
normal that haunts their relations. In a passage of Gide's
Journal for August 1887, transcribed and perhaps a little
adorned in the *Cahiers d'André Walter* (it is presumably
the fictional André writing of his Emmanuèle), we read:
"You and I are alone in your room, bewildered and feverish with love. . . . Pressed together, so close that we quiver
as one, we sing the May night with extravagant words,
and then, when all words are spoken, we wait together as
if the night were infinite, our eyes fixed on the same star,
letting our tears blend on our close cheeks and our souls
mingle in an immaterial kiss."

It was in part the strictness of Madeleine that furnished the inhibition. "Your mind!" complains the André of the *Cahiers,* "ah! how I used to resent it; your poor mind so afraid of the disturbances of your soul, trying so hard to calm its transports. What ceaseless struggles to resist yourself!" But Gide accommodated himself readily to the situation. When, during the winter months, they were separated, she remaining in Normandy and he going back to Paris, contact was maintained by a full and constant correspondence which was so satisfying that it threw a little constraint on their relations when they met. His love of his cousin and his devotion to God merged naturally; sometimes he almost preferred to have her, like God, invisible, like Him a distant point of aspiration. At other times she was like a mother for him. He loved her beautiful hands, their touch upon his head laid in her lap:

> To lie at your feet and lay my head on your knees.
> Those dear hands that were mine,
> Those hands, those worshiped hands,
> Their cool shade on my eyes,
> Their silence on my thoughts . . .
> To sleep—the soft folds of your dress.
> To dream—to forget that I am alone . . .
> Emmanuèle.

These lines from the *Cahiers* inevitably suggest "Les chères mains qui furent miennes," of Verlaine; suggest too Rupert Brooke's much later "Retrospect"—

> Wisdom slept within your hair,
> And Long-Suffering was there,
> And, in the flowing of your dress,
> Undiscerning Tenderness—

with the conclusion:

O mother quiet, breasts of peace,
Where love itself would faint and cease!
O infinite deep I never knew,
I would come back, come back to you.
Find you, as a pool unstirred,
Kneel down by you, and never a word,
Lay my head, and nothing said,
In your hands, ungarlanded;
And a long watch you would keep;
And I should sleep, and I should sleep!

Gide, Verlaine, and Brooke are sounding a single universal note. Man's yearnings have always had a systole and a diastole, an "outward bound" and a "home thoughts from abroad"; what is expressed in these poems is the swing homeward, and in the haven of return the Woman-Mother and the Father-God stand very close together.

All this is normal enough; but Gide was not normal. The revelation of the rue Lecat was not the first incident to arouse his horror of sex. He had received solemn warnings about the Passage du Havre in Paris, by which he might have occasion to pass on his way to or from school, and which was said to contain "bad company"; there had been a later encounter with a brazen prostitute, before whom he had flinched and blushed, and who had laughed hoarsely and jeered, "You mustn't be afraid like that, pretty boy." Sex—the natural kind, for homosexuality was too utterly beyond the pale for mention—came to arouse in him a repulsion which he took for virtue, and the Devil, wrote Gide long afterward, lying in wait, rubbed his hands in glee. He assures us that he never felt the slightest physiological curiosity about the opposite sex; when taken to a museum of sculpture it was the male nudities that caused him to linger, to the scandal of the maid in whose

charge he was. He got curious sensual ecstasies from sweet
and piercing melodies, from a profusion of colors, from
accounts of breakage and damage, from a harmless story
of George Sand which told of the transformation of a boy,
who had jumped into a river to escape his cruel brothers,
into the branch of an oak tree. The nightmare of the
fevered André Walter may well have been his own: it
seemed to him that *She* came to him, very beautiful and
richly dressed. And then an obscene monkey hopped up
and started to lift the hem of her dress. As André tried
vainly to turn away his eyes, *She* suddenly laughed and
threw the skirt up over her head, and beneath it there was
nothing, nothing at all. Gide was unwilling to pollute his
love by erotic imaginings, that is clear; perhaps, too, he
could not. The tortured history of his sex life is certainly
no recommendation of his separation of love and desire;
and yet it is not everyone who, in all honesty, all wilful
romanticism aside, can write as he did, after more than
thirty-seven years of marriage, "Every time I see her again
I recognize anew that I have never really loved anyone
but her; and even, at times, it seems to me that I love her
more than ever."

At the age of about sixteen Gide began to plan his book,
a great work which was to lay bare as never before the
secrets of the human heart. He could not think of it as
merely the first of a literary career; it was rather his
utmost, his final word, beyond which he could only
imagine madness or death.

The specter of madness was for him at this time no
mere figure of speech but an actual threat, and its occasion was the remorse which tormented him over relapses
into the solitary vice of his childhood. To his aspirations

toward God and toward Madeleine the flesh was an en-
cumbrance, but when he tried to exclude it, he suffered
its revenge: the more exalted his religious fervor, the more
riotous and depraved became the imaginings which the
repressed flesh prompted. He had no adviser, religious or
lay, to tell him of the inevitability of this psychological
compensation. He had to struggle and to suffer alone; but
he did begin to wonder what secret dramas lay behind the
surface appearances of people he knew. "What would I
not give," mused the André of the *Cahiers*, "to know
whether others, whether those I love, have suffered from
the same torture.—Oh no! I would have seen it in their
look, I would have felt it in their words, they would not
talk as they do of these things, with that carelessness; they
would not laugh as they do. That is why I should like in
this book to cry out what I have in my heart—for myself
alone—or perhaps, if there are any, for those who have
endured the anguish I have endured and who like me are
in despair, believing that they are alone in their suffering. . . . One should dare to say these things."

That he was not alone in his suffering he became convinced, for he said later, "At the time when I was writing
it, this book seemed to me one of the most important in
the world, and the crisis I was depicting as of the most
general, the most urgent interest. . . . The state of chastity, I was forced to conclude, remained insidious and
precarious; every other outlet being forbidden me, I fell
back into the vice of my early childhood, and despaired
anew each time that I succumbed. With much love, music,
metaphysics, and poetry, that was the subject of my book."

Although in his sixteenth year he had begun keeping a
Journal, with the expectation of using it for his book, he

did not feel ready for the actual composition of the great work until he was twenty. Meanwhile there was his education to consider. In addition to class work and tutoring in preparation for his baccalaureate examinations he did much reading and thinking of his own. One summer he wanted to take a walking trip alone. His mother suggested Switzerland, and while she was willing to let him go without her, it was only on condition that he attach himself to some group of tourists of the Alpine Club. Such hearty company was a revolting prospect to the esthetically minded youth, and in place of Switzerland he proposed Brittany, which Flaubert's *Par les champs et par les grèves* had made attractive. But Brittany, thought his mother, would not be safe for him alone; she must go with him. Finally a compromise was reached whereby André would walk alone in Brittany and she would follow him from the middle distance, meeting him at preëstablished points every two or three days.

The journal which he kept during this tour, much reworked, became the substance of his first appearance in print, under the signature of André Walter, in the literary review *Wallonie*. Gide called his contribution "Reflections from elsewhere—little studies in rhythm," and it is as an exercise in style that the little piece strikes one today. "Already I was experiencing the greatest difficulty in clearing my thought," he said later. "More and more everything that I could have expressed easily seemed to me banal, without interest." Rhythm, suggested by the subtitle, was not his only preoccupation; painting, both literal and figurative, also interested him. "Yesterday," we read, "(for during the last three days the idea has been pursuing me) the idea of painting had become an obsession. At every

new vision I worried about translating it; it seemed to me
that if I had had paints with me I would have found as if
instinctively the blends and harmonies which reveal out-
wardly that something which we think is incommunicable,
when we feel that it thrills so deeply in our soul." And,
appropriately enough, at a small village inn he stumbled
across three painters, whose apparently childlike but intensely glowing canvases filled him with stupefaction.
Later he was able to identify two of them as Séruzier
and Gauguin.

He passed his examinations and cleared the decks, but
still he was not quite ready to launch on his career. In the
fall of 1889 he was back in Paris, studying a little with a
former professor of his in the École Alsacienne, dreaming,
making plans for a literary review. At this same school he
had met Pierre Louis, who later, in *Aphrodite* and *Les
Chansons de Bilitis,* spelled his name "Louÿs." They had
been drawn together by a common love of literature and
the arts, and by competition for first place in their literature class. Now he and Louis looked over rooms that might
serve for meetings of a literary club, and were much taken
by an attic location in the rue Monsieur-le-Prince, with a
view over the rooftops of Paris. "And we both dream of the
life of a student in a room like this, poor but with just
enough money to assure freedom of work. And at his feet,
in front of his table, Paris. To shut oneself in there, with
the dream of one's book, and come out only when it is
finished. The cry of Rastignac, overlooking the city from
the heights of the Père Lachaise: *Et maintenant,—à nous
deux!"*

By spring he felt that the time had come to write his
book, and he set out in search of solitude. At first he tried

the vicinity of the little lake of Pierrefonds, near Com-
piègne, but within two days Pierre Louis had tracked him
down. Evidently he must get farther from Paris. He went
to Grenoble, and combed the vicinity and to the south;
finally he found at Menthon, in the Haute-Savoie and on
the shore of the lake of Annecy, two rooms in a charming
cottage surrounded by orchards. Needing music for relief
and inspiration, he had a piano sent out from Annecy.
His meals he arranged to take at a summer restaurant
nearby where, at this season and for the first month of his
stay, he was the only customer, and in the solitude of his
rooms he tried to keep himself in the state of lyric fervor
which he then felt to be indispensable to literary composition. Under these conditions he wrote the whole of the
Cahiers d'André Walter.

At first he had seen his work as "melancholy and
romantic," "metaphysical and profound," inconsecutive,
without plot. Then, through fear of empty declamation,
he decided to include in it the story of "our love,"—the
love of both Andrés, both Emmanuèles. His own deter-
mination was settled: to marry his cousin at the earliest
possible date, overcoming the opposition of both families
and the resistance of Madeleine herself. In addition to
being a confession and a bid for glory, his book was to be
a move in his courtship.

At the opening of the first section, "the white book,"
André Walter lyrically addresses his soul after a fall into
sin: "Wait, until your sadness is a little more rested,—poor
soul whom yesterday's struggle has left so weary." Then
he recounts, with liberal extracts from Gide's Journal and
many scriptural quotations, the story of his love. André
Walter's hope for a successful issue to his suit is gone: at

his mother's deathbed he and Emmanuèle have stood together and heard her sentence that she should marry another; and the sentence has been carried out. André Gide had not yet asked for Madeleine's hand, not yet been formally refused.

Throughout the first section the loosely knit recapitulation is interspersed with prayers, the record of struggles for purity, metaphysical distress, and literary problems. The second section, "the black book," tells of the march to disaster, ending in "brain fever" (the romantic catastrophe so beloved of nineteenth-century novelists) and death. The last notation of the dying and imbecilic André Walter is, "The snow is pure."

One can readily understand the mortification expressed in Gide's preface to the 1930 edition of the *Cahiers* at republishing it unaltered. In contrast to his later standards of classic simplicity, understatement, clarity, this early work is turgid, ejaculatory, and full of a self-confessed confusion. "The emotions," we read, "are in a constant reciprocal dependence, they evolve in parallel: religious love and the love of Her often merge; at least there is between the two a constant correlation—as there is for the fervor of thought and study—and, still more, for the ardor of the insubordinate flesh; perhaps, even, all depends on the latter; perhaps it, in its turn, depends on springtime, how should I know?"

The division of mind is paralleled by a division of characters. André Walter writes at once his own story and that of his creation Allain, at times even dividing his page so that he can write two books concurrently. In the second section it becomes a race to see which character will arrive at madness first, and Allain's victory, by a hair, is announced to the accompaniment of the already insane laughter of his creator. Similarly Gide used André Walter, pushing his fictional character before him experimentally, as if trying out a potentiality of his own nature. This exorcising of his own demons in a work of art, preparing the way for a swing in the opposite direction, was to become a characteristic of much of his work to come; the critic within the work is perceptible in several of his subsequent books, and reaches full embodiment twenty-five years later in the Edouard of *Les Faux-Monnayeurs*.

In fact all of the Gide to come is implicit in the *Cahiers*, which in its very confusion is more revealing than the chastened art of his maturity. Here we see him struggling to escape from the labyrinth of his obsessions—upward toward God, outward toward nature and his fellow creatures. In the mood of escape to God, he was a spiritual being, possessed of free will, called to higher things, and all that was in the world—"the lust of the flesh and the lust of the eyes and the pride of life"—was sin. When the urge was outward toward achievement and experience, he felt that he was part of a natural order, and could Nature be wrong? In this mood, free will was an illusion, his sublime aspirations merely physiological—"dogs also bay in the moonlight." But then he would swing back: "Forgive me, Lord, I am only a child, a little child, lost in treacherous paths." His efforts in either direction were nullified by the doubts suggested by its latent opposite. And so he tried to accept both tendencies, and to maintain the precarious paradox of belief in unbelief: "Chimeras are better than realities. . . . The illusion is good and I mean to keep it." Again, "Free will: reason denies it.—Even if it does not exist, one should still believe in it." And again: "If I had known thee, Lord, I would have loved thee with my whole soul.—And I love thee still, not knowing thee; I love thee even if thou art not."

André Walter's Emmanuèle had no patience with such sophistry as making untruth into truth by believing in it. "O André," she cries, "if it were as you say, faith would be a swindle; only truth is worthy of belief, even if it brings despair. I prefer to suffer from unbelief than to believe in a lie." "Protestant!" comments André, but her position was the stronger one, and her hold on him unshakable. She was on the Lord's side, of course, but unlike the Lord she could not be talked away. She might be deluded, but she was herself no delusion: she was a woman of flesh and blood, waiting with cool hands to lay on his head when he returned from his wanderings.

Gide's ultimate decision was forced, not chosen. If he could, he would have taken the Lord's way, but the concept of Sin defeated him. The Lord's way, he could not help thinking, imperatively demanded moral behavior, or more accurately moral abstentions, self-denials. The commandment "Thou shalt not" immediately magnified the forbidden thing into an obsession, a fall became inevitable, and the succeeding remorse provided the exact climate needed for a new temptation, another sin. There seemed to be no escape but in getting rid of the concept of Sin; as he noted in the preface to the 1930 edition, "It soon seemed to me that the wisest triumph, on this field of battle, was to let oneself be conquered, to cease opposition to oneself."

Arguments to make the new position respectable were promptly and obediently supplied by his mind. "Free the soul by giving the body what it wants," a friend had once advised; the counsel was rejected at the time, but now it seemed to have possibilities. It accentuated the cleavage between body and soul: "Each goes its own way; the soul dreams of ever chaster caresses, the body abandons itself to the current." Then Ribot (a current psycho-physiologist whose *Maladies de la volonté* purported to show that the "will" as a faculty was nonexistent, that it was never a cause but merely a name for an observed effect) contributed his bit: "Emotions lead men, not ideas." If that was so, why make resolutions? If emotions were to have the last word anyway, why not admit it at the outset, and give them their head? Then there was the idea of "representing," of "making manifest": "We live to make manifest, but often involuntarily, unconsciously, and for truths which we do not know, for we are ignorant of our own reason for being." Perhaps chastity, so pursued and so elusive, was only a snare: "It is a pride in disguise; to be able to believe oneself superior, noble, above others. . . . All right if you win, but you don't; the Evil One, as soon as he is tracked down, transforms himself, like Proteus of old; you only conquer his multiple forms one by one. . . . Depraved continence! What a subtle perversity!"

The end of the road pursued by Allain is marked by the epitaph written for him by André Walter: "Here lies Allain who became insane because he thought he had a soul." Gide, pushing Walter before him to the same conclusion, himself stops short; Walter has served his purpose as an example of the end of a tendency, as a warning; his creator, with a resurgence of vitality, shakes off his impotence. "Awake thou that sleepest, and arise from the dead!" To express his inmost nature, whatever it may be, is his new objective, and ardor his watchword: "Life in intensity, that is the magnificent state."

Exalted by his new energy, exasperated by his solitude, Gide chafed at the limits of Menthon and Lake Annecy, dreamed of "the unknown road fleeing into the distance, the road I might have followed, farther, farther, new streams, mountains, snows, forests, villages," calling in his heart for a companion to share his odysseys. His travels, like his erotic satisfactions, were still accomplished in imagination only, and three years more were to pass in hesitation before he could shake off the past; but with the completion of the *Cahiers* the outcome was not in doubt.

Ambition seized him again. His book—confession, manifesto, song of love—was complete. Now to Paris, and glory: "To arrive suddenly, unexpectedly, and give my trumpet call!"

3

The Artist and the Saint

IN THE MIDSUMMER OF 1890, BURSTING WITH HIS MESSAGE and fearful that someone might speak it before him, Gide hurried back to the literary capital. Change, he felt, was in the air. Naturalism, attacked by de Vogüé in his preface to *Le Roman russe* in 1886, seriously shaken by the manifesto of five former disciples of Zola against his *La Terre*, was in full retreat, and Symbolism was carrying the banner of revolt. Paul Desjardins was preparing his proclamation of the "present duty" of all good citizens to shake off negativism and apathy, to come to life, to believe, to act.

As a matter of fact Naturalism was less routed than it seemed; the plea of Desjardins' *Le Devoir présent* for a return to action based on the old faith and morals had little in common with Gide's new orientation except its energy, and Symbolism, never a very vital movement, had passed its peak. Moreover, nobody in particular seemed to be waiting for Gide's message, let alone forestalling him. He made preparations for two editions of the *Cahiers* (his mother supplying the money as "expenses for André's career"): a beautifully printed limited edition and a large ordinary one. The plain edition was out first, and instead of creating a sensation, as he had confidently hoped, it fell completely flat. Mortified, the young author saved out a few copies for publicity purposes and sold the rest by weight, glad enough to get a little money in exchange for his waste paper.

The effect on Gide of this first check was to be evident for the rest of his career. "I have passionately desired fame," he admitted, but he was readily persuaded that success with the multitudes was a poor passport to a durable literary reputation. Thenceforth his books were to be issued in very small editions; if they created a demand—and for many years they did not—he was not averse to subsequent larger printings, but his first bid was to be modest.

His new attitude toward success fitted well both with his own disposition and with the tenets, exquisitely disdainful of the mob, of the Symbolists with whom he now became associated. Through the good offices of Pierre Louÿs, who had more assurance than himself, he was brought to meet some of the leading literary figures of the day: Henri de Régnier, then at the height of a celebrity that has greatly declined; Heredia, whose work, almost exclusively in sonnets, was, with its meticulous versification and the physical objectivity of its subject matter, more Parnassian than Symbolist, but who was on friendly personal terms with the leaders of the new school; above all, the master Mallarmé, whose celebrated Tuesdays in his apartment in the rue de Rome had a lasting effect, direct or indirect, on such writers as Valéry, Suarès, Proust, Claudel, as well as on Gide, men so diverse in most ways but bearing in common the mark of Mallarmé—

a love of the ideal and an indifference to changing popular standards.

In the course of his career Gide often stated his opinions on the subject of literary influence. To fear the effect on one's precious originality of another man's work was a sign of weakness, he maintained, not of strength; periods of great literary vitality, like the Renaissance, were times of large borrowings and importations. One should use the works of others freely, and as freely confess the debt, not in slavish imitation but with fruitful assimilation and re-creation. He was often accused of interpreting the books of others to suit his own ideas, and he usually replied by half admitting and half protesting the charge. Each writer has his own particular angle of vision, his own individual message, and among the works of others he is drawn in the first place to those which will meet his needs. More-over, "is it not the characteristic of a perfect work of art that one can see in it more than the artist designed to put?" On the other hand, deliberately to distort another man's words was a sin against integrity, of which critics of himself were often guilty and which he was scrupulous to avoid.

In his own case one of his earliest and most decisive influences was that of the Greeks, but he drew them to himself, took from them what corresponded with his own experiences and intuitions. He read the *Bacchae* of Euripides just at the time when he was struggling with the puritanism of his upbringing; in the resistance of Pentheus to Dionysus he recognized his own, and was encouraged when Pentheus discovered that the Bacchae were peaceful and the earth around them fruitful if they were allowed to worship the god in freedom, and became mad only when constrained. In the Greek mythology to which he so often in the course of his career had recourse for embodying his ideas, what interested him was not its origin and history, but its applicability to man today, its still valid psychology.

Like the Greeks, Goethe, whom he began to read at eighteen, did not deflect him from his course but encouraged him to pursue it. From Goethe, Gide learned that man can discard the swaddling clothes of his early beliefs and yet not feel naked; from him that God can be approached through the physical world as well as through religious devotion; from him, too, that nothing great has been attempted by man but in revolt against the gods.

Goethe prepared him for Nietzsche's new tables of the law and the superman. Nietzsche, the first of Gide's "four-starred constellation" (the others, in chronological order of impact, being Dostoevsky, Browning, and Blake), was not for him an initiator, a former of his mind, like the Greeks and Goethe, but rather a witness to ideas which he himself had already formulated. For many years Gide maintained that he had not read Nietzsche until he had half completed *L'Immoraliste,* that is, about 1899; and although he later admitted that he must have had some acquaintance with his work much earlier, and forgotten the fact, it still remains true that his debt at first was unconscious and in part indirect. At the time when he was working out his principal ideas, he did not look to Nietzsche as a master, as he did to Goethe.

The three years following the completion of the *Cahiers d'André Walter* Gide later recalled with humiliation as the most confused, the most trivial of his literary life. Partially released from the despairing preoccupations out of which his first book had been formed, he now gave himself over to self-cultivation. He pictured himself as a Goethe on his first trip to Italy: at last he knew himself for what he was, an artist. He liked to write on a dressing table bequeathed him by Miss Shackleton, and between sentences he would gaze long at his image in the mirror, trying to find artistic expression for the unique individuality that lay beneath that interesting countenance. He studied his gestures, the tones of his voice, the expression of his face, in the effort faithfully to represent his inmost personality.

Duty, morality, he felt, were not the same for everyone; perhaps God himself disliked the uniformity toward which the Christian ethic, in its effort to subjugate nature, tended. To submit to the common morality, Gide now thought, was to betray one's individual mission and so to commit the sin against the Holy Ghost for which there was no forgiveness.

He carried these preoccupations into the literary salons he was now frequenting, but found it hard to express himself. If, as occasionally happened, someone appealed to him directly for an opinion, he was apt to be disconcerted, then confused and angry at what he found himself saying. For the most part, however, what these men of letters wanted most was the opportunity to talk about themselves and their own ideas, and Gide made himself popular by following his own bent, listening everywhere with the closest and most flattering attention, seldom speaking himself, but trying hard to look like an artist. To maintain his footing he set to work in 1890 on a treatise, having recourse for the first time to the Greek mythology that was later to serve him so well and so often for the framework of his ideas. In 1891 a small edition of the *Traité du Narcisse* was published.

The myth of Narcissus seems an appropriate choice for the state of mind he was then in, but his handling of the material was surprisingly philosophic and impersonal. He set out to explain and defend the basic doctrine of Symbolism: that the forms of the visible world, the phenomena, are but the changing external symbols of eternal verities that lie behind them—noumena, Platonic Ideas; and that the business of the poet is to penetrate beyond surface appearances, which he handles in such a way as to make them suggest the eternal Ideas they represent. Narcissus, bending in the traditional posture over the surface of the water, discovers not only his own reflection but the moving panorama of life to which he had been blind. The spectacle of this unceasing change makes him dream of its timeless predecessor—Paradise, the Eden of the Ideas; it was individual desire, he learns, that broke the original harmony and gave birth to time and change. Paradise lost is still everywhere present, and can be regained by the sacrifice of self.

In this beautifully written (if somewhat oracular) essay the most interesting statements are in a footnote, written close to Gide's twenty-first birthday and rich in implications for the rest of his life. "Every phenomenon," we read, "is the symbol of a Truth. Its only duty is to manifest it, its only sin to prefer itself. . . . Every representative of the Idea tends to prefer himself to the Idea which he makes manifest. To prefer oneself—that is the fault. . . . The moral question for the artist is not that the Idea which he makes manifest should be more or less useful for the majority; the question is that he should manifest it well.—For everything must be made manifest, even the most baleful things: 'Woe to that man by whom the

offence cometh,' but 'it must needs be that offences come.'
—The artist and the man who is truly a man, who lives for
something, must in advance have made the sacrifice of
himself. His whole life is but a moving in that direction.
And now, what should one make manifest? One learns this
in the silence."

Among the various elements of his Christian upbringing
against which Gide was battling, the principle of self-loss
—dying in order to live—remained unconquerable. But
competing now with self-loss was his newer discovery of
faithful representation, of making manifest one's inmost
self, and for this too he found authority, more ambiguous
but still scriptural: "Everything must be made manifest."
What he is doing in the *Narcisse* is attempting to conciliate
self-loss and manifestation, thereby justifying his literary
ambition and veiling its self-assertive egoism. He had felt
a religious vocation; now, abetted by turbulent desires,
unsatisfied senses, and the failure of his efforts toward
personal purity, he felt called to be an artist. But self-loss
still held good, and he needed the support of his conscience; he was therefore to be a dedicated, a selfless,
artist.

Was it possible? Leaving aside the question of money,
which he did not need, was authorship possible without
the spur of desire for fame? Was manifestation merely a
pretentious name for self-assertion, and at the opposite
pole from self-loss? To be an artist is to express oneself,
to deny oneself is to be a saint; is it possible to be both?

Some thirty years later his answer to the question was
to be a categorical negative: it is impossible to be both,
one must choose. But for the present he was not so sure.
There was Mallarmé, who was for him much more than

a literary master; in his simplicity, his serenity, his single-minded devotion to the Idea, his indifference to success and failure, Mallarmé seemed to stand out above other literary men as the example of the artist who was also a saint. And yet there was something missing. Deeply as Gide admired his work, he could not but feel oppressed by its deliberate obscurity, its remoteness from life, above all by the artistic sterility into which the poet kept sinking, and from the contemplation of which, paradoxically, he extracted some of his best poems.

On the other hand there was Oscar Wilde, who, not yet the pariah but radiant with success and preceded by his shrewdly constructed legend, descended upon Paris one day in 1891. Gide met him at a restaurant dinner for four, where he and Wilde got along very well together each by following his own bent: Wilde talking incessantly and Gide listening closely. "You listen with your eyes," said Wilde to him when they were alone together later, "and that is why I shall tell you this story." It was but the first of a long series, for the two met again frequently. "I don't like your lips," said Wilde again; "they are straight like those of a person who has never lied. I want to teach you to lie, so that your lips may become beautiful and twisted like those of an antique mask."

Wilde was the champion of the pagan ideal, but was troubled by the opposing ethic of Christianity, to which he paid the tribute of constant attack, and in a form of fable that was like an inverted Gospel parable. Self-loss was the antithesis of all he stood for, and he knew it. When later he wrote *De Profundus* he said that he had learned a secret which had lain within him like a treasure hidden in a field: humility. "Promise me one thing," he said to

Gide after his release from Reading Gaol, and à propos of Gide's *Nourritures terrestres*, "never write 'I' again."

"Wilde, I believe, has done me nothing but harm," wrote Gide before the end of this early contact. "With him I had forgotten how to think." The harm was not due to Wilde's morals, about which Gide was then uninformed, nor because of his anti-Christianity or his views on art, on both of which subjects his sayings aroused a sympathetic response, but because he was a wit and a storyteller, whereas Gide felt that his own talents required deeper thinking and a more intellectual organization. He had a strong, if intermittent, thirst for knowledge which competed with his ambition for creative writing, and he pursued one or the other in accordance with the uppermost desire. When intake had produced satiety he would turn to writing, and when blocked there by difficulties or a sense of sterility he would turn back to study. When both failed him, his dormant but indestructible religious aspirations would seize him again. And in whichever direction he set his face he was harassed by a sense of guilt over the abandonment of his immediately preceding pursuit.

In his Journal for 1890-93, which reveals these oscillations, there are large gaps, occasioned partly by abstention from writing in it (as he sometimes tells us at the next entry) and partly by his destruction of large parts of it just before his departure for Africa, and of still more after his return. But with what we have, and with what the mutilated record suggests, we learn much about this crucial period of his life.

On his *Traité du Narcisse*, planned while he was still writing the *Cahiers*, he set to work immediately on return-

ing to Paris in the summer of 1890; but before the end of
the year, probably because of the distracting effect of his
assiduity in literary salons, he found himself at a dead
end, and laid the work aside. Follows a six months blank
in the Journal, at the end of which he finds himself again
seething with ideas, urging himself to production, to
single-mindedness. He is, moreover, at the opposite pole
from Christian renunciation. "My mind," he says, "is becoming voluptuously impious and pagan. I must exaggerate that tendency." By July 10 he has started writing
again, but interrupts himself "through lack of will." Then
he is further diverted by a trip to Belgium with his mother,
during which he talks with Maeterlinck, derives (and
rather pedantically records) a certain profit from looking
at masterpieces of painting, but is bored by the sights,
which he cannot enjoy without Madeleine. Travels in
France follow those in Belgium, but "in fact," he says,
"I haven't traveled"—having been wholly absorbed in
Tolstoy and Schopenhauer. Then a creative mood catches
him again; back at La Rocque in September he writes at
a stretch the series of poems that are to be published the
next year as *Les Poésies d'André Walter*, and in October
reattacks *Narcisse*, this time bringing it to a successful
conclusion.

At Christmas time he is at Uzès, a season and a place
favorable to the return to religion which we feel to be
about due. On December 29, still at Uzès, he writes:
"Lord, I return to thee, because I believe that all is vanity
save knowing thee. Guide me in thy paths of light. I have
followed tortuous ways, and have sought to enrich myself
with false goods. Lord, have pity upon me." Next day the
mood still holds: "There is only one possession which

makes rich: God." But on the thirty-first appears the competing attraction: self-manifestation in art, clothed in its appropriate virtue of sincerity: "The hardest thing when one has begun to write is to be sincere. . . . The fear of not being sincere has been tormenting me for several months and preventing me from writing. To be perfectly sincere."

The religious phase is not quite over, however, for he writes on January 3, 1892, "Shall I always torment myself thus and shall my mind, Lord, nevermore find rest in any certainty? Like a sick man in his bed, tossing in search of sleep, from morning to night I am disquieted, and at night too I am awakened by unrest. I am anxious at not knowing who I shall be; I do not even know who I want to be; but I well know that I must choose. . . . Lord, grant me to want only one thing and to want it without ceasing." January 11: "My dilemma is between being moral and being sincere." January 20: "Adoration kills the individual. The God takes his place."

Yet by this time the pendulum has swung, specifically toward learning rather than creative writing, for on the same date we read: "I had begun again to work a little at my mediocre verses of September. It bores me. Today I have discovered such marvelous fields of learning that all the joy of production is canceled by the furious joy of learning. It is a wild lust. To know." At Easter he still wants to know; he has been reading Goethe, Edmond de Goncourt, Banville, Constant, and has been trying to study philology. But "I feel that in a short time I shall throw myself back into a frenzied mysticism."

The familiar dilemma which threatens to recur is modified by a trip to Germany in May, and he writes in Munich:

"I am less and less interested in myself, more and more in my work and my thoughts. I no longer ask myself every day, every hour, whether I am worthy of my God." But also in Munich he writes a note which says: "The other things! When I have sufficiently tasted their vanity I shall withdraw into study. Just a little longer, but first I want to exhaust their bitter flavor, so that afterwards no desire for them will trouble my peaceful hours."

The summer of 1892 he spent at La Rocque on a new work: *Le Voyage d'Urien*. In later years he looked back on this time as the most despairing of a desperate period; uncertain of his direction, discouraged, turned in on himself, he relapsed into the solitary vice that had been the chief cause of the torments of André Walter: "At La Rocque . . . I almost went mad; nearly the whole time I spent there I was cloistered in my room where nothing but my work should have kept me, and toward my work forcing myself in vain (I was writing *Le Voyage d'Urien*); obsessed, haunted, hoping perhaps to find some escape in excess itself, come out into the clear weather beyond, exhaust my demon (I recognized in this his advice), and exhausting only myself . . . until there was nothing ahead but imbecility, but madness."

Perhaps it was the memory of this obsessive summer that made him look back with some disfavor on the book that came out of it: "I have written no book without having felt a profound need of writing it, with the single exception of *Le Voyage d'Urien*; and even there it seems to me that I put a great deal of myself and that for one who reads aright it too is revealing."

For anyone who has been following Gide's problems to this point it is not hard to read the book's revelations. The voyage of Urien is symbolic (as Mallarmé, who had feared it was concerned with real travel, was relieved to discover), a voyage through the "pathetic ocean," a "Sargasso Sea," toward the "frozen sea," a voyage undertaken as relief from the "bitter night of thought, of study, and of theological ecstasy." The insubstantial shores and cliffs that drift by Urien's ship in the pathetic ocean while the passengers learn "to distinguish the passing things from the eternal isles" are scarcely more unreal than the "real" world sometimes appeared to Gide—in June 1891, for example, when he wrote: "I can never succeed in entirely convincing myself that certain things really exist. It has always seemed to me that they ceased to exist when I stopped thinking about them. . . . To me the world is a mirror." When certain of Urien's companions go ashore and bring back magnificent fruit which Urien regards with suspicion, they taunt him: "Will you not dare to taste even fruit, from fear, and will your sterile virtue always consist in abstinence, in doubt? Will you always then doubt?"—and their voice is the voice of the repressed side of Gide's own nature. The stagnation of the Sargasso Sea is no less easy to interpret: "O temptations which we used to deplore and dread; desires! at least when we resisted you our souls were occupied; we did not yield; we wished that the temptations would go away, and now that they are gone, boredom stretches endlessly over the gray sea!" The voyage through the frozen sea, the march toward the pole, are the search for the spiritual world, and at its end, "here in despair," a former explorer has carved his own epitaph: *Hic desperatus.*

Hope deferred makes the transparent allegory of *Le Voyage d'Urien* more desolate even than *Les Cahiers d'André Walter.* The Emmanuèle of the *Cahiers,* who at least had a solid original, has been replaced by Ellis, the elusive wraith about whose identity Urien is in doubt, and who at the end speaks like a disembodied voice: "Urien! Urien! unhappy brother! Why have you not always dreamed me? . . . Why did you try in your lassitude to compose my chance image? . . . I await you beyond time."

But there are faint signs of a rebirth; a deliberately and humorously incongruous note, for the first time in the musical lamentations of Gide, puts in an experimental appearance, slightly in the sketch of the manners and customs of the Eskimos, but chiefly in the person of Ellis. She appears to Urien on an island of the Sargasso Sea, where she has been seated for fourteen days under an apple tree; she is wearing a polka dot dress, carries a parasol, a vanity case, and a plaid shawl, and is engaged in eating an escarole salad while reading *Prolegomena to all future metaphysics.*

Urien is a transitional book: the past is not quite dead, the future not yet born. "I was afraid," says the author in an Envoi, "to shout too loud and to spoil poetry by telling the Truth, the Truth which must be heard; preferring still to tell lies and to wait—to wait, to wait. . . ."

Up to now Gide had been trying to live by sets of rules for the conduct of his literary and personal life; periodically he drew them up in his Journal and as regularly, but unintentionally, abandoned them. Now, after this wretched summer at La Rocque, he resolved "to strain powerfully toward joy and to give myself up to life, which I had told myself was good." But by the next summer he was back on his rules of conduct; in La Rocque again in July 1893, he notes: "I have lost the habit of lofty thought;

this is a *most regrettable thing*. I live in a facile way. This must not be; everything in life must be resolved, and the will constantly stretched like a muscle." For now he has another work to produce, which he calls *La Tentative amoureuse*—an "attempt at love" even more personally revealing than the *Voyage d'Urien*.

Of this new work he says in his Journal, "I was sad because a dream of unrealizable joy was tormenting me. I relate that dream and, taking the joy out of the dream, I make it mine." And in the foreword to the *Tentative* he writes, "Our books will not have been the very truthful story of ourselves—but rather of our plaintive desires, the wish for other lives forever forbidden, for all impossible acts." Luke, his hero, desired love but feared the carnal act: "Unhappy upbringing that we had, that made us foresee as tearful and heartbroken, or else as morose and solitary, a pleasure which should be glorious and serene." And then Gide breaks off: "No, after all! Luke was not like that; for it is an absurd mania to make whomever you invent like to yourself.—So Luke possessed this woman." But he is none the happier for accomplishing what Gide could not; physical love brought boredom, and the happiness for which he and Rachel were seeking is symbolized by the closed park beside whose walls they walk seeking admission, and when finally they obtain it they find—just an abandoned park.

Gide's closing note, however, is a foretaste of the doctrine of *Les Nourritures terrestres:* "No things are worthy to turn us aside from our way; let us embrace them all in passing, but our objective is beyond them. . . . Rise quickly, winds of my thought, and scatter these ashes."

Francis Jammes (a then unknown young poet in the provinces whose acquaintance Gide had made by letter and whose first steps to celebrity were greatly aided by Gide's personal and financial intervention) wrote of his friend's early work: "Ah! how I love your poetry. But how much more I will love it (excuse me, for I have a horror of criticism) on the day when, freed of hospital bandages perfumed with incense, it will reflect your soul, in love with the strange, but healthy." There is indeed a pathological note in Gide's early work, but it reflected a condition which was to prove an advantage for his books to come. As he said in a note on circumstances favorable to literary production, "To be well. To have been sick." Convalescence may bring an intensity and a realization of living more acute than is known to uninterrupted good health.

His sickness of soul, he realized, was in large part due to being immured within himself, battling enemies which he himself had created: "It is characteristic of the Christian soul to imagine battles within; after a time one no longer understands why. For, after all, whatever is defeated is still a part of oneself, and the result is waste. I have passed my whole youth in setting against each other two parts of myself that perhaps asked for nothing better than a reconciliation."

At this time perhaps more clearly than later he realized the discrepancy between his desire to get into contact with others and its attainment. "I try to discover," he wrote early in 1890, "what affection is and I doubt whether I love anyone. And yet my heart quivers with pity, oh! an infinite pity, at every unhappiness that I meet." And three years later, retrospectively: "Sometimes it seemed to me that others around me lived only to accentuate in me the realization of my personal life."

Yet already he was capable of seeing and briefly sharing the viewpoint of another: "I always see almost at the same time the two sides of each idea and my emotion is always polarized. . . . And when I am talking with a friend, nearly always I am concerned only with telling him what he thinks, and I myself think only the same thing." This sort of sympathy, however, had in it more cool lucidity than warmth. What he needed was to go out to people and to the world of things freely, joyously, without fears or inhibitions. "We are a misunderstood harmony; we think we can go our own way, alone, and at once we are in opposition to ourselves. . . . Scrupulous souls, timorous souls, self-oppressors; they fear joy as they would a too dazzling light."

He was sick of self-absorption, weary to death of the fatuity and futility of his life among vain men of letters interested only in their own work and unable to appreciate any other because it seemed like competition. Already he was planning to satirize them in a book which was to become *Paludes,* where Tityrus, the author, lives in a tower surrounded by stagnant water and emerges only in quest of admiration. He carries a notebook; some scene arouses an emotion, and he writes down some such phrase as, "Tityrus smiled"; then, satisfied, he puts away pencil and paper until the next visitation of the muse.

Of books Gide had had enough: "We have passed our life without seeing it. We were reading." The haunting lines of Mallarmé he made his own:

La chair est triste, hélas! et j'ai lu tous les livres.
Fuir! là-bas fuir! . . .

He experimented in cultivating bodily fatigue and
thirst, so as to savor the exquisite refreshment of rest and
a sherbet. And above all, "Other lives! other lives: all that
we can live of them, *ourselves.*"

His self-imposed isolation from the physical world and
the life of the senses was accentuated by the fact that
Madeleine had received his first book, on which he had
founded his hope for love as well as for glory, without
comment; and his formal request for her hand had been
met by a categorical refusal. He declined to consider the
rejection as final, but he was in a measure cut loose,
authorized, he could not but feel, to adopt the policy here-
tofore only considered of making a separation between
love and pleasure. Now he must set himself to the hard
task of learning to live in the senses.

For three years now he had been nerving himself for
the break which he had planned in 1890. At that date he
had also decided on his traveling companion: Paul-Albert
Laurens, a painter and of exactly Gide's age. The father
and brother were painters too, and with this family he felt
particularly congenial, having seen them increasingly both
in Paris and at their seaside home at Yport, where he wrote
a part of *La Tentative amoureuse*. In 1893 fate gave the
awaited signal: Paul Laurens received a fellowship for
travel, and Gide, who needed no such financial assistance,
decided to accompany him. "I have lived," wrote Gide, "to
the age of twenty-three completely a virgin and depraved,
frantically searching everywhere for a morsel of flesh on
which to plant my lips." Paul Laurens was in much the

same state, and although, unlike Gide, he was normal in his desires, they were agreed, each in his own way, upon emancipation into experience and upon North Africa as the scene of their adventure.

Determined to make a complete break with his past he abandoned his daily custom of Bible reading and prayer; he read over his Journal and destroyed much of it, but preserved, inconsistently and significantly, "certain devout and pure pages. . . . What pleases me most in my former self are the moments of prayer." And his farewell to the God of his childhood is itself a prayer: "O God, let this too narrow morality burst and oh! let me live fully; and oh! give me the strength to do so without fear and without always thinking that I am about to sin."

When at last, in October of 1893, he set out with his companion for the South, it was with the sense of abandoning himself to his destiny. "I now believe," he wrote, "that man is incapable of choice and that he always yields to the strongest temptation." But there was a certain voluptuousness in this letting go, this giving up of his everlasting rules of conduct; was this then, perhaps, the true self-loss? At any rate it was a love of one's destiny— *amor fati* his future master Nietzsche would have called it.

As if in honor of their new independence, the Mediterranean naval base of Toulon greeted them with dressed ships and illuminations: France was entertaining the fleet of her new ally Russia. Paul Laurens went to an evening fête on one of the warships, but Gide, unhappy and worried by a severe cold, lingered in the city, watching, with horror and fascination, scenes of debauchery and drunkenness, which represented, to this puritan in revolt, at once Sin and his duty.

Gide's health had for some time been uncertain; twice he had been deferred for military service, and on the third examination was definitely invalided out, and "tuberculosis"—the disease from which his father had died—was inscribed on his record. Now, with his debilitating new cold, he wondered whether he was wise to leave France, and whether it would not be better, not to abandon, but to defer the trip. But *amor fati* won out; the die was cast, and for better or worse he abandoned himself to his destiny. He said nothing of his fears to Paul Laurens, and a few days later they set sail from Marseille for Tunis.

It was breathlessly hot in their cabin, and the second night Gide went out on deck. The sky was lurid with flashes of heat lightning; to the south, ahead, lay Africa—drawing, inviting, yet terrifying.

4

Education for Freedom

TUNIS CAME TO MEET THEM LIKE A PAGE FROM THE
Arabian Nights. Bands of red-gold fish spurted from the
water at the ship's side, grave fantastic camels silhouetted
themselves along a spit of land enclosing the harbor, chat-
tering gesticulating merchants of shoddy wares submerged
them. The young travelers walked happily into all traps,
followed the ragged urchin who offered himself as guide
(they would have been indignant at any suspicion of his
disinterestedness), and drank the sweet coffee of the
merchants with wonder at their generosity.

The native city had as yet been little touched by the
occupation, and beyond the trees and shade of the French
quarter it blazed in the sun, bare and severe, its whiteness
unrelieved by the touches of winter moss and mold which
the dry season had burned away. But this was only the
face which Tunis turned to the African sky; beneath
teemed the shadowy odorous swarming *souks.* One entered
them through a narrow passage shaded by a jujube tree;
first came the leather workers' section, then the perfume
bazaar where authentic amber and essence of apple blos-

soms were dripped by pipette into tiny flasks, which were then wrapped and rewrapped, each new covering seeming to add to their rarity and price. Through these and other marvels Gide and Laurens picked their way, feasting eyes and ears and noses and lightening their pocketbooks—but by how little, they thought, in return for what they got!

They had come armed with letters of introduction—often useful, but sometimes, as it turned out, encumbering—to military and administrative officers, and now a captain placed at their disposal army horses. Gide's first ride was like a parable of his life. Like other carefully brought-up children of the well-to-do he had had riding lessons—round and round the riding ring on a sedate plug and under the critical eye of the riding master, posting carefully and observing the traditional ritual. But here he was given a fiery little Arab mount which at first, fearfully, he tried to curb, then, abandoning himself once more to his destiny, he gave the horse its head. Soon he had lost both his way and his companions and was galloping westward toward the distant mountain of Zaghuan, past ruins of an ancient aqueduct and salt pools turned blood red by the setting sun, into a new life, a new freedom.

Gide and Laurens had planned to spend the first part of the winter at Tunis, but their officer friends convinced them that they should do their traveling before the definite onset of the rainy season. So they set out in a monstrous four-horse landau, enveloped in their newly acquired Arab costumes and accompanied by two ferocious-looking Maltese as coachman and guide. And now Gide began to measure the physical cost of his adventure. He had always been particularly sensitive to changes of temperature and careful about sweaters and shawls, but now, weak with his heavy cold, he could not keep up with the climate. First the blazing sun would reduce him to a wet rag and then the roaring wind would chill him to the bone. At Zaghuan, the first stage of their journey to the west and the south, he arrived exhausted, and immediately prepared for bed at the inn. But the military, notified of their arrival, hospitably insisted on their moving to the encampment, and would take no refusal; not only so, but they proposed making a night of it in the Moorish cafés. And when the travelers pleaded fatigue, one of their hosts politely insisted on prolonging the evening in the camp, discussing Arab dialects and reading long extracts from his new book on the subject. When at last Gide was free to collapse into his canvas cot it was only to make the acquaintance of bedbugs, and he spent much of the remainder of the night outside the hut in the disembodied delirium of exhaustion.

On the following days they passed through Enfide and Kairwan, and when at last they reached Susa, where they were to dismiss their carriage and attendants, Gide was really sick and breathing with great difficulty. The doctor whom Laurens called in took a serious view of the case, but the prospect of death left Gide indifferent. He took the doctor's medicines but refused to stay in bed, preferring to wander feverishly about wrapped in his shawls. He wanted Laurens to go on with the trip alone, but of this his loyal friend would not hear, and for six days they rested at Susa.

It was here that occurred the first incident in fulfilment of his long-established secret desires. At certain hours Laurens went out on a painting expedition, and Gide, left to his own devices, would allow himself to be captured by

one of the Arab boys who hung about the door of the hotel
in hope of employment. One of their number, whom he
had already noticed as more reserved and attractive than
the others, led him one day into the dunes, and there the
puritan finally nerved himself to casting off his inhibitions.
That evening the lingering reverberations of his experience produced in him a state of exaltation which was not
lost on Laurens, though he was too discreet to comment.

They moved on to Biskra, destined to remain an earthly
paradise in Gide's imagination, and they decided to winter
there. The Hotel de l'Oasis put at their disposition an
apartment surrounded by terraces; it had been prepared
for the visit of a cardinal, and the cardinal's bed became
Gide's. Instead of taking their meals with the other guests
of the hotel they were served in their own dining room
by a young Arab named Athman, who also made himself
useful to them in other ways. He was honest, spoke
French, enjoyed the easy-going ways of his new masters,
and was a natural artist. One morning they found him
seated in the open air surrounded by a circle of alternate
vases of flowers and burning candles, busily shining their
shoes and singing something that sounded like a religious
chant.

Sometimes they separated in search of entertainment,
Laurens going with the doctor's wife to the newly opened
French casino and Gide preferring a dim Arab café that
Athman called "the little casino." And then there was the
"holy street" of the Oulad Nail, dancer-prostitutes of the
famous tribe that sends out its daughters at nubility to
earn their dowries; they danced in the cafés that were in
the same street, and at other times sat each in front of her
door, adorned like an idol in its niche. In this street Gide

wandered and looked and wondered, but preferred observation to participation.

His illness proved stubborn. The congestion seemed
finally to settle in a part of one lung and then, to the
stupefaction of the local practitioner, abruptly shifted to
the other. He was very weak, and even a few minutes of
piano playing made him breathless. One day he had a
hemorrhage, and Laurens, seriously alarmed, wrote to his
parents, who in turn communicated with Gide's mother.
And so it came about, to the consternation of the young
men, that a telegram arrived announcing that Madame
Gide and her elderly maid Marie were on their way.

By this time Gide was in much better condition, and
because of a treatment which he thought more efficacious
than the complicated prescriptions of the doctor. Paul
Laurens had come in one day in great excitement announcing that he had made contact with Meriem ben Atala, an
Oulad Nail, and that she was coming to the apartment
that night; she was to make her escape (for the Oulad,
though not difficult of access, were surrounded by regu-
lations) and meet Paul in a park. The young men gave
Athman an evening off and made great preparations, but
that night, after a long wait, Paul returned alone, and they
went to bed greatly downcast. Soon, however, they were
roused by a scratching at the window. It was Meriem; she
had been delayed, but had run into Athman, and he had
shown her the way to the apartment.

Gide had already seen Meriem dancing at a café in the
manner of the Oulad: hands moving, the torso erect and
motionless save for the tremors communicated to it by the
rhythmic stamping of the feet. But his eyes had been more
drawn by the boy Mohammed, one of the musicians, who

was banging his tambourine in a transport of lyricism and joy. And that night, with Meriem in his arms, it was of Mohammed that he thought. Yet the experiment was a success, and when the next morning Athman passed before the cardinal's bed with downcast eyes and a prudish "Good morning, Meriem," the needed comic touch was added. He was relaxed, his illness was almost forgotten, and life was good.

But his mother and Marie, inopportunely, were coming; what was to be done? Gide and Laurens took counsel, and agreed that come what might there was to be no change in their way of life and no concealment. And so it happened that Madame Gide and Marie arrived on a day when Meriem was expected. Gide kept his own door shut, Meriem went to Paul's room, and that night scandal did not break loose. But the next morning Madame Gide, up betimes, saw Meriem leaving, and shortly afterward she summoned her son for an accounting. Gide made no attempt at explanation or denial, and even insisted that if Meriem came for Paul she came also for himself sometimes. His mother's reaction was not indignation but tears, deep and long continued weeping that was harder for Gide to withstand than any anger; but he stood firm.

Whatever her horror at her son's behavior, Madame Gide had come to take care of him and to release Paul, and care for him she would. The prospect for Gide was not heartening, but out of consideration for his friend he was willing that she should stay. It was Paul who saved the day; again he would not hear of deserting André, so that in the end it was Madame Gide and Marie who packed and left.

The winter at Biskra passed, and new life stirred vaguely

in the oasis and in the awakened senses of Gide. Children played in the gardens, birds sang, the air was heavy with new perfumes, and Gide, emerging from the shadow of death, felt his heart tremulous with adoration for the spirit of life in nature. "Take me!" he cried, "take me wholly. I belong to you, I obey you, I abandon myself. In vain I have struggled against you, but now, your will be done. Take me." And with his face bathed in tears he entered into a new life. It was at once a resurrection and a religious conversion.

In the spring they planned to go to Tripoli by way of Malta, but on the first leg of the voyage they were so seasick that they decided on the much shorter crossing from Malta to Sicily. Through Syracuse and on to Naples and Rome they hurried, Gide still so encumbered by his habitual health precautions that he could enjoy nothing, regretting Biskra, almost ready to relapse into his illness. In Rome, still conscientiously in pursuit of release, they entertained "the lady," a woman of easy but expensive virtue. Gide, however, found her elegance and pretentiousness unbearable. Meriem was a little savage who made no pretense of romantic love, but with "the lady" he felt that he was profaning what was most sacred in his heart.

At Florence the two friends separated, and Gide went on to Geneva to consult Dr. Andreae, a friend of his uncle Charles Gide. The doctor quickly convinced him that his trouble was now chiefly a nervous disorder, and that what he needed was to stop coddling his body, take long walks, expose himself to sun and wind, and when he came to a body of water throw off his clothes and jump in. As a first step in the cure, he recommended a course of hydrother-

GIDE IN AFRICA

apy at Champel, to be followed by a winter in the mountains. Gide followed the prescription to the letter, with
the greatest benefit to his health. His *Nourritures terrestres*, that hymn of joy to the senses, had been germinating
within him since the spring in Biskra, but it was Dr.
Andreae, with his recommendation of meeting nature
freely and fearlessly, who made the book possible.

Between the cure at Champel and the winter in the
mountains Gide returned to Paris and Normandy. The literary circles were unchanged; the self-satisfied littérateurs
did not notice his fresh vitality and were as indifferent
to his new message as they had been to the old. Decidedly
the air of these salons was unbreathable, and to take his
final leave of all these men of letters (always excepting
the revered Mallarmé) he made a start on *Paludes*, so far
only vaguely considered; it included a passage unmistak-
ably in parody of Mallarmé, but offense was neither intended nor taken, and Gide remained on friendly terms
with the master until his death a year later.

He arrived in Normandy in time to be with Madeleine
through the last days of her sorely tried father, Gide's
uncle Émile. As they stood together at the deathbed he
felt that he was now her natural protector and took hope
for the future, for his adventures had not in any way
weakened the feeling he had long entertained for his
cousin.

In the fall he returned to Switzerland, not yet to his
proposed winter quarters but to Neuchâtel. He found a
room near the lake in a "temperance house" largely inhabited by old maids in straitened circumstances; in the
dining room a small card advertised "raspberry lemonade,"
and a much larger one declared "The Lord is my shepherd,

I shall not want," as if to serve notice that in this house spiritual consolations took definite precedence over mere earthly food. In spite of the austere setting, or because of it, Gide spent here some happy weeks, released from the old bondage to puritanism and not yet enslaved by his new god. He worked steadily on *Paludes*, although it no longer corresponded to his mood; read Leibnitz, Fichte, Lavater, a biography of Lessing; and for relaxation took long walks, not, as in later days, feverishly and goaded by a demon of unrest, but in relative tranquillity.

The autumn woods, the fall plowing, the walnut gathering turned his mind back with a pleasant nostalgia to similar seasons at La Rocque where, after a long walk, he used to change to slippers and settle down to tea before the fire in his favorite green armchair and with a volume of Dickens or George Eliot (in translation, for he did not yet read English); his mother too would be reading, casting her shadow across the big table; and only the welcome sound of the dinner bell would break the studious atmosphere. Were those days gone forever?

The pendulum had swung again, but with less than the usual accompaniment of remorse. God returned to the pages of the Journal—this time, however, more nearly on Gide's own terms. He aspired to an ethic of unity, and would have none of a God who could not be worshiped with his whole nature, with his body and its riotous urgings as well as in the piety of his soul. Desires, he wrote in his Journal, are natural, and "when the young soul has resisted them long enough to be rightly proud of itself, it should turn to silencing them or profiting from them, for there is profit in desires and profit in the satisfaction of desires; but what is not good is to excite desires by too long a resistance; for the soul is thereby disturbed." And again: "Laws and morality are for the state of childhood: education is an emancipation. . . . The wise man lives without morality, in accordance with his wisdom. We must try to arrive at the higher immorality. . . . You cannot lose God from sight, whichever way you turn. . . . *Take on as much humanity as possible.* That is the right formula."

There can be little doubt that Gide was sincerely searching for a satisfactory way of life on the basis of accepting desire, and the satisfaction of desire, as right, a part of nature and hence of God. And yet there is a rationalizing note in his arguments. He had been unable to keep his old rules of moral conduct, so now he said, "The wise man lives without morality"; when desires were too strong he told himself that prolonged resistance had a bad spiritual effect. And he did not always have the courage of his new convictions: "Lord, I must hide this from all others, but there are moments, hours, when everything in the world seems to me without order and lost, when every harmony that my mind invents falls apart, when even the thought of the search for a higher order is tedious. . . . At some moments I say to myself: I shall never find my way out. It is impossible. Lord, teach me!"

With the coming of winter he moved to La Brévine, a little village on an icy peak of the Jura Mountains, near the Franco-Swiss frontier, and settled down in three pleasant rooms of a farmhouse on the edge of the village. The snows and sub-zero temperatures did not bother him in the least. He faced the icy blasts to go out for his meals and at night slept with the window wide open, snugly wrapped and hooded and with his feet at a stove, and he thrived on the regime.

Here he finished his book, keeping almost wholly to himself—not on account of his work nor because of a preference for solitude, but through the unsociability of the inhabitants. Calls on the pastor and the doctor, with letters from Dr. Andreae, did not encourage him to repeat the experiment; the reserve of the villagers approached hostility, and he decided that Rousseau had invented nothing when he told of persecution by the stranger-hating people of this region. "Every Swiss," said Gide, "has a glacier within him."

But the opulently modeled Swiss girl who came to take care of his rooms seems to have been an exception to the national rule of ice within. While she was one day telling Gide at length all about her fiancé and he, unwisely, was tickling her neck with his pen, she suddenly collapsed in his arms, panting amorously; he managed to trundle her to the couch, and only escaped from her embraces by pretending to hear someone coming.

By the end of the year *Paludes* was finished, and in January 1895, after a short visit to his uncle Charles Gide in Montpellier, he set out again for North Africa, this time to Algiers. He was disappointed in the city, and Blida, a little to the southwest, at this season proved unattractive. The wind and the rain extinguished his ardor; he was lonely, and ready for home. He returned to Algiers, and three days later he packed and sent his luggage to the station. As he was standing in the foyer of the hotel awaiting his bill his eye chanced to fall on the slate which bore the names of the guests: the last two names were those of

Oscar Wilde and Lord Alfred Douglas. Immediately and instinctively he took up the sponge and effaced his own name from above them, then left for the station. But on the way he began to think that perhaps Wilde had already seen his name and would be hurt: for he was no longer the popular social lion of a few years before, but the subject of gossip, a man whom people avoided for fear of being compromised, and on the eve of his disastrous suit against Lord Alfred's father, the Marquess of Queensbury. Gide was in no mood for Wilde, but to disavow a friend whom it was compromising to know was the last thing of which he would care to be guilty. So he shipped his bags back to the hotel, and his name reappeared on the slate. But the full reasons for putting it back, and for rubbing it out in the first place, were obscure to him; he was acting more by instinct than reflection.

To Gide, Wilde seemed at this time to be a man under the cloud of an impending destiny: his laugh was loud and strained, his wit brittle, almost tragic. "I have gone as far as I can in my direction," he said, "I can go no farther. *Something* must happen." As for the egregious "Bosy," Gide failed to find him as beautiful as he appeared to the infatuated eyes of Wilde. He was brutal, cynical, and made atrocious scenes which Wilde endured meekly and with a look of dumb suffering.

The pair led Gide on a round of dubious cafés where hashish was smoked and where the principal attraction was beautiful boy musicians. In one place a languorous flute player caught Gide's attention. "Dear," whispered Wilde, "would you like the little musician?" Choked by emotion Gide managed to articulate "Yes." Some arrangements were concluded with a hideous go-between, and to the accompaniment of the diabolic laughter of Wilde, they wound through dark alleys and brightly lighted squares to a disreputable hotel where Gide spent the night with the flute player.

"Ah, from what a hell I was emerging," added Gide to his account of this lurid episode; he must have known that to his reader it would sound more like a descent into hell. But he was remembering the desperate summer of two years before when he had been writing *Le Voyage d'Urien*, and he had seen no escape from his solitary obsession but madness or death. Now at least he had broken from his imprisonment, had attached his passion to something outside of his fevered imaginings; if in the eyes of others his emancipation bore the name of perversion, in his own it was nature.

Shortly after this night, Wilde left for London where his fate awaited him, and Gide, anxious to shake off Douglas, set out for the deliciously remembered Biskra. But on the way, at Setif, a telegram from Bosy urged him to wait; he was on his way with his latest fancy, a sixteen-year-old Arab boy. Gide, always liable to irrational reactions and curious about the boy, waited, and later accompanied Douglas and his companion to Biskra. But if he yielded to curiosity and the perversity of doing what he had just been trying to avoid, his moral reflexes were soon back in order, and he found Bosy, with his poetic affectations and the obsessive return of his conversation to the subject of homosexuality, intolerable. He preferred to go on long walks, by himself or in the company of his old friend Athman; and sometimes he remained in his room and worked, with a feeling of virtuous superiority.

He played with the idea of taking Athman back to

France with him, and even suggested it to the young Arab, who was overjoyed; but the reaction from home was not encouraging. His mother not only objected herself, but marshaled in support of her opinion that of other relatives, and even of old Marie the maid, who wrote him that on the day Athman should set foot in their house she would leave it forever. Gide yielded, and Athman's disappointment was acute; on the day his patron left he disappeared and, as the train left Biskra, Gide saw him sitting on the dunes beside the track, his face in his hands and the picture of despair.

Unable yet to tear himself away from North Africa, Gide dallied further days in Algiers; but at last the frenzied appeals of his mother, urging him to "break off" (she thought he had a mistress) succeeded in their aim, and he left for Paris, where he arrived two weeks before she planned to leave for La Rocque.

Relations between mother and son had come to such a critical pass—she always trying to keep him in line, supervising his conduct and all details of his life, doling him out an allowance, he struggling always for more independence—that both were aware of the need for conciliation and compromise, with the result that the two weeks of life together in Paris brought more peaceful relations than they had known for a long time. She did not, it is true, approve of the title *Les Nourritures terrestres,* already selected for the newly planned book—perhaps she would have preferred something like *Bread of Heaven;* but she heroically refrained from personal criticism, and he in his turn, having been away from her so much, was able to view her with more tolerance and show her the affection which constantly underlay his irritations.

Then she left for La Rocque, and Gide went to visit a friend. They were to meet at La Rocque in July, but before that time a telegram from Marie informed him that his mother had had a serious attack. Gide found her in the large room which he used to use as a study, propped up in bed but incapable of clear speech and only vaguely aware of her surroundings. The habits of a lifetime were still strong upon her however—the obsession of things to be done, arrangements to be made, advice to be given. And before her she had a large notebook on which she constantly traced indecipherable scrawls with a pencil; when her son, thinking to give her rest, took the book and pencil away, her fingers continued the writing motion on the sheets. She could not let go of the dutiful activities which had been her life.

Some years before, when she had been trying to introduce him to "society"—her society, not the world of artists and writers which he would have preferred—Gide had been struck by how easily, naturally, and sensibly, by contrast with some others in the salon, including himself, she played her role; and on coming out he told her so, impulsively. She said nothing at the time, but that evening she allowed herself a rare moment of sentiment. "Was it true, what you said to me?" she asked. "Was I—all right?" And on his redoubled assurances she continued, "If only your father, just once, could have told me—" tears checked her, but at last she brought out, "—that he was pleased with me."

Thinking of these things, and of the unremitting effort which her life had been to serve and to bring the best according to her lights to those about her, and how they had taken her for granted; remembering how those fingers, now scrabbling senselessly at the sheets, had once run so lightly on the piano, and how, in her own way, she had loved all the arts but had been too busy with her self-imposed duties to give them the attention she would have enjoyed—thinking of all this Gide was overwhelmed with tears, not from a feeling of personal loss but from a sense of sublimity.

The death of his mother left him in a state of moral exaltation not unmixed with panic. The restrictions against which he had chafed were gone, the liberty which he had been pursuing was suddenly in his hands, and "terrifying," as he said in his *Nourritures terrestres*, "is a liberty no longer guided by duty." No sooner was she gone than the duty of service which she had represented seemed desirable, necessary; he wanted to strip himself, to give. The estate at La Rocque, now his, comprised six farms and large areas of woods, and extended over several communes. He would have liked to give it all away, but that would not have been her way; he must accept it as a trust, an obligation to serve. Other things, however, he could give: the jewels, the little mementos of his mother that he would have liked to keep, and all the more for that reason, he sent in various directions, some to distant relatives who certainly could have cared little to have them.

Now more than ever Madeleine was necessary to him, for she represented attachment to family and home, and his love for her was part filial, part protective, part comradely: he wanted to come back to her and lay his head in her lap, and at the same time he wanted to shelter her; again he wanted to share with her all his experiences, show her the things he had seen, go out with her, as on those early morning walks in the woods, hand in hand on an

ever fresh voyage of discovery—not discovery of the physical world alone, but of a way of life, of the truth, of God.
No danger seemed too great, no obstacle too high, for his
present ardor.

The situation was now more favorable to his hopes than
at the time of his first rejection. His mother, alarmed by
the apparent wildness of her son and impressed by the
contrasting constancy of his devotion to his cousin, had
begun to think that perhaps Madeleine after all would be
his best anchor, and while he had been away she had come
to consider her a daughter. Uncles and aunts too showed
themselves less opposed than they had been. As for Madeleine herself, Gide had never doubted that she loved him,
and he had convinced himself that she needed him even
more than he needed her. Bit by bit the remaining difficulties were overcome, persistence won the day, and Madeleine consented. On October 8, 1895, they were married
and set out on travels that were to cover much of Gide's
itinerary of the past two years.

He has left us in no doubt as to what was in his mind
when he took the crucial step of marrying his cousin, nor
as to the outcome.

He had wanted to break with his puritan past, he had
cut himself adrift, and the result, though exhilarating, had
been frightening. Now he wanted to come back to safety,
reattach himself, and yet without the sacrifice of his hard
won freedom; the dilemma was to be solved by marrying
Madeleine and setting out again, but this time with her
support and companionship. Not for a moment did he
suppose that she would countenance his homosexuality,
nor did he want her to. He was making a choice in favor
of what, despite his emancipation, he considered the better

side of his nature, with which her image was associated.
For her he would sacrifice his abnormality; the freedom
which he sought and to which he wanted to initiate her
was to be of a moral sort and yet was not to involve "immorality." How he was to achieve this somewhat paradoxical objective was not clear in his own mind. "A fatality
was leading me," he wrote at the close of the story of his
youth, "perhaps also the secret need to defy my nature;
for in Emmanuèle was it not virtue itself that I loved?
She was the heaven that my insatiable hell was marrying.
. . . I thought that I could give myself to her wholly, and
I did so without reserve."

Before marriage Gide consulted a specialist on sexual
problems, telling him both of his homosexual proclivities
and of his love and desire to marry. The doctor reassured
him. "Get married without any hesitation," he said. "You
will quickly discover that all the rest exists only in your
imagination."

But the specialist was wrong; Gide's marriage was never
consummated. "The spiritual strength of my love," he
wrote long years later, after his wife had died, "inhibited
all carnal desire. I was able to prove elsewhere that I was
not incapable of the urge (I mean of the procreative urge)
but on the condition that nothing intellectual or sentimental should be mixed with it."

At no time in their marriage was there any discussion of
the situation; it merely existed in silence. It did not occur
to the young husband that he was depriving his wife of
anything, for despite his efforts to free himself from puritanism, despite the latitude of conduct he had allowed
himself, sex was evil in his eyes and desire was inconceiv-
able in the virtuous women he had known: his mother,

Miss Shackleton, his aunt Claire, Madeleine herself. From her there was never a word of complaint. The most she permitted herself was a touch of gentle irony such as she showed on one occasion when Gide was reading her the manuscript of his *Immoraliste* and came to the sentence, "Marceline confessed to me *(m'avoua)* that she was pregnant," and Madeleine interrupted him. "My friend," she said with a tender smile, "that is not a *confession,* it is at the most a *confidence;* one *confesses* what is reprehensible; what you want here is 'confided to me' *(me confia).*" And her suggestion was incorporated in the published work.

Not until after her death in 1938 did he fully realize that his wife had had a normal woman's desire for the physical love of her husband and for the children that would have followed. Such advances as her modesty permitted she had made, and when they met with no response she blamed herself for not being sufficiently attractive.

On October 23 Gide wrote to his friend Jammes that after the difficult period of his engagement he was beginning one of "indefatigable repose, beside the most tranquil of wives." But he soon found out that however tranquil his wife might be, he himself could not long remain so, and with the discovery began the opening of his eyes to another mistake in the assumptions on which his marriage had been based.

He had known that Madeleine was frail and timorous, but that had been part of her attraction for him: he wanted to drag her from her hiding place, give her courage and vitality, make her live. He did not realize that what she needed first of all was security, and he had no conception of the depth and tenacity of her instinct of retreat.

The physical and moral adventures he offered did not stimulate, they froze her, made her instantly want to protect herself against them.

A revealing incident occurred while they were still in Switzerland and Gide had managed to persuade her to accompany him on an excursion in the mountains. At one dangerous stretch on the snowy mountainside, where the narrow footing overhung a precipitous drop and they were traveling in single file roped to their guides ahead and behind, Madeleine insisted on holding her stick on the precipice side, thereby endangering both herself and those to whom she was tied, and no remonstrance from her husband or the guides could make her change; she simply had to have something between herself and the void. If a device of self-protection proved more dangerous than meeting the threat directly, there was no help for it; she stubbornly clung to apparent safety. And so it was in moral situations: before anything shocking or painful or brutal her first reaction was retreat; she affected not to see, she averted her eyes.

But they were eyes that had already seen much. They had seen that her husband, bored and restless in Switzerland, suddenly came to life when their carriage drove into the towns of Italy and was surrounded by troops of boys. Gide was not anxious to discuss his abnormal inclinations, and if Madeleine chose to pretend not to notice his reaction to the Italian boys he was quite content to follow her lead and pretend there was nothing to notice. And so the long and painful comedy began, in which Gide was deceived by his own acting of his role. Nearly twenty years later he thought, or said that he thought, that she knew nothing of his homosexuality. Not until after her death did he realize that she must have known almost from the start, but had preferred to avert her eyes.

They arrived in Florence in radiant weather, but in the night a violent thunderstorm came up with wind and hail, against which the early morning bells of the Advent season could scarcely be heard. Chilly overcast days followed and Gide, always adversely affected by the disappearance of the sun, relapsed into lassitude. He dutifully trailed around the museums with his wife but reacted tepidly to the paintings; in the Santa Maria Novella he found nothing to admire, and the guide was unbearable. In the next few days conversations with Roberto Gatteschi and d'Annunzio afforded some diversion, and Donatello's nude bronze of David aroused his enthusiasm. But by December 31 he was gloomy again, depressed by the short days, the black cypresses, the bare boughs of the other trees. He wished that the little cloister of San Marco had been full of roses, and dreamed of the African sun: "Obsessions of the Orient, of the desert with its ardor and emptiness, of the shade of the palm gardens, of the loose white clothes—obsessions in which the senses go mad and the nerves become exasperated, and which at the beginning of every night make me think sleep impossible."

It was New Year's Eve. Madeleine, tired and unwell, went to bed early, but Gide, unable to sit still, went out for one of his solitary rambles and yielded to his mania for trailing some youths who had caught his eye. It was a first step toward admission that he could not change his nature, and that evening reaction set in. Friends came in, there were noisy games, and every sound stabbed him with remorse at the thought of Madeleine, deserted and unwell. "Instead of this dancing and shouting at the approach of this particularly moving time I longed for prayers together, a service, or simply a serious waiting. . . . What was Em. thinking of all this while?"

At Rome the step foreshadowed at Florence was taken. In the public squares young male models offered themselves for hire to artists, and Gide, leaving Madeleine to make the round of the sights by herself, had some of them come up to his apartment on the pretext of "artistic photographs." At first he really did take pictures, carefully explained to his wife why he wanted to take them, and showed her some of his first prints. But she did not care to look at them. She was not deceived, nor were the models, and soon the pretext was abandoned.

On January 19, 1896, he wrote to Jammes, "Rome is still the horrible city, where life seems more unbearable than elsewhere. However," he added—was it from a deceitful loyalty or was it the truth?—"this year, thanks to my wife, I am standing it fairly well."

He was restless again, and nothing would do but to push on to North Africa and show its marvels to Madeleine, with stops along the way at Naples and Syracuse. Tunis in its winter green seemed wonderful once more, but in the evenings he deserted Madeleine and wandered through somber native cafés where there were boy musicians and the obscene pantomimes of the traditional Caracous.

And so it went. Two years before, it had been he who dragged limply from place to place and Madeleine, well at home, had been worried about him. Now he was filled with insatiable energy and Madeleine was ailing. On this journey he did not sufficiently learn his lesson, for the next year they were together at Ravello, she keeping to her room in the hotel and he trying to exhaust his energy by

overlong walks in the mountains. "Em. is still languishing," he wrote to his friend Eugène Rouart, "and I am
particularly anxious because she is beginning to be resigned to it and does not seem to remember that one can
be in better health." Later in the year, on leaving Alençon
after a visit to Madeleine's married sister, he wrote to the
same correspondent, "Em. tries to hold back her tears and
succeeds only at the price of giving herself a sick head-
ache."

In the end he had to yield to the evidence: this companion, without whom his experiences seemed incomplete,
was disturbed and distressed by travel. Not in Italy, nor
North Africa, not even at La Rocque, could she be her
quietly radiant self, but only on her home ground of
Cuverville. Eventually they settled down to what was to
be their characteristic arrangement: she busying herself
steadily and cheerfully at her Cuverville duties, he standing it for as long as he could and then setting out again
on his travels, alone or with a male companion.

He would have felt easier about departure if Madeleine could have brought herself to approve, to bid him
Godspeed; but that she could not do. Of his leaving for
the trip that was to result in *Renoncement au voyage* he
wrote (a year after the event): "So I resolved to set out.
I nearly killed myself in explanations to justify my conduct; to set out was not enough, I had to have Em. approve
of my departure. I ran against a hopeless wall of indifference. Or no, I did not run against it, I sank, I lost footing,
I was swallowed up. . . . A deplorable misunderstanding
[was] caused by this deliberate (and yet almost unconscious) abnegation (I can find no other word) on the part
of Em. It contributed not a little to my demoralization."

In a considerably later incident of the same sort her self-abnegation was less effortless: "A few words from Em. plunge me back into a sort of despair. As I finally make up my mind to speak to her of the plan for spending the winter in Saint-Clair, she says: 'Yes, *I owe you that*,' with such an effort of her whole being, which at once makes her face so sad, so grave, that I immediately give up this project like so many others."

So he got out of the way of discussing his movements with her. He simply left, a little remorseful at the tears his departure called forth but secretly happy to be away; and he returned with an equal though different kind of joy.

Divergences in ideas also early appeared. While they were still in Switzerland the review *L'Ermitage* asked him for a contribution and he responded with a piece later incorporated in *Les Nourritures terrestres*. In it Ménalque, a character invented by Gide to be the prophet of his gospel of nonattachment, told of his years of vagabondage and inveighed against the attachments of home, love, friendship: "Families, I hate you! closed homes, shut doors, possessions jealous of happiness." The piece appeared in January 1896, and Gide called it to the attention of Jammes, who reacted at once.

Jammes had a childlike nature, and when he was not in the depths of depression he could be charming, bubbling over with good humor and authentic wit. But he was supremely confident of his own gifts and would keep repeating, in effect, "I am a poet, a poet! Isn't it wonderful? I am a poet!" and anyone who did not at once recognize his superiority thereby revealed himself as an envious dunce. "Aren't you irritated," he wrote to Gide, "at this string of grotesque nonentities who trail after us, these

Paris types that one finds in Bordeaux too? . . . these crea-
tors of new art, these individuals who snivel their emptiness in crazy rhymes. . . . It's pitiful. Talent? Go on! Only
You, Griffin, Régnier, and I know what talent is. . . . And
Mallarmé, because he stirred up the ideas of the age"—
the persons mentioned being precisely those who had
praised his own *Un Jour,* whose publication Gide had
paid for.

Jammes was in fact a very gifted and original poet, but
it was a little annoying to keep hearing him say so. He
was incapable of accepting the slightest criticism of his
own work, in prose or in verse, but was always ready with
tactless comment on the shortcomings of others. Perhaps
his lack of a detached critical faculty was a part of his
being a fine lyric poet, but in the realm of ideas, to which
Gide's tale invited him, he was sadly deficient. He had
surrounded himself with a series of clichés and stock symbols, a troop of household divinities to which he paid un-
critical homage: "my old pipe," "my faithful dog," "the
solitude of my woods," Motherhood, the Pure Fiancée,
the Devoted Young Wife, Innocent Childhood (bodied
forth by nephews and nieces in their better moments);
among these fetishes, and on the same footing, God himself took his place—not the serious God of later days, after
Claudel had worked over him, but a *bon Dieu portatif,* as
Gide called him, a portable divinity that was a projection
of his own emotional satisfaction with things as he found
them.

With this character and this mental furniture, Jammes
naturally bounded with indignation on reading Gide's
"Ménalque"; he sat down at once to write a reproving
letter to his friend, in which he professed to believe that

Gide was presenting Ménalque ironically, with tacit disapproval, but whose indignant tone belied his own as-
sumption. Not content with this, he wrote a reply to
Ménalque for the *Ermitage*, where it duly appeared; and
in both the letter and the article he called himself, somewhat paradoxically, the "faun," and Gide the "shepherd."

Thus Gide began his career of idol smashing, calling
forth at the outset the furious protests of the defenders of
tradition. And it is interesting to note that to his reply to
Jammes, full of an affectionate good humor of which
Jammes in like case would have been incapable, Madeleine added a word in her own hand: "Good faun, thank
you! The wife of the shepherd salutes you." Thus at the
beginning of their marriage she marked an implicit resistance to any tendency on the part of her husband to
flout ideals to which, once and for all, she had given her
allegiance.

The incident, however, is exceptional; more typically she
received his books, as she did his first one, with no comment whatsoever. And she once said to a cousin, "I do not
think I have the right to influence in any way his thought
and would reproach myself if I thought that out of regard
for me André did not write exactly what he thought he
ought to write."

In the spring of 1896, the wedding trip over, they were
back in La Rocque, Gide's childhood home—once a refuge,
now a care. He did not want to know its boundaries, not
because they would have limited him and made him desire more, but because to have a private claim on nature
seemed somehow wrong. He was walking in the garden
one day with Eugène Rouart and Madeleine when Robidet, the overseer whom he had inherited with the estate

from his mother and who, like most of the Normans of the vicinity, was motivated solely by material interests and a respect for a set of closely associated proprieties, approached with the triumphant news that Gide had been elected mayor of the commune. It had not happened by accident; Robidet—not disinterestedly, for he hoped to be the power behind the throne—had been working toward that end for some months, and waiting only until Gide should reach the legal minimum age of twenty-five (as he had the previous November) and until the previous incumbent should retire. Rouart, practical and politically minded, at once foresaw for his friend a career: mayoralty, General Council of the Department, Chamber of Deputies —it was all clear and practically inevitable. The overseer, watching Gide and expecting to see his face light up with excitement and ambition, was astonished to observe that it was becoming progressively more downcast; that there was such a thing as a disinterested love of nature and that it could be threatened by such axiomatically desirable things as power and possessions were ideas beyond the range of his comprehension. Madeleine understood much better, but with her the sense of duty was paramount; André, she urged, owed it to the common good to accept the post. And Gide, vulnerable from that angle, reluctantly yielded. For three years he conscientiously carried out his duties, but at the end of that time his disenchantment was complete. Continually torn between what seemed to him naturally right and customs rooted in the sense of private ownership, he could see about him in his small commune nothing but greed and alcoholism. And his sorry cares interfered with his true work, his writing.

For by this time he was really launched on his life work.

The pale foreshadowings of his early writings were ready to assume the firmer outlines of his mature thought. His major steps in education—by books and by life—had been taken. He had a stock of material that was to last him for a decade and out of which were to come many of his best books. He had found a measure of freedom and he had voluntarily limited it by coming home and by marrying, and in so doing he had, with his customary reaction, made freedom seem more desirable, and supplied himself with a unifying theme for his work: the conflict between spontaneity and discipline, between the God of Nature and the God of Christianity, between self-assertion and self-loss.

5

To an Unknown God

THE NEXT FEW YEARS WERE CHIEFLY SPENT AT LA ROCQUE, with breaks at his apartment in Paris. Despite the cares of his estate and his duties as mayor, it was on the whole a happy time. The main dwelling at La Rocque was a château dating in part from the sixteenth century, surrounded by a moat but with the drawbridge permanently down. Here he delighted to receive and entertain friends: Henri Ghéon (for many years his most intimate companion), Rouart, the composer Raymond Bonheur, Marcel Drouin (a close friend since childhood who became the husband of Madeleine's sister Jeanne), the young Belgian writer André Ruyters, Francis Jammes (whose acquaintance in the flesh he and Madeleine had finally made at Biskra through the good offices of their common friend Rouart). The visit of Jammes in the fall of 1898 was long and happily anticipated; he was to meet the Gides at Alençon, where they would be visiting the Drouins, and together they would proceed to La Rocque. In his letter of plans Gide wrote: "If the sky is not too overcast, the moon which will then be half-full will encourage us to arrive at night; marvelous will be the entry into this deep country; the dogs will bark, not recognizing us; the people from the farm will hurry up with lights; you will say 'My dear Gide, ah!' and I will embrace you, and I shall be deeply moved, if I weren't so much so already in advance."

The visit proved to be momentous in more ways than one. According to Jammes's somewhat embroidered account a wasp nest hung from the ceiling of the drawing room, left there out of respect for animal life, and in his isolated turret room he claimed to have found a young owl nestled in his slipper. There were half a dozen guests besides himself, most of them young men of letters, and the days passed in literary or political talk, music, trout fishing, mushroom gathering, long walks, drives to Trouville, games. One of their amusements, at which Jammes (and not by his own testimony alone) was particularly proficient, was inventing new names for things and finding unusual analogies: a peach with an ugly insect hole, for example, he proclaimed to be exactly like the curé's ear— to the scandal but amusement of Gide's elderly Aunt Claire. And on one of their long walks they visited an abandoned domain which inspired Jammes's fine Fourth Elegy, and, several years later, Gide's *Isabelle*.

Gide was happy in these years because he was productive; except for travel notes, his Journal, repository of his hesitations and broodings, was suspended until 1902, the best of his writing energy going into creative work. Between 1896 and 1902 he wrote *Les Nourritures terrestres*, two plays, *Philoctète*, *Le Prométhée mal enchaîné*, and *L'Immoraliste*, besides *El Hadj* and other echoes of travel, and considerable criticism. And in all of this work his seriousness of purpose—even in the humorous *Prométhée*

—is noteworthy; through it all one can see his intense preoccupation with his search for a philosophy of life. "You are too grave," wrote Jammes after their meeting in Biskra. "I am not so grave. I admire you. You are a sort of monk. Your arms and your head thrown back are as if you were reading a work of piety." Gide himself became aware of the effect his austere appearance made on others, of how they felt a certain constraint in his presence and were careful about too great license of speech—and this despite his occasional real joyousness. In one of his acute self-estimates he called himself "a small boy amusing himself, combined with a Protestant minister who bores him."

With his propensity for seeing simultaneously two sides to every question, perhaps too with the fondness of his German masters for *das Problem,* Gide's seriousness took the form of thinking in terms of a succession of antinomies. First it was sincerity and morality: how could one honestly represent one's inmost nature and at the same time not offend against the principle of self-subordination to a larger good? Then the terms shifted a little and the opposition was between liberty and culture, for society, and for the individual between spontaneity and discipline. And a third transformation of the problem confronted art and realism, art appearing as a constraint imposed upon the raw material of reality. But through all these shifts in formulation he was searching for an ethic and a sanction: he needed a God to explain and to justify a way of life.

Les Nourritures terrestres, published in 1897 and the doctrinal point of departure of his series of speculations, was not conceived and planned in advance but grew out of notations of experience during the years 1895 and 1896.

As a record of development it has an autobiographical character and indeed parallels many passages of the Journal which preceded it; and yet the "I" of the book does not quite coincide with Gide (as he warned in the preface to the 1927 edition); it is rather an offshoot of his nature, almost a character in a novel. Gide is behind the "I," tacitly; it is as though he said, "These have been my experiences, and this is what they mean; this, accentuated, is where they would lead." "Ménalque"—that Virgilian name so thoroughly appropriated by Gide that its French form seems more appropriate for our purposes—is not Gide either: he is a further accentuation; he is to the explicit "I" what that "I" is to the author.

The book developed into a manual of emancipation; to Nathanael, the imaginary young reader to whom it is addressed, Gide said in effect: "This has been your servitude and this is your way of escape. But when you have delivered yourself, throw away this book. You must not obtain freedom from one master at the price of giving yourself another." And he followed his own advice. Before the book was finished he had voluntarily surrendered a part of the liberty he had been seeking and was examining with detachment the possible destination of his trend.

In the *Nourritures* Gide looks back on his initial state of torpor and recognizes that through it all a new life was developing obscurely within him, like a chrysalis in a cocoon. Then he traveled, he fell sick, and in his convalescence the new life broke out of the cocoon. With fresh awareness of the physical world, he reëxamines his old insensibility, and the causes that led to it. There was his puritanism, from which he must escape by suppressing in himself the idea of merit—that "great stumbling block for the spirit"; by acting without an advance judgment as to whether the act is good or bad; by embracing desire and cultivating fervor, instead of considering them temptations and trying to conquer them. A further bond he must cast off is studious abstraction; now he must "wash himself from the contamination of books."

Yet he carries over into his new state his inalienable seriousness. He will not be a mere sensualist, for, as he was to write a few years later, sensuality "consists simply in considering as an end and not as a means the present object and the present minute"; joy is not to be considered as a relaxation of effort but as a new duty. The comparatively trivial occasion of a desire must not be allowed to limit one's fervor, which must be transferable and unending. And what is this burning, transcending love of all things but God himself?: "Do not distinguish God from happiness"—"God is what is ahead of us"—"Understand that at each instant of the day you can possess God in his totality." His conceptions no less than his sensations must be enlarged: "Do not seek, Nathanael, to find God elsewhere than everywhere." To search for God is to hold oneself perpetually stripped of attachments, ever ready for new departures.

But this ardor cannot, he realizes, be in fact unending: it is essentially a product of youth "which man possesses only for a time and the rest of the time recalls." There is also such a thing as coming too late to the feast: "Spoiled fruit! you have filled our mouths with a poisonous insipidity and you have deeply disturbed my soul." And endless desire, endless wanderings, can bring a longing for rest: "Oh! for an immense repose, I long for salutary death. . . . Desire! Desire! What can I do to you, what will you have? Will you never be weary?" "All humanity wearies itself between thirst for sleep and thirst for pleasure . . . like a sick man turning in his bed for relief from suffering."

At the close of the book Gide is back at home; his intoxicating sensations and his delirious desires are the figments of a dream that is past. Now he is faced with "convictions that are too great; anguish of thought. What shall I say? *True things*." And he realizes the danger of egoism in his doctrines: "OTHERS—the importance of their lives; to speak to them."

In a "Hymn in the Guise of a Conclusion," dedicated to "M.A.G." (his wife, who after her marriage signed herself "Madeleine André Gide"), "she" meditates on the stars, which burn with ardor but follow each its ordained course in intimate dependence upon the others. The fervor which he has been advocating can only be maintained, he suggests, by following one's destiny with gladness and recognizing one's relation to others.

Jammes—somewhat surprisingly, considering his earlier reaction to the piece about Ménalque—was the first to see in the *Nourritures* something more than a hymn to Pan: "Never had I dreamed of a less pagan work. Never had one reached such a degree of almost religious abnegation. . . . Each of your thoughts carried in itself, DIRECTLY, its own refutation. . . . Neither the appreciations I have been able to read of your book nor what I have thought others might think of it can change my impression. . . . I have the very clear feeling that I can only read it in reverse, as if I were turning each page up to a glass to read it from right to left. It's strange. I read *another book*." But Jammes was not insensitive to the anti-Christian aspect of the *Nourritures*, for he wrote later: "You have sacrificed the beauty of your soul to a burst of anger which the fierce dogma of theologians had built up in you. . . . Why have you spoiled (if I dare say so) your book by geometrically religious arguments which should be left to Richepin? Don't you believe that our souls expect of you consolation? Why this childish exaggeration?" Gide was much struck by these comments at the time, and thirty years later confirmed them in his preface to the new edition by calling attention to his early exaggerations and insisting that they carried with them their own refutation.

Also deeply impressive was Wilde's injunction, after reading the *Nourritures*, never to write "I" again; Gide mentioned it in a letter written in 1897, and said further: "It is very hard for me to talk to you about myself. . . . *I* does not exist any more. . . . What I was looking for in the pages of my *Nourritures* has come, a blessed state: I am nothing more than comprehension, affection, passion, sensation, even action, a work to write, and anything else you choose—to all this I no longer oppose myself, I don't oppose myself to myself and for that reason I say that I am no more: I live in the third person." The state of mind which he is here struggling to express (with abundant use of the first personal pronoun) and which he admits to be a tendency rather than an achievement, is a subject to which he was frequently to recur later—in passages of the Journal, for example, in the *Symphonie pastorale*, in *Dostoevsky*. And in "Printemps," a piece first published in 1941, he says: "As soon as the air is sufficiently mild and the sky blue, I want to evaporate into the whole of nature, carried off by the passing breeze, floating here and there without further ties. Oh to be only somewhere, to be only someone!"

The state is sufficiently recognizable and could be called, somewhat paradoxically, an impersonal emotion, achieved by a displacement of the sense of self from the instrument of enjoyment (the body) to a larger entity of which the true "I" is a part. In this way, from this new vantage point, one can see one's body, one can understand one's human destiny, as things for which the larger "I" has responsibility, but which do not constitute its identity, to which it is not irrevocably attached. The charm of this nature mysticism for Gide (and perhaps for anyone) is that it is a form of self-loss, of escape from the burdens of individuality.

Criticism of his doctrine of following desire, subordinated and almost hidden in *Les Nourritures terrestres*, is uppermost in Gide's next work and first play *Saül*, begun before publication of the *Nourritures*, but—his hopes for an immediate performance having been disappointed—not published until 1903. It carries the story of Saul, first king of Israel, from shortly after his anointing to his death, and includes the incidents of the slaying of Goliath, the love of David and Jonathan, and the consulting of the witch of Endor; the drama is furnished by the mysterious fatality hanging over the king, preventing realization of the hopes he had aroused at the time of his anointing. The "secret of the king," about which people whisper and laugh, though nowhere explicitly revealed, is clearly homosexuality: Saul hates his queen and kills her, is somberly attracted by the youthful David and jealous of the more than fraternal love of David and Jonathan. This aspect of the play is interesting as representing Gide's first cautious step toward frankness on homosexuality, but by no means constitutes the chief significance of the play. As Saul himself says: "They want to know my secret; but do I know it myself? I have several." The central situation, to which homosexuality is only accessory, is revealed by the king in the first act. Recalling the days of his happiness and success he says: "Every morning the priest told me what I was to do: that was the whole future, and I knew what it was. I made the future. The Philistines came, I became anxious, I wanted to question God myself; and from that time God ceased to speak." In other words, and to generalize the problem, as long as one believes in a revealed and organized religion and trusts its authorized representatives, life is simple and duty clear; it is when this naïve dependence no longer satisfies and we seek the truth for ourselves that God eludes our grasp and troubles begin.

Deprived of his support in the prophet Samuel and unable to find God for himself, Saul finds himself in a state of brooding vacancy which makes him an easy prey to the demons—grotesque, facetious imps who recall their originals in the medieval mystery play and who represent anger (or madness), lust, fear (or doubt), domination, vanity (or immodesty), and Legion, who summarizes all the rest; by his mistaken kindness to what at first seem like weak and shivering creatures Saul gives them power over him, and ceases to be master in his own house. The moral of the situation is spoken by the dying witch of Endor: "Close your door! shut your eyes! stop your ears—and let the fragrance of love . . . no longer find access to your heart. Everything that charms you is hostile to you. . . . Deliver yourself, Saul!"

The play contains only the statement of a problem, not its solution. Its significance lies in its being the antiphon of the *Nourritures:* the earlier work had shown the tyranny of puritanism and had extolled desire, and *Saül* pointed out that desire too can become a master. Where, it asks in effect, will a liberty "no longer guided by duty" lead? Can God be found outside of the formal religion which reason and the senses alike reject?

Similar problems are raised in two pieces published in 1899: *El Hadj* and *Philoctète. El Hadj*, the "treatise of the false prophet," is based on a true incident which Gide turned into a parable for his own ends. It tells of a prince who leads his people into the desert in search of a paradise. He rides in an enclosed litter to which only El Hadj, a singer and teller of tales, has access. At last they come to the shores of a sea, beyond which, they feel sure, must lie the promised paradise, but on the orders of El Hadj they camp for the night without approaching the sea. And in the night El Hadj reconnoiters: the water is an illusion, merely the salt bed of a vanished lake. The prince dies, and El Hadj, concealing the fact from the people, leads them back to fertility and civilization by means of the empty litter; it is he now, El Hadj, who has become the prophet and who leads the people in full awareness that he is deceiving them. "I know now," he says, "that if there are prophets it is because they have lost their God. If it were not that He is silent, of what use would be our words?"

The piece was an experiment in a poetic prose form, and it utilized, in addition to the incident on which it was founded, Gide's recollection of the Chott el Djerid, near Tunis, for the vanished lake. The allegorical intent is surely pessimistic: it seems to mean that the other world is an illusion, that God is gone, and that one is caught between the equally undesirable alternatives of pursuing a soul-fortifying but in the end fruitless march into the desert, or abandoning aspirations and returning to the fleshpots.

A more hopeful view of the unseen order appears in *Philoctète,* the "treatise on the three moralities." It is a tale in dramatic form based on the classical legend of Philoctetes, the Greek archer who set out for the Trojan War bearing the bow and poisoned arrows of Hercules, and who, having accidentally wounded himself with one of the arrows, becomes unfit for service and is abandoned by the others on an island. In Gide's story, Ulysses and Neoptolemus return to the island to obtain by stealth the bow and arrows without which, they have discovered, the Trojan War cannot be won. But Philoctetes, unseen, over-hears their plan, and at the end freely gives up his bow and arrows. He has meanwhile explained the changes which have come over him in his solitude. "The man who lives among others," he says, "is incapable of a pure and truly disinterested act"; alone, he has learned the beauty of behavior without ulterior motive. The cries which the pain of his wound caused and which were intolerable to the other Greeks have become, since there has been no one else to hear them, disinterested and consequently beautiful. Every day, moreover, he has become less a Greek and more a man. The three moralities whose ex-istence he now recognizes are three devotions: to Greece, to the gods, to what is above the gods. Devotion to Greece is devotion to other men, "of all forms the most sense-less," for in sacrificing oneself for other men one does it with a feeling of merit, with a sense of superiority to them. To make the gods the object of devotion is still to limit oneself to Greece; for the gods are a national appanage, a projection of Greek aspirations, and as such limited and partisan. The devotion to what is above the gods now alone claims the allegiance of Philoctetes, but when asked what it is that is above the gods he can only say: "There is . . . I don't know any more. I don't know. . . . Ah! ah! Oneself! . . . I don't know how to talk any more, Neoptolemus." The suggestion "oneself" is allowed to pass by Neoptolemus, and Philoctetes does not return to it; later he professes complete inability to explain: "I devote myself, but it is not for the fatherland . . . it is for something else, understand; it is for—what? I do not know."

The obscure aspiration of Philoctetes comes close to being devotion for its own sake. The precise object of his veneration may not be known, but belief in it produces a psychological effect almost as definite as a sensation. The service to "what is above the gods" demands total disinterestedness, the abandonment of all attachments; when this requirement has been met, the painful but precious ego is displaced, and one emerges into a larger being. Whether or not the intellect can frame a satisfactory definition of this devotion is irrelevant; to possess the state is enough. For Philoctetes the last attachment is to his bow and arrows; when they are gone he achieves serenity, and nature itself bears witness to the truth of his faith: "His voice has become extraordinarily beautiful and sweet; flowers pierce the snow around him, and the birds of heaven descend to feed him."

In allusions to the fatherland, the gods, and what is above the gods one can see a reflection of the Dreyfus Affair, which was at its height when Gide was writing. To those who claimed that Dreyfus, innocent or guilty, must be sacrificed to the good of the country, he replied, by implication, that there was an honor, an integrity, a devotion, that stood above France and her army and her church. But this incidental reflection on the Affair, which as his letters of the time show did deeply concern him, did not divert him from using the Greek legend for a purpose closer to his heart: that of bearing witness to the obscure divinity—more natural than the God of Christianity but more austere than Pan—which now claimed his allegiance.

Le Prométhée mal enchaîné, also published in 1899, overlaps to a certain extent with Philoctète in that it touches on the problems of disinterestedness and service to others; but it is richer in suggestions, and is, moreover, presented with a sustained humor which had only been faintly suggested in Gide's earlier works. "A sheaf of wild tares," he called it in his dedication to Paul Laurens, in which he hoped that readers might find some good grain. It has three loosely correlated themes: the gratuitous act, the symbolism of the eagle of Prometheus, and a parable of personal application put into a speech by Prometheus at the close. And the whole is a sort of legend of Prometheus in modern dress, with a few other classical elements thrown in for good measure.

The gratuitous act is illustrated by Zeus, an all-powerful banker of Paris who, having unlimited fortune and not being bound by the mercenary motives of other men, wearies of the tiresomely inevitable concatenation of cause and effect in human conduct and decides to inject a new element. He therefore puts a five-hundred-franc note into an envelope, goes out into the Boulevard de la Madeleine, and lets fall a handkerchief. A passer-by restores it to him, and Zeus asks him to write on the envelope the first name and address that come to his mind. No sooner has the man complied than Zeus gives him a resounding slap in the face, jumps into a passing cab, and disappears. The envelope containing the five-hundred-franc note is eventually delivered at its destination, and a gratuitous situation has been injected into society: one man, who has designated himself by a polite gesture, receives an unmerited slap in the face, and another, selected by this man, obtains an unearned sum of money.

For both, the results are momentous. Cocles (named after "one-eyed" Horatius of bridge fame), the man who received the slap, now has a grievance which ultimately changes his whole social status; Damocles, the man who received the money, has, as a sword hanging over his head, a debt payable he knows not when nor to whom, which at the end brings about his death.

Meanwhile Prometheus, finding himself a little cramped by his chained position in the Caucasus, gets up and walks down the Boulevard de la Madeleine. Astonished at the apparently purposeful haste of passers-by, he sits down in a café and asks the waiter where they are all going. "In search of their personalities," replies the waiter.

This waiter is a philosophical soul who loves nothing better than to bring into relationship customers who have previously followed separate orbits; in this function, the waiter believes, he is performing a disinterested, a gratuitous act which may have interesting results. As a preliminary to the operation of conjunction the waiter must know something of the history of his customers. Prometheus shows himself a little reticent about his past —understandably, for he was a manufacturer of contraband matches, and consequently an offender against the state monopoly; but the waiter discreetly lowers his eyes, and the delicate topic is dropped.

Through the agency of the waiter, Prometheus, Damocles, and Cocles become acquainted with each other. After the other two have told their stories Prometheus, still evasive, explains that he has an eagle, and on being challenged to produce it, gives a cry, the boulevard is darkened by great wings, and the eagle crashes through the glass, destroying an eye of Cocles (destined by his name to be one-eyed) and settling on the side of Prometheus. Viewed from close by, the eagle is less imposing, and seems mangy and ill nourished. The customers depreciate him: "That, an eagle? At the most it is a conscience." Others say they all have eagles, but it is bad taste to wear them in Paris, and particularly so to feed them on one's liver in public, as Prometheus is now doing.

The cost of the three dinners, of the plate-glass window, and of a glass eye for Cocles, plus a tip for the waiter, exactly uses up five hundred francs, and Damocles delightedly rids himself of his unearned note, thinking thus to rid himself of his debt. He is mistaken, however; he still owes money to somebody, and now he has not even got it to pay. He is so worried by this situation that he sickens and dies. Cocles too is caught by his fate: the story of his slap and lost eye brings publicity, a subscription is started, money rolls in, and eventually he founds an institution for the benefit of the one-eyed, and names himself director. He becomes a public benefactor and a pillar of society.

Meanwhile Prometheus, denounced to the police by the kindly offices of the waiter, has been thrown into prison for infringement of the state match monopoly. His prison is like a tower, open to the sky, and within it he neglects his destiny and becomes fat. One day in his boredom he remembers his eagle, gives his cry, and the bird, still thinner than before, wings slowly and weakly to him. Day after day Prometheus restores it with his liver, and as the eagle gets stronger he himself grows weaker and lighter, until at last the eagle is able to lift him into the air and out of the prison.

"Prometheus delivered" decides to give a public lecture about his eagle, whose presence he guarantees, promising that it will make a few turns about the hall between the points of his discourse. Not feeling confident of his powers as a public entertainer Prometheus holds in reserve, for the amusement of bored listeners, a few rockets and a pack of obscene postcards.

At the funeral of Damocles, Prometheus delivers another address, the story of Tityrus, which seems to have no particular point. "Let's put it that I have said nothing," he says in apology. He now seems well fed and light hearted: the fact is that he has killed his eagle, and after Damocles' funeral he invites Cocles to dine on it at the café, the waiter taking the vacant seat of Damocles. The eagle proves to be very good.

The "gratuitous act," which emerges as one of the serious ideas behind this foolery, was a subject to which Gide had already given some thought. It is touched on in *Paludes*, where already it appears that the act which is truly responsible, representative and expressive of one's personality, must be gratuitous. The ordinary act, born of the conjunction of outer circumstances and the inner recognition of self-interest, has a necessary, a mechanical character: it cannot express individuality because its causes produce the same effect in anybody. The gratuitous act also has causes (otherwise it would be unthinkable), but they lie deep in the character of the individual; the source of spontaneous behavior, like that of art (itself gratuitous), is in the unconscious.

In *Paludes* what Gide has to say about the gratuitous act is undermined by the satiric character of the book; everything anybody says or does in it is a subject of mockery. The fanciful incident of the millonaire and the five-hundred-franc note in *Le Prométhée mal enchaîné* is apparently still less serious, and we may be quite sure that in his later *Caves du Vatican* Gide did not intend the gratuitous murder committed by Lafcadio to be taken as a model for behavior. In thus taking refuge behind a barrier of facetiousness he is tacitly admitting that his speculations about spontaneity are difficult if not impossible to put into practice. Yet in themselves these speculations have both seriousness and depth.

Naked materialistic self-interest was for Gide an insufficient motive; indeed by the time he had reached manhood one of his most settled attitudes was to suspect it in himself and to act against it. But the disguised self-interest of acquiring merit by self-denial was a more pertinent problem, and he set himself, as recorded in the *Nourritures,* to "suppressing in himself the idea of merit," and to "acting without advance judgment whether the act is good or bad." Yet wholly to let himself go was for him an impossibility; something within him, a root of his nature, an inner necessity, called for restraint. Some of his thoughts on the subject at the time of writing the *Nourritures* appear in the Journal:

I arrived at a sort of feeling of certainty; yes, my acts seemed to me to flow happily and fully as from a certain source. Their beauty appeared only later; I even became quickly convinced that, in order to be perfect in my eyes and to please me, the beauty of my acts must not be prepared, must be scarcely even foreseen, by me up to the moment of the act itself; my most beautiful acts, or at least those which seemed so to me, were those whose beauty surprised me. And the intoxication which I then suddenly felt filled me with that special lightness which permitted the forgetfulness of self, with that strength also which made me capable of any accomplishment. In these moments I felt, as if in spite of myself, that my whole being was tensing, stiffening, hardening; I became cruel to myself and found joy in treating myself roughly. Sometimes . . . I thought almost spitefully of abandoning myself to myself, of relaxing my will, of giving myself respite and leisure. I never could do so, and I understood that with me constraint was more natural than abandonment to pleasure with others, that I was not free not to will, to relax, to cease to resist; and I understood at the same time that from this very absence of liberty arose the beauty of my acts.

There is an attempt here to harmonize a contradiction. On the one hand there is the desirable objective of spontaneous, disinterested, unpremeditated action; on the other, the inexorable demand of his deepest nature, which it is his duty to represent, for resistance. The gap is ingeniously bridged by the principle of self-loss: because for his particular nature to be spontaneous *is* to be restrained, to lose his superficial self (which would follow the dictates of calculated self-interest) in the nonrational (but necessary, right, and hence beautiful) demands of his deeper nature for restraint. Spontaneity lies in acceptance of one's destiny, in *amor fati.*

This brings us back to Prometheus and his eagle. "I do not love men," says the Titan; "I love what devours them." Every man carries within him the egg of his eagle, the potentiality for the passion which will give him no rest. In a generalized form the eagle is the belief in progress (and that was the gift of Prometheus to mankind); but each man has his own particular tormentor—a virtue, a vice, an activity—to which he must submit if he is to follow his destiny. You can kill your eagle and consume it, in which case you become heavy, sluggish—and happy. Or you can allow the eagle to feed on your vitals; then you become worn and thin, but the eagle becomes strong, capable of lifting you out of your earthly prison house.

The parable told by Prometheus at the grave of Damocles, although not obviously related to what precedes, is not entirely gratuitous. Tityrus, that old friend with the Virgilian name who served as the central character in *Paludes*, lived, as in that book, alone and surrounded by marshes. One day Ménalque came along and "put an idea in the brain of Tityrus, a seed in the marsh that was before him. And this idea was the seed, and this seed was the Idea." From the seed sprang a great oak, and its care required the help of others, and so, bit by bit, a community grows up around the tree, with police, courts of law, cashiers, accountants; the business of society becomes so heavy that Tityrus takes an assistant, whereupon he himself automatically becomes mayor of the commune. He installs a circulating library, whose custodian turns out to be none other than Angèle. At last Tityrus wearies of his responsibilities, and he and Angèle desert their community and walk up the Boulevard de la Madeleine. Here they find a great crowd assembled to greet Meliboeus (another name out of Virgil), who plays seductively on a shepherd's pipe. To the embarrassment of the now conventionally minded Tityrus, Meliboeus is entirely naked, but Angèle finds him delightful. He tells her (in Latin, which she does not understand but finds charming) that he is going to Rome; then he starts to play his pipe again, crooks his arm, and Angèle takes it, abandoning Tityrus without further ado. That evening the papers announce that Angèle has gone off with "somebody naked who was going to Italy," and Tityrus awakes to find himself alone again, and surrounded by marshes.

"Don't try to find too much meaning in all this," advises Prometheus, but what meaning there is, is clear enough. An idea, even if it is the gospel of nonattachment, can become a vested interest; when this happens Angèle (the muse of Tityrus, perhaps?) leaves her patron and attaches herself to someone who is more nearly stripped of entanglements. Thus Prometheus, who, having killed his eagle, is now sleek, happy, and uninspired; thus Gide, who has been exploiting the doctrines of *Les Nourritures terrestres* and now finds himself with a vested interest.

In *Le Roi Candaule* (1901), Gide's second play and the first to be performed, he returned to his old problem of conciliating morality with sincerity. It is based on an incident in Herodotus about Candaules, king of Lydia, who exposed his wife to Gyges, who, in turn, on the instigation of the outraged queen, killed the king and succeeded to the throne. In Gide's play Gyges is a fisherman who has found in the belly of a fish a ring of invisibility which enables him to become the lover of the queen while she thinks she is embracing her husband; and Candaules is motivated by the inability to enjoy his possessions (in-

cluding the queen) unless he shares them with another.
Further ideas for the play came, as Gide tells us in the
preface, from a phrase of Nietzsche, "Generous to the
point of vice," and from an article in favor of "moral
liberty," in which the author urged his colleagues to edu-
cate the people by sharing with them ideas which had
previously been considered too abstruse or too scandalous
for the generality.

Gide urged his readers not to look for "symbols" in his
play, but simply "an invitation to generalization." But
behind the general problem proposed (the conciliation
of morality with sincerity) lay Gide's own personal situation. His writing career was founded on the premise of
the duty of "representation," of having his writing faithfully reflect the particular truth of which he alone was the
custodian. It did not matter whether what was within him
was in the conventional sense "good" or "bad," nor even
whether his own judgment approved: what was within
him was there, given, and it was his duty to make it manifest. He believed that he now knew a part at least of what
lay within: the state of moral exaltation in which he had
married was past, and he was now prepared to admit (to
himself) that he was a homosexual. To make this admission publicly seemed logically and in accordance with his
own principles the next step; but he was not the only one
concerned in this inmost truth about himself: there were
friends, family; there was above all his wife. Candaules
in the play violated the modesty of his queen by insisting
on revealing her secret beauties to Gyges: would he, Gide,
be committing a similar offense against Madeleine if he
told all the truth about his own nature? Again his problem
is stated, not solved; many years were to pass before he

nerved himself to the final acts of self-revelation. For the present all he could do toward frankness was to throw off hints.

Undoubtedly the most important work of this prolific period is *L'Immoraliste,* finished in October of 1901 and published the following spring. To Jammes, who did not approve of the book, he wrote: "Don't try to persuade me any longer that I was wrong in writing my book; you wouldn't succeed. It lived in me more than five years and I took two years to write it. It was no more possible for me not to write it than it is today not to have written it. . . . Don't you realize that if I had not written *Paludes* I could not have written *Saül?* That my *Prométhée* cleared the way for my *Candaule,* and that but for my *Immoraliste* —I was in danger of becoming one? I purge myself. And not for the last time." Similarly he wrote in another letter: "I write it so as to pass beyond. I write books as one has sicknesses. I now respect only a book that the author almost died of."

The autobiographic element of *L'Immoraliste* is indeed conspicuous. Like Gide, Michel is the only child of wealthy parents, his father a professor and scholar, his mother a puritanical Protestant. In accordance with his father's dying wish (his mother is already dead) he marries Marceline (the phantom of Madeleine), stating that "not yet knowing myself I thought I was giving myself wholly to her." He has weak lungs, sails from Marseille for Tunis, develops tuberculosis, has hemorrhages, comes close to death, is loyally tended by the ever more loving Marceline, is reborn at Biskra where he is fascinated by the Arab boys, like Gide moves northward to Italy via Malta and Syracuse, and again like his creator learns to expose and harden himself. As Michel grows stronger Marceline becomes weaker; moving in their opposite directions they meet at a mid-point: the marriage is consummated the night after Michel has physically chastised a drunken coachman who has endangered his wife. Then they go home to La Morinière (La Rocque).

Meanwhile Michel has learned that morally he is not the same man as he was before his physical rebirth, and that his "new being" is the "old man" whom Saint Paul (and Christians generally after him) put off with all his works. Michel is like a palimpsest: beneath the inscriptions of Christian civilization lies a more ancient writing which he must now try to decipher. The man whom Marceline loved and married was the civilized man; the new man (in reality more primitive) whom she begins to see alarms her, and Michel, to protect his new tendencies, finds himself committed to a policy of deceit, which, under the circumstances, seems natural and right.

Back at La Morinière, Michel finds his possessions encumbering and unnatural, and his overseer Bocage—who, like his original Robidet, can understand no motivation but material self-interest and deeply respects the conventions of property—becomes his natural enemy; poachers and foot-loose characters are his new friends.

Before his physical rebirth he had already made a brilliant beginning in historical scholarship; now, although like his father he becomes a professor, the precocious achievements of his past seem to him futile. Formerly he treated historical events like pieces of a mosaic; their dead and unchanging character pleased him because it enabled him to handle them with greater facility. Now all that seems worthy of attention in the past is its

living character; the past is a transposed present, it is not
history as such but a timeless psychology. Moreover,
among historical characters it is not the just and prudent
rulers who interest him but the turbulent rebels, not the
sowers but the scatterers, not the Romans but the Goths.
Into the atrophied academic world Michel brings the
secret of a man raised from the dead, and the professorial
fossils naturally do not understand.

But in the audience at his first lecture is his (and our)
old acquaintnce Ménalque. Certain aspects of Ménalque's
doctrine and the fact that he is said to have been concerned in a "scandalous" suit, whereby his reputation has
greatly suffered, have led some readers to identify him
with Oscar Wilde. But Ménalque is more symbol than
man, more the personification of an idea than a fully
delineated character. Furthermore the Idea he represents
is neither pure hedonism nor the gospel of art; he is the
dedicated servant of a vital urge, and his service involves
an austerity (he neither drinks nor smokes, for example,
except on special occasions) that was foreign to the character of Wilde.

In any case Ménalque, interested by Michel's lecture,
renews relations with him, and the night before his departure on a dangerous government mission (again how
unlike Wilde!) he spends with his old friend, at just the
time when Marceline, who has been unwell, has a mis-
carriage.

And now Gide's demon of unrest takes charge of
Michel's life. He can scarcely wait to break away from the
encumbrances of professional friends and their incomprehension, of the stodginess that seems to dog all recognized
honorable careers, of his social stake in possessions; and

on the pretext of her health he drags Marceline away on travels. At Neuchâtel, like Gide and Madeleine, they are briefly happy, but repose, so needed by Marceline, is intolerable to Michel. In the Engadine, where Gide wrote the story of Ménalque for the *Nourritures* and disquieted Madeleine by his new doctrines, the health of Marceline steadily improves, but her husband, rationalizing his unrest, argues that what good the mountain winter can do for her is already done, and that what she now needs is the warmth of the South. They push on into Italy—Florence, Rome, Naples, Syracuse—always in search of hot sun and finding only a damp chill much harder to endure than the dry cold of the Alps. "Your doctrine may be beautiful," says Marceline sady, "but it suppresses the weak." And Michel with involuntary brutality breaks out, "That is what is needed." And so they go on to North Africa, Michel dutifully trying to be kind to his ever weaker wife, but in spite of himself revolted by illness and the shadow of approaching death. At night, after he has seen her safely to bed, his demon is too much for him, and he goes out to wander somberly through dim Arab cafés. The inevitable happens: he comes back one morning to find that Marceline, all alone, has had a serious hemorrhage; and the next day she dies. Michel is left alone with an intolerable sense of guilt, confusion of mind, and paralysis of will; and it is in this state that we take leave of him.

Scarcely less obvious than the detailed parallels between this story and the life of Gide is the fact that these resemblances are trivial in comparison with its central theme, which is Gide's own problem: what God is one to serve? The events and the cruel behavior of Michel are accentuations of happenings and tendencies he has observed in his own life; he is immeasurably kinder to his wife than Michel to his, but he like Michel leaves her, to wander at night in dark quarters, he too reproaches himself for neglect. Michel—as small but insistently recurrent details make clear—is like his creator homosexual by nature; but homosexuality is accessory to the situation, not central; it is one of several types of revolt against convention. The real question remains: what is, who is, this vital urge which compels us to burn what we have adored? Is it good or evil, god or demon? If the rule "By their fruits ye shall know them" is a trustworthy guide, Gide's answer (ignored by his hostile critics) is clearly that the fruits are bad and that the tree on which they grow is consequently at best dubious. "I give this book," he says in a foreword, "for what it is worth. It is a fruit full of bitter ash; it is like the colocynths of the desert which grow in spots burned dry and offer to thirst only a more intolerable parching, but which, on the golden sand, are not without beauty." And to a friend he wrote: "That there is in me a bud of Michel goes without saying. . . . How many buds . . . we carry in us that will never blossom except in our books! . . . To create a hero my receipt is simple: take one of these buds, put it in a pot by itself, and you arrive at an admirable individual. A piece of advice: choose by preference (if indeed one can choose) the bud which bothers you the most; you get rid of it by the same stroke. Perhaps that is what Aristotle called the purgation of the passions."

Gide is well aware of the destructive aspects of the tendency he has isolated in Michel. It involves the Nietzschean exaltation of a master morality over a slave morality, with the consequent suppression of the weak; the great man becomes "the great guilty one," who has the courage to defy the conventions of slave morality and to live by his own rules which his might makes right—an idea developed before Nietzsche by Dostoevsky in the Raskolnikov of his *Crime and Punishment*. It prefers barbarism to culture, and opposes to the artistic ideal of balance and harmony a joyous fanaticism of vitality. "Art," says Michel, "is leaving me, I feel—to make way for what else? It is no longer, as formerly, a smiling harmony. . . . I do not know what dark God I serve. O new God, grant me to know new races, unforeseen types of beauty."

The power of the new God is enhanced by the weakness of the old, who seems to be in unholy alliance with materialism and complacent self-interest. The whole machinery of civilization, blessed by religion, cultivates torpor and greed. And what if religion itself is a conspiracy, an invention of priests who take advantage of credulity and superstition to consolidate their own power? What if the heavens are empty?

It is the case of the devout Marceline, rather than of the free-thinking Michel, that raises the question of the nonexistence of the Christian God. When Michel is at death's door and discovers that Marceline is praying for him, he proudly asserts that he would rather die than owe his recovery to any power outside of himself. Later, when she herself has begun to be ill, she asks him for her rosary, and he ironically puts it in her hands. At the end, when his demon is driving him deeper into the desert, he notices that Marceline also looks with avidity at the blazing emptiness, but the fierce strength of the new God is too much for her debility. On her deathbed Michel again puts the rosary into her hands, but this time, with unmistakable intent, she lets it fall to the ground; for her too the old God has lost his power, but she has not the courage for the new.

Yet Michel is not the stuff of which the Nietzschean superman is made. Despite his occasional brutality he finds in his heart pity and love for Marceline—slave virtues, Christian flaws unworthy of the superman; and he is disturbed by discovering in himself a preference for what, by his old standards, is evil: thieving, debauchery, crime. That he can think in these terms shows that the old standards have not for him lost their force; it is precisely because evil seems evil that it attracts him.

The problems which prove too much for Michel are accepted by Gide as a necessary part of man's complexity. "My value is in my complexity," his Saul had said; "Who shall say how many mutually hostile passions and thoughts can live together in man?" asks Michel. With his aptitude for seeing both sides of every question Gide wants to seize the new without letting go of the old; perhaps the problem of the opposition of barbarism and culture can be solved by a rhythmic alternation. Arising originally out of a superabundance of vitality, culture gradually detaches itself from life, hardens, and checks its own source, until at last it is cracked and overthrown by an upsurge of new barbarism containing in itself the promise of a new culture. For the individual the art of living is contained in "the perfect utilization of self by intelligent restraint."

This position is not far from that of the early Nietzsche in *The Birth of Tragedy*. The new God, who is an old God forgotten, is Dionysus; the art which depends on the inspiration of Dionysus but gives it intelligent restraint is Apollo; the enemy is the Socratic spirit, the rationalizing intelligence which has lost contact with its vital source. As for the later Nietzsche, Gide is like the old saint in the forest, mentioned at the beginning of *Thus Spake Zarathustra:* he has not yet heard that *God is dead.* (In this context it is interesting to note that as late as June 22, 1930, Gide wrote in his Journal: "For the seventh or eighth time (at least), attempted *Also sprach Zarathustra.* IMPOSSIBLE. The tone of this book is unbearable to me. And all my admiration for Nietzsche cannot succeed in making me put up with it.")

Since the Renaissance there had been a trend from theocentrism to anthropocentrism, and Nietzsche—like Feuerbach, Comte, and Marx—followed it to its logical conclusion. For such thinkers a revised Christianity, or the theism of the Enlightenment, or even eighteenth-century atheism, were not enough; what was needed was a resolute break with the past and the substitution of a vital faith in man for an outworn belief in a supernatural God. At this extreme, Gide balked—not wholly from timidity or too close attachment to his origins, but because a complete godlessness did violence to his still unconquered transcendentalism. With Nietzsche he was ready to ask, "What is the measure of a man?," but while man remained man, that measure, he believed, was on this side of Godhood. In the *Nourritures terrestres* he had declared that his puritanism had been wrong, that his old theology which opposed God and Nature was inadequate; yet God was still there, He was "what is ahead of us." The perplexities and the doubts of his new position he set forth in *Saül*, in *El Hadj*, in *Le Roi Candaule*, in *L'Immoraliste*, even—by implication—in *Le Prométhée mal enchaîné*. Yet he still believed what he had said in *Philoctète:* that above and beyond the old gods, outworn concepts, there was something not himself to which he could aspire and which he could reach by total self-surrender.

6

The Lean Years

FOR GIDE THE YEARS OF FURIOUS PRODUCTIVITY INSPIRED by his emancipation ended with the publication of *L'Immoraliste* and were succeeded by a period of sterility, as the lean kine in Pharaoh's dream ate up the fat kine; and with the advantage of retrospect one need not be a Joseph to interpret the portent. Effort and rest, advance and retrenchment, assimilation and output: the familiarity of such complementary terms bears witness to our recognition of a basic rhythm, not only in art but in all life as we know it.

Broad historical considerations, however, are of small help to the single individual, at a given point of time, facing a particular problem. The fact staring Gide in the face was that the source of his inspiration had dried up. "Since the 25th of October 1901," he wrote late in 1904, "the day on which I finished *L'Immoraliste*, I have not seriously worked. . . . A mournful torpor of mind has made me vegetate for three years. Perhaps working too much in the garden with plants has made me contract their habits. The least sentence is an effort: talking more-

126

over is almost as much of an effort as writing." He had flashes of joy, but for the most part there was a monotonous succession of days spent merely in getting older.

But neither joy nor monotony advanced his work or eased his self-reproach for its neglect. Time and again he got up feeling fit after a good night's rest, with a sunny day before him and the prospect of few interruptions, thinking, "Now at last I shall get ahead"; but the day passed and somehow the writing did not get done.

What was the matter? He twisted and squirmed in his explanations like a man who knows in his heart what the trouble is but will not face it, blaming Cuverville, the weather, his diet. Thinking that his depression might have physiological causes, he consulted doctors, tried various cures, but without noteworthy improvement. The remedy of travel was only briefly efficacious; as soon as he got back from a trip he sank once more into lethargy.

It occurred to him that North Africa, which he had visited five times, might have become an obsession with him, and that he could get rid of it by the method he had tried in literature: making a book out of it. And so, after elaborate efforts at self-justification, he set out in the fall of 1903 for a sixth visit, planning to buttress his recollections with precise researches into economic, ethnological, and geographic materials; but all he brought back was a journal which he published as *Renoncement au voyage*—a farewell to travel; and as a motto on the flyleaf he put: "I was at the age when life begins to have a more dubious taste on the lips, when one feels each instant fall into the past from a little less high."

On his trip in 1893, youth, a fresh first contact, and convalescence from a serious illness had combined to give him an experience so rich that the recollection of it impoverished present sensations. "I go back into the heart of my youth," he wrote in Biskra. "I replace my feet in my footsteps. Here are the charming contours of the path I followed when, still weak, emerging from the horror of death, I sobbed, drunk with the pure astonishment of *being*, with the ecstasy of existing." But—"It is useless. One can see the same place again twenty times, but never again as something new. One looks more, one sees less. One understands better perhaps—but without the ravishing astonishment."

The idea of the desert still attracted the man surfeited with the sown, but the reality was disappointing, like the wild pomegranate which he picked from the tree and found intolerably puckery: "Even in its wild state the fragrance of the fruit is revealed, but it needs to be sweetened, softened, and tempered by long cultivation. However, I stubbornly persisted, bit again. . . ."

Southward the unknown beckoned imperiously, but now he was jaded enough, disillusioned enough, to realize that the invitation was empty and its charm limited to itself. Humanity as well as nature spread before him specious allurements. An Ouled Nail seated before her door in Blida calls to him, but the glimpse of a cool dark garden behind her has greater attraction. He is drawn by the atmosphere of evil mystery in a dark alley, into which penetrate a faint light and the tinkling of a native guitar from a Moorish café: "Shall I go in?—To see what? A squalid hut, twelve prone Arabs, a musician who is very probably ugly? I shall stay here, and let night come into me, insinuating itself with the music." To another café he returns repeatedly, fascinated by a cellar door within, through which, periodically, an Arab mysteriously disappears. "Oh, to know, when that dark heavy door opens before that Arab, what will greet him beyond! I should like to be that Arab, to have what awaits him await me." In still another spot he experiments with smoking the forbidden *kief*, feels a fleeting sense of well-being, not from the satisfaction of desire but from its restful disappearance. A hideously painted doll hangs from a hook on the otherwise bare wall of the café. "The devil," whispers his guide, nodding toward it.

Sometimes he feels as if he hated the country. He deserts the top of the diligence because it is too distracting, and he can read better within. He mentally runs through a Schumann symphony, immerses himself in his beloved Virgil, wishes he had a La Fontaine. At the tip of the Algiers breakwater, where spindrift blows through the interstices of heaped cement cubes, he wishes for a wave to carry him away, engulf him in its green bitterness.

Back at Cuverville he briefly savors the odor of fern and cut fields, the coolness of the evening mist that seeps up from the Channel. What more can he ask than he has already, at home? "On these warm days I dream of the flight of nomads; oh, to flee elsewhere and yet to stay here! To evaporate, be undone, be carried away, dissolved in a breath of the blue sky!"

Then the mournful torpor closes over him again. He has tried to escape, but he cannot distance that implacable pursuer—himself.

The obvious—but to him insufficient—explanation of his sterility was discouragement over the failure of his books. The five-hundred-copy edition of *Les Nourritures terrestres* still had a remainder and the small critical attention it had received showed an almost complete incomprehension of its message. *Saül* had not been played at all in France, and the preface to his *Roi Candaule* betrayed a bitterness, almost a spitefulness, that is rare indeed in his published work: "Uncertain of the reception that will be accorded to [this play], I may, I must, suppose anything—suppose even that it might be applauded. That would result from a misunderstanding. For in view of the noisy success that the public has given the plays of M. Rostand, for example, I cannot for a moment claim that, if my play is applauded, it will be for its literary merits." As it turned out, *Le Roi Candaule* aroused neither acclaim nor noteworthy condemnation; it was quietly smothered by the indifference that had met his other works.

When it came to publishing *L'Immoraliste,* into which had gone intimate experience and the best of his literary art, he wrote in his Journal: "Why do I print only three hundred copies of *L'Immoraliste?* To disguise from myself a little my bad sales. In an edition of twelve hundred copies it would seem to me four times as bad; I should suffer four times as much." And a few months later he wrote to Jammes:

Sometimes it seems to me that all one can do is to turn the crank of an old barrel organ, all of whose tunes are too well known, until the concierge drives you off or until, from the window of a much higher floor, the millionaire tosses you a penny or cries, "When will you be through with your music? You keep people awake." But not even that happens. I don't know what tune to play nor in which direction to turn the crank.

There was some consolation in taking refuge in a disdain of popular success. As he had said in one of his critical

Lettres à Angèle: "I hate the crowd; it respects nothing—tenderness, delicacy, precision, beauty, all are warped by it, broken, mortified. . . . Do not see pride in my words: when I am in the crowd I am a part of it, and it is because I know what I become in it that I hate the crowd." As for a play—made, dramatists normally admit, to be performed, to be delivered up to the crowd—he adds: "And yet I cannot consider drama as subjected to the audience, no, never; I consider it rather as a struggle or rather as a duel with it—a duel in which scorn for the audience is one of the principal elements in victory. The great mistake of our modern playwrights is not to have sufficient scorn for their audience. They should not try to win it over but to conquer it. A duel, I say, from which the audience should emerge both beaten and satisfied."

Despite his disclaimer, there is a stubborn pride in these words; pride too, but recognized, in his insistence in the following passage (about a conversation with a man who worshiped material success) that the critical silence about his work was intended by himself:

Through fatigue I let myself say words of the sort which in writing I should at once cross out with shame. I take on in his eyes the appearance of complaining (the appearance one forgives, which I forgive myself, the least). So why should I talk of the silence that surrounds me to one who, were he to live three times over, could never understand that *I myself have made* this silence? I tell Thadée that neither the *Ermitage* nor *Vers et Prose,* nor the *Occident* have said anything about my *Amyntas.* I should have liked him to understand that I *did not want* articles in a place where praise was almost obligatory. But Thadée immediately starts to console me! I leave him to meditate at length on the distress of appearing in a false position. I say "false position" because the *beauty* of this attitude will have no validity unless I have the courage (and the strength) to maintain it to the end. And it is a mistake to talk of *attitude* without at once adding *natural,* for it is when I abandon this attitude that I give a wrong impression of myself and put wrinkles on my face, and I never do so except when I am tired.

In the passage about the small edition of *L'Immoraliste* he admitted that he wanted success, and a success measured to some extent by the number of copies sold. Now he reproaches himself for allowing it to appear that he is hurt by the neglect of the critics. He *is* hurt, of course, but at the same time he is quite sincere in not wanting côterie acclaim; he would like his work to attract attention on its own merits. This attitude is surely "natural" enough, and it would acquire "beauty" if, confident of the merit of his work, he had the strength to await, serenely and consistently, the verdict of time.

Yet a contemporary success—if not with the multitudes then at least with the happy few—would have given him some assurance that he was on the right track; but even the élite seemed to deny him a hearing, and, as he said in a lecture at Weimar (an occasion which for a moment gave him such a hearing), "The artist cannot do without a public." He must feel that he is communicating with someone, and if he takes refuge in the idea of writing for posterity he loses contact with life and lays himself open to self-deception.

To be a voice crying in the wilderness is at best an ungrateful role, but if you do not fully believe in your message it is intolerable. Even in the heat of happy activity Gide had been by no means sure of himself; such doctrines as he had developed bore the stamp of compro-

mise with an unsatisfactory situation. He had been trying
to follow the way of art as he understood it, the way of
"intelligent restraint," of Apollo utilizing but dominating
Dionysus; but it had proved neither materially successful
nor morally satisfying. "Why don't you understand that I
detest *my thought?*" he wrote to Jammes at the time of
the publication of *L'Immoraliste*. "I wear myself out fighting against it; but I cannot deny it except by its own
means, as one casts out a demon by Beelzebub, the prince
of demons." And to the same correspondent he had said,
while he was writing *Saül:* "All the demons of Judaea
inhabit me, feed off me, torment me; if I did not cherish
them a little I would be much more unhappy, but I should
not be so sick. I am haunted"—and not, he went on, by
heaven alone, as Jammes seemed to think.

He cherished his demons to get rid of self-esteem: "I
applied my ingenuity to losing it and it was not hard. . . .
I gave myself up to debauchery, and was not unwilling
even to do it systematically, I mean to work hard at it. . . .
I despised nothing in myself so much as my self-esteem; I
proposed to make it impossible, and took pleasure in de-
basing myself, driven to it by the fear of cowardice. When
something in me held back I was afraid it was fear, and
I went ahead. At present I care little what I am or am
not. I no longer worry about that."

This indifference was partly due, he believed, simply to
getting older. To exorcise his demons of unsatisfied desire
and the insomnia they caused, his standard recourse had
been night wanderings, undertaken in the half-recognized
hope of seeing and trailing some youth, preferably ragged
and with the air of not being a disciplined and functioning
part of the social machinery. Sometimes the hope was ful-

filled, more often not; but in either case the result was physical exhaustion, disappointment, and further restlessness. By the beginning of 1902 he believed (prematurely, as it proved) that he was getting the better of the habit, not from increase of self-control but from decrease of desire. On January 8 he wrote: "Last night I stayed quietly at home, finishing *Lamiel* and meditating. I foresaw that it would be *indispensable* for me to go out. I did not, and am none the worse for it (I even had a rather good night). Two years ago I should have had to stay out until three o'clock in the morning, after having wandered on the boulevards since ten o'clock. I seem to be behaving more wisely; the fact is, I am older."

But he was not always reduced to taking, or trying to keep from taking, unhappy night walks; sometimes his desires seem to have found their target, and his only melancholy is at the thought of the transitoriness of experience. On a warm spring night of 1905 he writes: "My brain is clear, not too frivolous, my flesh in repose, my heart firm. I should make an admirable lover tonight. . . . I should like not to have met M. before yesterday, not to have been able to speak to him before today. If I threw myself from the balcony tonight, it would be with the thought, 'It's the simplest way.' . . . On a night like this four years ago I should have roamed all night."

This mention of "M." (and there are many such veiled references) brings up another aspect of his psychological progression. He continued to maintain a distinction between "love" and "pleasure," and it is undoubtedly true that the tender and enduring feeling which he had for Madeleine and for which (when he thought about a distinction) he reserved the word "love," was of a wholly different character from what he felt in his ephemeral sexual adventures. But it is also clear from the Journal that his homosexual adventures were not of a single type. There was the genuinely ephemeral type, where he sought "pleasure" and found sometimes relief (not untouched by remorse) and sometimes frankly admitted disgust; and there was a more durable kind, smaller in number, in which a variable degree of sentiment was involved. What are we to call relationships in which are found the anguished combination of fear and hope, obsession and a tender concern for the welfare of the other, if not affairs of the heart?

Take a passage like this, written in Cuverville in July of 1905: "Today I learned what suspense is: not the impatient kind that makes a horse froth at the bit, but that horrible anguished suspense in which the heart struggles from beat to beat as if working against clots. There on the road, on the bank, in full sunlight, I wait, wait for the passing of X's carriage. It is late. Probably it has taken the other road." And a day or two later: "I still have in me an enormous sum of joy that I do not know how to expend. Will nothing calm the frightful beating of my heart? The whole summer oppresses it. Yesterday I took a long bicycle ride, more uplifted than overwhelmed by the heat. . . . The return journey was magnificent—apparent serenity of the harvesting, the solemn onward march of evening. I wander like a madman in the midst of this peace more arid for me than the desert."

Quite as important then as his purely literary difficulties, and underlying them, was his personal moral problem: what good and what evil, how much nature and how much sheer perversity, were there in his developing tendencies?

At times, with propitious weather and good health, he would feel self-confident, ready to abide by his rationalized destiny; at others, more numerous in this period of his general discouragement, he was prepared to admit that he was a wandering sheep, almost ready to return to the fold.

On September 1, 1905, for example, he wrote: "Again I am losing my footing, letting myself be rolled along by the monotonous flood, be carried away by the current of the days. A heavy somnolence dulls me from getting up until night. . . . I compare what I am to what I was, to what I should have liked to be. . . . Sensuality permeates everything, my greatest virtues are deteriorating, and even the expression of my despair is blunted. How should I find absurd a morality that would have protected me against all this! My reason both condemns it and calls for it—calls for it in vain. If I had a confessor I should go to him and say: Impose on me the most arbitrary of disciplines, and today I will call it wisdom. If I cling to some belief that my reason finds absurd it is because I hope to draw strength from it against myself." But then, significantly, he adds: "As soon as I have a day of good health I shall blush to have written this."

It seems likely that even at this time he obscurely realized, in his heart of hearts, that "one thing was needful," that a faith which could be immediately and satisfactorily rationalized was not the indispensable first step, that like his own Philoctetes he could surrender his self-will, the cause of so much torment, in favor of something which he could not define but in which he could with his whole heart believe. "He that loseth his life shall save it"—how often, in season and out of season, had he not quoted and stretched and misapplied but still come back to these haunting words?

As in 1893 he had hesitated, temporized, awaiting the stimulus of an external event to crystallize his decision to abandon puritanism and embrace Dionysus, so now he drifted unhappily and looked for a sign that would precipitate a religious conversion. And it was while he was in just this state that there burst upon him the overwhelming personality and the unshakable religious conviction of Paul Claudel.

The two men, nearly of an age, had met in the days of Mallarmé's Tuesdays (though not actually at Mallarmé's), when both had been young beginners. Then Claudel had gone abroad in pursuit of his diplomatic career, and they had exchanged rather formal compliments and copies of their respective works. They met again in 1900, when Claudel was on leave in France, but again without notable result other than that Gide, feeling in the other a force hostile to his ideas and way of life, kept on the defensive.

His frame of mind was quite different in May of 1905, when he first glanced at Claudel's *Ode aux Muses:* he was discouraged, and his guard was down. "The few sentences that I read while walking," he wrote in his Journal, "take instant possession of my thoughts. My whole being is shaken; it is like the *warning* that I have been awaiting for almost a month." The following September he wrote to Claudel, who was again in France, "*I thank you*, Claudel, for having written the *Ode aux Muses*. This nourishment has really sustained me this winter."

The fervent Apostle of the Faith, scenting a convert, replied at once with a brief but cordial note suggesting a meeting, and followed it up (apparently in reply to one of Gide's that has not been preserved) on November 7 ("Feast of the Immaculate Conception") with a long and earnest letter in which he said, in part:

We cannot all become Saints, but we can always at every moment of our lives honestly do what we can; and to tell the truth that is what sanctity is, a filial preference of the Will of the heavenly father to our own. So how can you speak of a pagan sanctity, which is a detestable pride, a spiritual lust of the creature turned in on itself and rejoicing in its strength and its beauty, as if it were itself their origin. . . . It is for you, my dear friend, to see at what moment of your life you have arrived, to have no illusions about the exigency of the voice which summons you, to measure the strength of the obstacles which check you. . . . It is before God that you must examine yourself in the sincerity of your conscience.

On November 30 they met at the house of a common friend, and the next day Gide described the man he had not seen since 1900:

In his youth he looked like a nail; now he looks like a pile driver. A rather low but wide forehead; a face without nuances, as if blocked out with a knife; a bull neck running straight up into the head, which you feel will become readily congested by a passionate rush of blood. Yes, I think that is the dominant impression: the head is continuous with the trunk. I shall look at him more closely next Tuesday (he is lunching with us); I was too busy defending myself and only half responded to his advances. He looks to me like a frozen cyclone. When he talks it is as if a release mechanism clicked inside him; he proceeds by sudden affirmations and maintains a hostile tone even when one is agreeing with him.

At the Tuesday luncheon Claudel continued his proclamations of the truth, talking steadily and relentlessly and, if interrupted, waiting until the other was through and then resuming his talk at the point where he had left it. Once, however, when Gide indicated that he understood, Claudel retorted, "Then why don't you become converted?" And Gide let him see that he was disturbed.

That same evening Claudel pursued his advantage with another letter, part apologetic and part peremptory:

What would you have? You must take me as I am, and a Claudel no longer a zealot and a fanatic would no longer be Claudel. How I should have liked to be more eloquent! Alas, it is in such moments that one perceives how terrible it is not to have responded to the absolute duty of being a saint. . . . We must see each other again; I have many things to say to you and I am afraid I scandalized you by speaking rather succinctly about certain things.

But Gide found an attraction in Claudel's intransigence, as his prompt reply showed:

Since you love souls, you will understand that there are some to whom nothing is more repugnant than a practical and temperate religion, and that after having made, at the beginning of my life, of the Bible my daily food and of prayer my first need, I preferred . . . the sharpest break with my first beliefs to some tepid compromise between art and religion. . . . *For the first time* the day before yesterday (but already I glimpsed it in your works) I was able to see, enlightened by you, not a solution—absurd to hope for—but a new, an acceptable position for battle.

And do you know what tormented me now: the difficulty, the impossibility perhaps, of attaining sanctity by the pagan route, and when you spoke to me, Claudel, of "the absolute duty of being a saint," did you foresee that no word could draw me back more violently?

The old problem of the artist and the saint was on the carpet again. At the time of writing the *Traité du Narcisse*

Gide had believed that one could be both; now he was much closer to his ultimate conviction that the combination was impossible and that a choice must be made. To the worldly mind, even to the Protestant mind, there is something both pretentious and ridiculous about wanting to be a saint: the very word evokes an outmoded asceticism, a martyrdom no longer opportune, miracles performed by relics, the medieval ceremonies of canonization, whereas the aspiration to be a literary artist is generally respected and admitted to be legitimate. Although Gide was not the man to be deterred from following a conviction by fear of ridicule or contempt, he recurred, like most men, to an average frame of mind in which the illuminations of his rare exalted moments seemed like abnormal extravagancies. Furthermore he could without undue vanity lay claim to having literary gifts; was not their possession in itself a calling?

Yet Gide did not deceive himself about the fundamental issue. When Claudel said "We cannot all become Saints" (with a capital S) but spoke in a subsequent letter of "the absolute duty of being a saint," the contradiction was only apparent: what he meant was that not everyone could be canonized but that all, without exception, were under the obligation of striving for the essence of sanctity—the subordination of the personal will to that of God. For Claudel such subordination could only be achieved in the Roman Church; for Gide the issue was a living one only because Claudel's words reasserted his own conviction of the spiritual necessity of self-loss. The uncompromising affirmations of Catholicism had an appeal when he was feeling weak and discouraged, but their only abiding significance for him was as markers for one way (among possible others) of losing his life to save it.

Claudel too had faced the problem of the artist and the saint. "For a long time," he said to Gide at their luncheon meeting, "for two years, I went without writing; I thought I must sacrifice art to religion. My art! God alone could know the immensity of this sacrifice. I was saved when I realized that art and religion must not be antagonists within us. That they must not be confused with each other either. That they must remain as it were perpendicular to each other; and that their very struggle nourishes our life."

But his problem was somewhat different from Gide's. For one thing, he faced it from a solidly established position of faith, whereas Gide was still drifting. For another, Claudel, notwithstanding the profundity of his literary work, was quite capable of self-deception. His words reported by Gide—"I was saved when I realized that art and religion must not be antagonists within us"—can be taken at face value: he made a genuine discovery of truth, quite independently of his own desires in the matter. But it takes something less than the subtle perceptions of Gide to find in these words the distinguishing marks of a rationalization. Claudel has an intense desire to write and a strong faith which he fears may be in opposition to this desire; is it not almost a foregone conclusion that sooner or later he will make the discovery that art and religion are not, after all, in conflict? The only question is whether he is going to catch himself in the act of rationalizing. He did not; Gide, in similar cases, almost invariably did.

All this without prejudice to Claudel's discovery in

itself; it brought him peace of mind and it has much to recommend it in general. There seems to be no fundamental reason why art and religion should be in opposition, since both, at their best, are efforts at self-transcendence; they conflict only because desire for fame and pride in one's work—which so commonly accompany artistic production that one is tempted to call them inevitable—are obstacles to the self-surrender demanded by high religion. Of course Claudel took pride in his work, but he claimed to have disciplined it to the status of the concern for good workmanship of a skillful cabinet maker; to literary glory he professed to be indifferent, and worked, he said, only for the glory of God.

Gide, like most cultivated readers, saw in the poetry of Claudel the workings of a mind at once lofty and profound and of a magnificently implemented sensibility. He saw also the no less evident flaws which, by a paradox of which there is more than one example among great writers, were those of extreme simplicity of mind. Claudel simply did not know when genuine eloquence turned into mere sonorous verbiage; he was sublimely unaware of another viewpoint than his own—unaware, for example, in his later war poem, "Tant que vous voudrez, mon général," that the generosity of this noncombatant with other men's lives might seem excessive to the man in the trenches. It is written that to enter the Kingdom of Heaven one must become as a little child; but does this requirement include egocentricity, the infatuated assurance of being exclusively in the right? And "religious certainty," wrote Gide, "gives this robust mind a deplorable infatuation."

Claudel carried the same assurance into his judgments of literature. He was not a great reader, claiming to know a good book from a bad intuitively and at a glance. Not only many of his talented contemporaries but Montaigne, Kant, Rousseau, Renan, and other illustrious figures of literature and philosophy fell under his anathema; and even Pascal, grudgingly admitted to have a mild interest for a mind in process of formation, was pronounced unnecessary and even harmful for one who had attained the absolute and exclusive certainty of Roman Catholic faith. "He lays waste our literature with a monstrance," said Gide. "The greatest advantage of religious faith for the artist is that it permits him a *limitless* pride."

Confronted by Claudel's dynamic assurance Gide always felt inferior, futile, on the defensive; he seized upon flaws in the monumental personality as weapons to equalize the contest. Yet Claudel continued for so long to dominate because he could again disarm his opponent by a disconcerting candor and humility. "I have only too much self-reproach," he wrote to Gide from China in 1906, "for having been indiscreet and clumsy with you. However, one expresses oneself as one can. It is not conviction and the desire to do right that I lack. But also it is not with sonorous words and confused ideas that one wins souls. You are an honest man and some day you will meet the one you need. No, Gide, it is not the wretched rigmarole of this poor Claudel that you like, it is what you manage to decipher behind it."

Gide's broad humanistic culture was revolted by the summary literary judgments of Claudel, his intelligence rebelled against his claim that the truth "resides solely and exclusively in the teachings of the Catholic Church," and his taste and common sense objected to the "limitless pride"; yet it was not because of these, one is forced to conclude from the record, that both now and later he eluded not only Claudel but the more telling idea in his own mind which Claudel reawakened; fundamentally it was because he was not prepared to pay the price of a change in his way of life, he was not ready for the surrender of his personal will.

The most concrete result of Gide's encounter with Claudel and of the inner turmoil which preceded and accompanied it was the composition of *Le Retour de l'enfant prodigue.*

Although in January of 1907 he had been working for nearly two years on his next major production *La Porte étroite,* he was finding progress increasingly difficult; the disorder of his new house at Auteuil but reflected, he felt, the disorder of his mind. In Berlin, preparations were being made for the first performance in German of his *Roi Candaule.* He considered attending the performance himself; his friend Maurice Denis was enthusiastic about the idea and proposed to accompany him, but Gide remained undecided: "Impossible to decide whether or not to leave for Berlin: impossible to decide even whether or not I want to go. Let myself be taken there? Yes, perhaps. At least my vacillating character has this advantage: it has no regrets. This indecisiveness is both an effect and a cause of my fatigue. Perhaps it would be better, then, to stay in Paris."

His days continued to be absorbed by small occupations which left him exhausted; he attended the reception of Barrès at the Academy and came out "demoralized with fatigue and melancholy. Another day like this and I shall be ripe for religion." Two days later, however, Denis "in a burst of laughter sweeps away all the arguments I had been building up against going to Berlin. Impossible to resist his cordial confidence." And the day following they set out for the German capital.

The most important event of the trip for him was not the performance of *Le Roi Candaule* nor a visit to the art gallery and the taking of notes on the pictures, but the inspiration to write *Le Retour de l'enfant prodigue,* the composition of which marked his emergence from the literary doldrums. He began work on it February 1, two days after his return to Paris, completed the first draft in two weeks, spent one more in revision, and by June was correcting proof for its publication in the quarterly *Vers et Prose;* never had he conceived and executed a literary project with such dispatch.

In length the piece is no more than a short story, in content merely an expansion of the Gospel parable of the prodigal son, but its beautiful form and its personal significance give it an importance beyond what its unpretentiousness would seem to warrant.

It is at once an act of contrition and a defense of his position, and a foreword makes clear both the duality of theme and its personal application:

Leaving scattered and mingled the double inspiration by which I am actuated, I do not seek to prove the victory over me of any god—nor my own victory. Perhaps, however, if the reader requires of me some piety, he would not seek it in vain in my painting, where, like a donor in the corner of the picture, I have put myself kneeling, as a pendant to the prodigal son, like him at once smiling and with his face bathed in tears.

That he is indeed in the picture, he makes still more plain by breaking the story, when scarcely begun, to say: "My God, like a child I kneel before you today, my face wet with tears. If I recall and transcribe here your urgent parable, it is because I know what your prodigal child was; because I see myself in him; because I hear in myself sometimes and secretly repeat those words which, in the depth of his distress, you represent him as saying: 'How many hired servants of my father have in his house bread in abundance, and I perish here with hunger!' " And once established, the parallel continues. "The son admits to himself that he has not found happiness, nor even succeeded for long in prolonging the intoxication which, in default of happiness, he sought." And on his return he says to his father, "I have changed your gold into pleasures, your precepts into whims, my chastity into poetry, and my austerity into desires."

The father is of course God, as in the original, and in Gide's version the House is the Church—the Roman Catholic Church, one must assume, for Gide would not concede orthodoxy to any Protestant denomination; and the elder brother represents collectively the Catholic faithful, or the priesthood. In the House it is he who, with the consent, up to a point, of the father, lays down the law, of which the principal precept is, "Outside of the House there is no salvation"; yet the father made not only the House but all the world; and after saying to the prodigal the words prompted by the elder brother he adds: "It was I who formed you; I know what is in you. I know what drove you out on the highways; I awaited you at their end. If you had called me, I was there."

Gide takes the point made in the original that, servitude for servitude, it is better to work for one's father than for a foreign master, and expands it to mean that the prodigal, since he had lost confidence in himself to the point of hiring himself to a citizen of the far country, did well to return, but that he would have done better if he had maintained the courage of his first convictions and gone his hungry way without selling his freedom for the husks that the swine did eat. And to carry out his idea the author invents a third son, the youngest, who at the time of the prodigal's return is in just the state of mind of his brother when he left the House; after a conversation with the prodigal and with his blessing he sets out, determined to emulate his brother's original ardor but not his capitulation.

Despite his warning to the reader not to read into the parable any attempt at proving the victory either of some god or of his own theory, it is surely obvious that what Gide is saying in his story is this: God made not only the House but the world, and whereas some can find Him and serve Him in the House, others may achieve the same end by pursuing the open road; in either case one must not sell one's soul for a mess of pottage.

Admirers of Gide have seen in *Le Retour de l'enfant prodigue* one of his most perfect works, and detractors find in it only hypocrisy. There is something to be said for both points of view. In language and in form it is a harmonious continuation of its classic original, but it bears the mark of personal emotion, particularly evident to one who knows out of what soul searchings it arose. It raises the old question of whether one can make literary capital out of individual experience without sacrifice of sincerity on the one hand or of universality on the other. It resurrects the issue of classic versus romantic, and Gide, despite his classic form, is essentially a romantic in his posture. To see himself in a corner of his picture as "smiling," but "with his face bathed in tears"; to make a public act of contrition, saying, "Father, I have sinned against heaven and in thy sight"; and then to point out the beauty of his former courageous independence: all this may be literature, but it is not true humility. As in *L'Immoraliste* he sought to rid himself of a destructive tendency, so in *Le Retour de l'enfant prodigue* he purged his repentence in esthetics.

7

The Strait Gate

THE FIRST IDEA FOR THE BOOK THAT WAS TO BECOME *La Porte étroite* dates back to 1891. It was inspired by the spectacle of the self-denying life and lonely death of Anna Shackleton, at one time the governess and later the companion of Gide's mother, and he thought of it under the title *L'Essai de bien mourir.* For many years the project lay dormant, probably because he was too much concerned with asserting the will to live to be attracted by a study of sacrifice and death.

Then fervor waned, repentance stirred, conversion loomed, and the essay on holy living and holy dying became more pertinent. He seems to have been thinking about it in 1903, but he did not get down to actual writing until 1905, and then only with many false starts and labored rewriting; his self-mistrust and confusion of mind were such that by the beginning of 1907 he was almost ready to admit incapacity to carry the project through. Then the rapid execution of *Le Retour de l'enfant prodigue* restored his confidence; he set in motion again the inert mass of his materials and finished the book in the fall of

1908. It appeared in 1909 after serialization in the newly founded *Nouvelle Revue Française*.

Meanwhile the source of his inspiration had shifted. The account of the last days and death of Alissa in *La Porte étroite* was still suggested by those of Miss Shackleton, but for the central theme of the book—a study in Christian abnegation—Gide had an example closer at hand in his wife. "She never quarreled," he wrote in *Si le grain ne meurt;* "it was so natural to her to yield to others her turn, her place, or her share, and she did it with such smiling grace, that you doubted whether she did not do it by preference rather than by virtue, and whether she would not have been putting a constraint on herself if she had acted otherwise."

"I am lost in admiration, adoration, veneration of Madeleine," he wrote to Jammes in 1897; "her gentleness is incomparable; she, so weak, contrives to be a protection." And in 1906, in the midst of physical and moral depression, he wrote in his Journal, "She is surrounded by a radiation of tenderness, charm, and poetry in which I warm myself, and my fretful mood melts."

But it was chiefly the remembered Madeleine of his childhood that Gide put into the portrait of Alissa, and in so doing he drew to such an extent on his recollections that in none of his works of fiction is there a closer parallel with persons and events of his own life. Jérôme, the male protagonist, is Gide, or rather occupies the position of Gide; Alissa, Jérôme's cousin, two years his senior, has the role of Madeleine; Gide's sister-in-law Jeanne Rondeaux takes the name of his mother Juliette; Valentine is not represented and the boys Edouard and Georges unite to become Robert in the novel. Jérôme's father, like Gide's,

has died, and at a corresponding period in the life of his
son; Miss Shackleton's part is played by Miss Ashburton;
Fongueusemare, the scene of much of the action, is Cuverville undisguised. The crucial incident of Gide's returning
to the rue Lecat and discovering the family drama that
was causing Madeleine such suffering is reproduced in
the novel with scarcely a change, and takes place as in
real life at Le Havre; and Jérôme's love for Alissa, clarified
like that of his creator by this event, has the same character of religious adoration and protective tenderness unmixed with physical desire.

Yet despite these striking parallels (and more could be
mentioned) Gide felt able to say many years later: "If in
L'Immoraliste I still put large segments of myself, I have
since then absented myself from my tales"; and he went
on to cite *La Porte étroite* as an example. The apparent
paradox can be justified by the fact that in this book, as
had not been the case in the earlier ones, the central
theme of sacrifice is not his own problem, and the interest
centers not upon Jérôme-Gide but upon Alissa-Madeleine.
Moreover Alissa, although obviously inspired by Madeleine, cannot be identified with her. As in *L'Immoraliste*
Gide isolated and studied a potentiality of his own nature,
so in *La Porte étroite* he took Madeleine's tendency to self-
sacrifice, suggested its implications, and pushed it to an
extreme not reached by the original.

In the story, Alissa's mother, after Jérôme's discovery of
her infidelity, runs away with her lover and on the following Sunday, Alissa and Jérôme attend church together and
hear the pastor preach on the text: "Enter ye in at the
strait gate: for wide is the gate, and broad is the way that
leadeth to destruction, and many there be which go in

thereat: Because strait is the gate, and narrow is the way, which leadeth unto life, and few there be that find it."

Both the young lovers are stimulated to ardent spiritual aspiration by these words, but in different ways. For Jérôme the strait gate suggests the door through which he passed to find Alissa on her knees in tears; to reach her suffering he had to lay aside his encumbering egoism. So it is with the strait gate: to pass through he must leave self behind, and yet Alissa is in the seraphic state beyond, and inseparable from its foreshadowed bliss. For Alissa, however, the gate which strips of egoism demands also, and necessarily, the abandonment of earthly ties; to pass into life one has to let go of the hand of the lover and move forward alone.

Not that Alissa is thinking consciously of her own solitary salvation: it is Jérôme she is thinking of, fearing that if he loves her too much, clings too closely to her hand, he will not be able to pass through the strait gate. At the time of hearing the sermon she does not foresee that she will eventually feel called upon to renounce Jérôme for his own good, but a little later she writes in her journal:

Alas! I understand it only too well now: between God and him there is no other obstacle but myself. If, perhaps, as he tells me, his love for me inclined him at the first to God, at present this love hinders him; he delays with me, prefers me, and I become the idol which restrains him from advancing farther into virtue.

But what Alissa has achieved at this point is not a true understanding but a rationalization of her motives in trying to alienate Jérôme. There are unconscious factors at work. With entire sincerity, but in obedience to unrecognized deep desires, she discovers a series of obstacles to

her union with Jérôme. She is too old for him; her younger
sister Juliette would make him a more suitable wife, and
Juliette already loves him (which is true). Alissa practically throws Juliette into the astonished arms of Jérôme,
but Juliette, unwilling to accept the sacrifice and with the
furious decisiveness characteristic of her, promptly marries
an unprepossessing middle-aged suitor and goes away with
him to the south of France. The marriage turns out better
than might have been expected, and with a flash of self-
understanding Alissa writes in her journal:

Why should I lie to myself? It is by a process of reasoning that
I rejoice in the happiness of Juliette. I really suffer at seeing
obtained so easily this happiness which I so much wanted, to
the point of wanting to sacrifice my own happiness for it. . . .
I clearly discern that a dreadful resurgent egoism is offended
that she should have found her happiness elsewhere than in
my sacrifice, that she did not need my sacrifice to be happy.

But this insight teaches her only that self is still not conquered, that she must try even harder to renounce Jérôme
in her heart.

She makes another discovery, and again it is more instructive to the reader than to her. One day when Jérôme
is standing close to her she feels a stirring of the senses
that frightens her: "So strange an agitation took possession
of me that I had to get up, in haste, while I was still
capable of doing so. I was able to leave the room for a
few moments, fortunately without his noticing anything."
A little later in her own room she lies down on the couch,
instead of sitting upright as is her usual custom, and finds
her thoughts turning to her mother. Her father, coming in
just then, is struck by her resemblance to her mother, and
tells her of it, to Alissa's distress. For her the awakening of

passion, the languor, the thoughts of her mother translating themselves into an actual physical resemblance, mean just one thing: she carries her mother's nature, the potentiality of her mother's sin, within her, as a sort of doom. "The sins of the fathers shall be visited upon the children." She must watch, she must pray, she must expiate. The reader, less dramatically, would say that the shock of discovering her mother's infidelity has given her an unreasoning horror of all sex.

Somewhat similar is her experience while visiting Juliette. Though she is twenty-five years old, this is her first journey, and she is astonished and troubled at the voluptuous warmth of the South: "I am almost frightened that here my feeling for nature, so profoundly Christian at Fongueusemare, in spite of me should become a little mythological." Early on the morning following her arrival she gets up and goes out into the grounds: "The sort of fear that more and more oppressed me was still religious. I murmured these words: *hic nemus.* The air was crystal clear; there was a strange silence. I was thinking of Orpheus, of Armida, when suddenly a single bird song arose so close to me, so full of pathos, so pure that it seemed suddenly as if all nature was waiting for it. My heart beat wildly; I remained a moment leaning against a tree, then went in before anyone was up."

In her fear of awakening the great god Pan she banishes from her life not only secular literature but even religious works if too well written and hence capable of arousing the wrong emotions. A part of the reason for this moral surgery is that the love of literature is a bond between her and Jérôme, and banishing from her shelves the books that he loves is like cutting him out of her heart. She wants also to wean him from herself, destroy what she is pleased to call his illusions. Defiantly she shows him her mutilated library; she manages to have the piano removed for repairs when he is coming for a visit, so that they cannot enjoy music together; she deliberately arranges her hair unbecomingly, wears the most unlovely dresses, converses only tersely and dryly.

At first these acts of mortification are performed not because she considers them meritorious in themselves but in order to alienate Jérôme. For a time, trusting to the protection of distance, she allows her repressed emotions a little expansion in her letters to Jérôme; but in the inexorable march toward total renunciation she reaches the point of forbidding herself to write to him at all, and takes refuge in her journal. Even here she tracks down the remnants of her love and destroys much of what she has written. Once she is on the point of burning the whole record; but she cannot bring herself to obliterate entirely the explanation of her apparently unloving coldness to Jérôme, and directs that after her death he shall read what she has permitted to survive of her journal.

Long before the end it is evident even to Alissa herself that her conduct is not to be explained solely on the ground of desire for Jérôme's spiritual good. "The reasons which make me flee from him?" she asks herself. "I no longer believe in them. And yet I flee from him, sadly, and without understanding why I do it." The love of beauty in all its forms, which she thought she was suppressing for Jérôme's sake, takes on for her the appearance of a vice to be crushed—why, she does not know, unless it be that she is driven to present herself before her Maker stripped of every conceivable attachment.

Her father, who, by his dependence on her, constitutes the last ostensible barrier to her marriage with Jérôme, dies, but she only retreats deeper within, living alone at Fongueusemare and growing daily weaker in body. As her hold on physical living relaxes, a rebellious desire for its rewards flares up again. "Poor Jérôme," she writes, "if he only knew that sometimes he has only a gesture to make and that sometimes I am waiting for it." She comes to believe that she will see him once more, and goes into the garden daily and calls his name. One evening he is there, and she finds the perverse courage to resist his appeal; but that night, when he is gone forever, her lips and her hands grope for him in vain.

In a final act of self-isolation she makes a will, leaves Fongueusemare without telling anyone where she is going, and hides herself in a small nursing home in Paris, where, abandoning and abandoned, she faces the solitary end of her path. In a sudden shudder of disenchantment she sees her whole life, realizes where she is, and that the walls of her room are bare. She is frightened, prays "Lord let me attain to the end without blasphemy"—and dies.

The immediate way to take this story, particularly after such a bare summary, is to see in it nothing but the description of a pathological case. Alissa has a masochistic craving for suffering, but this is not all: both she and Jérôme are natural solitaries, at their exalted best when separated and writing letters to each other, but constrained and uneasy when proximity summons them to translate their flights of imagination into the realities of personal relations. Alissa does not really love Jérôme, nor anyone else; all she loves are her own emotions, which she is trying to intensify by discipline and selection.

This interpretation is to some extent justified not only by the book itself but by the author's statement of his intentions. Gide meant to paint the portrait of a woman's soul, "of a Protestant soul in which is enacted the essential drama of Protestantism." This drama, impossible in authoritarian Catholicism, lies, as Gide explained to Claudel, in the fact that Protestantism "starts the soul on unforeseen ways which can lead to what I have shown. Or else to free-thinking. It is a school of heroism, of which I think my book brings out the error rather well; it lies precisely in a sort of higher infatuation. . . . But it can also be accompanied by true nobility."

This last sentence reveals the difference between the purely pathological interpretation and Gide's intention. In his view Alissa was mistaken but hers was a noble error; he wanted to show not so much the aberrations of an individual as the dangers inherent in Protestantism. Alissa was the victim of her religious education, and as such she had to enlist the sympathy, not the contempt, of the reader. "I was afraid," Gide continued in his explanations to Claudel, ". . . that detached from all exterior motivation this drama might appear paradoxical, monstrous, inhuman; hence the invention of the double plot, the fear of buying her happiness at another's expense—hence particularly the 'sin' of the mother, causing a vague need of expiation." And in a letter to another correspondent he called the book "a critique of Protestantism or of Christian abnegation, and critique does not mean satire—I use the word in the Kantian sense."

The book contains, in addition to its "double plot," an implicit dual judgment on its theme. We find, if we accept the author's evaluation, that Alissa's ideas contain something which cannot be immediately condemned and dismissed. They seem less like unadulterated errors than distorted truths; Gide is able to create this impression because he shares some of her beliefs and can present them with a persuasive sincerity. When Jérôme says of himself, "I sought of the future not so much happiness as the infinite effort to attain it," we are not particularly surprised at meeting one of Gide's basic attitudes because Jérôme to a certain extent represents him in the book; but Alissa too says much the same thing when she confides to her journal, "I wonder now whether it is indeed happiness that I want or a moving toward happiness." Gide's own also are her words, "We are not born for happiness," and her appropriation of the quotations, "God having reserved us for something better" and "All that is not God is incapable of fulfilling my expectation."

Another theme close to Gide's heart suggests itself and whether or not the reader accepts it he cannot help being seriously impressed by the question it raises. Is the quasi-religious character of youthful love merely a disguise for sex? When Jérôme and Alissa listen with exaltation to the solemn words about the strait gate are they only poeticizing a physical urge to reproduction? Or, without denying the little disputed observation that sex and religion are related, can one invert the relationship and say, not that the religious element in love is sex deflected, but that romantic love furnishes a temporary and illusory stopping place for the religious urge to enlarge the self, merge it with something beyond?

Claudel's answer to these questions is the one Gide wanted: "The gross literature of the past century is misleading on the subject of the deeper emotions. No, sexual satisfaction does not satisfy the passion of love, it shrinks it, it is sometimes the caricature of it, usually a deformation and always a transformation. The impulse to 'refusal' is deeply rooted in the heart of woman. . . . There is no richer or more complex dramatic subject, nor one more pathetic for the masculine soul; hence the interest for us of all the books where we watch the struggle of passion against duty, the most moving example of which is *Dominique*. The power of your book lies in the fact that there is no external duty, but only an inner voice."

Gide does not condemn Alissa's initial aspiration and he does not intend us to do so. On the other hand he does not condone the extremes to which her basically sound impulse led her, and in this unfavorable judgment lies his criticism of Protestantism. At the outset we have a basic character in which lives the broadly human urge to expansion beyond the limits of the self, and we have an environment which gives to the point of aspiration the name "God" and surrounds it with precepts of self-mortification. It is this environment which bends the young twig so that, instead of growing straight and true as nature intended, it ends in deformity.

Here is the charming early Alissa, waiting in the garden for Jérôme:

She was by the wall at the end of the orchard, picking the first chrysanthemums which mingled their perfume with that of the dead leaves of the beech grove. The air was saturated with autumn, the sun barely warmed the trellises, but the sky had an oriental purity. Her face was framed, almost hidden, in a large Zealand headdress which Abel had brought back from a journey and which she had put on at once. She did not immediately turn at my approach, but a faint start which she could not repress told me that she recognized my step; and already I was bracing myself, encouraging myself against her reproaches and the severity of the look she would give me. But as I drew close and as, timidly, I was already checking my pace, she, without at first turning her face toward me but keeping it down like a stubborn child, stretched out to me, almost behind her, a hand that was filled with flowers, and seemed to invite me to come. And as I, making a game of it, stopped at this gesture, she turned at last, took a few steps toward me, and raised her face, and I saw that it was full of laughter.

And here is the later Alissa in the same garden:

She was extraordinarily changed; her thinness and her pallor wrung my heart. Leaning heavily on my arm she pressed against me as if she were afraid, or cold. She was still in full mourning and probably the black lace which she had put over her head and which framed her face accentuated her pallor. She was smiling, but seemed to be about to faint.

There is no obstacle between them except her idea that God has reserved them for something better. She gives back to Jérôme her most prized possession, a small cross of amethysts that he gave her, and she tells him to marry someone else and give it later to his daughter. At this Jérôme breaks out, "Alissa! Whom could I marry? You know that I can love only you," and he seizes her in his arms and kisses her. For a moment she seems to yield; then her eyes close, and she says in a gentle voice, "Have pity on us, my friend. Do not spoil our love."

The contrast is sufficiently striking to suggest a doubt. Could the lovely natural girl of the beginning really have turned into the fanatical recluse of the end? Do the delicate music of Gide's style and the poetry of tender reminiscence which saturate the early part of the book lull us into accepting unnoticed a basic disharmony? Perhaps the sentimental interest of the story contributes to the same end: a deathless but unfulfilled love is always appealing, and in *La Porte étroite* there are two of them, Alissa's and Juliette's, both for Jérôme—though why that slack and moody young man should inspire such devotion is a little hard to understand.

Yet if we look more closely we become convinced that the total picture of Alissa is consistent. The potentiality of the fanatic is within the charming girl just as the skeleton and skull underlie her young flesh; her end can be foreseen from her early reaction to the sermon on the strait gate, and the progressive revelation of her motivation is both subtle and convincing.

But this is not to say, necessarily, that the ideas of the book carry conviction. Its charm lies in the early part, where Gide is recalling the scenes and even the events of his own youth, his own emotions and aspirations, above all his love for Madeleine. Here he is on sure ground. But also he is dealing with accessories; the real nub of the book, its theoretical justification, is in the later part, where tender memories are of no use to him. Madeleine was unshakable in faith and moral principles, but, as Gide later remarked, "her kindness tempered all this, and what I say about it would surprise those who have known only the gentle radiation of her grace. I have met fierce puritans: she in no way resembled them." Her self-abnegation was natural, not puritanical; what was negative and privative in it came from her character rather than from her religion. Her clinging to the home ground, her distress at travel, her emotional vulnerability, her instinct of retreat: these were temperamental weaknesses, not religious aberrations. In giving Alissa Madeleine's self-abnegation Gide cut it off from its original source, and to explain it anew he had to strike out for himself.

The resulting (but largely implicit) arraignment of puritanism is in its general terms an old story now; we have become satiated with such attacks. It is still interesting, however, in what it reveals of Gide's own problems, for it hinges on the question of sacrifice, and its relation to self-loss. Sacrifice undertaken from the motive of self-esteem, or as a move in the acquirement of merit, is poisoned at its source; it is only valid when it can scarcely be called sacrifice at all, when it arises spontaneously from the realization that there is no separate good, that the individual's happiness is, and can be no other than, the good of others. The gentle self-effacing Alissa was acting from selfish motives in trying to give up Jérôme to her sister; her later discontent revealed to her that she resented Juliette's being happy without her assistance. But Juliette, in taking the prompt step of accepting her middle-aged suitor, made an immediate and direct response to a situation; it was spontaneous behavior of the sort that Gide had been trying to inculcate in himself. It was not her fault that Alissa was not helped by her act, and her reward was that she achieved, not perhaps what would ordinarily be called happiness, but her own fruitful destiny.

The theoretical kernel of the book is in the journal and letters of Alissa, of which Gide wrote to a friend in 1909, "I am *very pleased* with the journal of Alissa and with nearly all her letters"; this satisfactory result was obtained, he later claimed, by subordinating himself to the demands of the character he had created:

The invasion of myself is natural and so complete that there is nothing, for example, that I have written with more facility, more transport, than the journal and letters of Alissa in my *Porte étroite;* it was so easy for me, so delightful, to yield her my place—yes to give place to a being less complicated than I and who, on that very account, expressed herself with less difficulty.

The account of Alissa's solitary search for God by prayer and meditation was objective in the sense that it did not correspond to a present preoccupation of the author; as he recorded while writing it, "It is an anachronism in the midst of all that we think, feel, and want today. No matter; I have to write it."

But Gide was no stranger to an effort like Alissa's; it was just such a quest that he had described in *Les Cahiers d'André Walter,* and the aspirations of his youthful hero ended, like those of Alissa, in doubt. There are of course great differences between the two books. *La Porte étroite* is immeasurably superior to Gide's first book in literary art, as is only to be expected. Moreover Alissa is morally superior to André Walter, and beyond the reach of his primitive temptations.

And yet there is a basic similarity between the two books. What André Walter wanted was a state of continuous religious exaltation, of which he had had foreshadowings but to which he thought his impurity was a bar. He therefore wanted in addition divine intervention in his temptations, and when it was not forthcoming he concluded that religious aspiration was illusory. Shorter-lived and more victorious is Alissa's struggle against sensuality; but self-love, which is its essence, is with her to the end, and happiness is for her, as for André Walter, the final objective.

For that matter it would be hard to prove that happiness in one form or another is not what everyone basically desires. But happiness may be repressive or expansive, separative or unitive. To seek for a happiness definable in terms of pleasurable emotions is quite a different matter from the mystic's longing for self-loss and union with the Absolute because it is a demand of his deepest nature without whose satisfaction he can find no resting place. When Alissa writes "'All that is not God is incapable of fulfilling my expectation.' O too human joy which my imprudent heart desired. . . . Was it to wring this cry from me, Lord, that you have reduced me to despair?"—she is far beyond the elementary petitions of André Walter.

And yet her appropriation of the mystical cry of Pascal is belied by the whole course of her conduct and preoccupations. Never does she forget herself, the state of her own soul, and she moves into a steadily shrinking area of sympathies and interests. The true mystic may be and often is physically isolated, and he always believes that the Kingdom of Heaven is within him; but a progressive spiritual isolation can result only in the defeat of his quest.

It is surely gratuitous to reproach Gide, as some have done, for having failed to give us a picture of true mysticism in this book, since his obvious intention is to depict false mysticism. The question of whether there is a true mysticism is simply not raised, and the existence of false varieties is not in dispute. Similarly unraised is the problem of the transcendent existence of God. Alissa dies in doubt, with perhaps a slight balance in favor of disbelief, but the author does not personally commit himself on his own beliefs. He has created a powerful atmosphere, he has made a credible character, and he has suggested certain problems, without answering them. Beyond that, in this book, he has not chosen to go.

But there is a very interesting real life epilogue to *La Porte étroite*.

Gide knew that his wife read the book, in fact he read a part of it to her aloud, but she never made the slightest comment and he never knew to what extent she did or did not recognize herself in Alissa. In his own mind, however, he was clear that Madeleine had served only as a point of departure for Alissa.

And yet, many years after the book was published, she began to resemble the fictional heroine more closely than she had when it was written. She began what looked like a deliberate effort to detach her husband from her. She ceased dressing and arranging her hair in the ways that he liked; she neglected the beautiful hands which he had venerated, exposing them to rough work and inclement weather until they became deformed and almost useless; she could find no time for the quiet sessions of reading aloud that they had both enjoyed and she avoided meeting him on their common ground of love of poetry and music. One day in 1922 she casually mentioned in a letter to him that she had given away the little cross she used to wear, the one which he had given her and which was the original of Alissa's in the novel. More and more deeply she immersed herself in religion and seemed to regret that she could not see her way clear to becoming a nun.

It was not the last phase of their relations, but what had been happening? Was she consciously or unconsciously imitating Alissa? Or had Gide assessed the quality of her self-abnegation, and forecast where it would lead, more accurately than he realized at the time?

8

Corydon

On the merits of *La Porte étroite,* as on so many other subjects, Gide was of two minds. At the time of its publication he told Jammes that he had put into it the best of himself. A few months later his judgment was more severe: "The book now seems to me like a nougat in which the almonds are good (i.e., letters and journal of Alissa) but whose body is pasty, badly made; however it could not be otherwise, given the narrator—the slack character of my Jérôme necessitates slack prose. So that, everything considered, I think the book is effective. But how I long to write something different! It will be ten years before I again dare use the words: love, heart, soul, etc." In March of 1913 he wrote: "Reread last night fifty pages of *La Porte étroite;* each time I take the book up again it is with an indescribable emotion." But the literary judgment he goes on to give does not materially differ from that of late 1909.

From these comments it appears that Gide did not so much change his mind about the book with the passage of time as have different reactions to different aspects of it. The writing in the name of Alissa was good, in the name of Jérôme, at least appropriate; as for the subject, he felt that he had outgrown it—at any rate he was heartily tired of it. When he said that he had put "the best of himself" into the book, he used the same phrase as he had to describe his love for his wife, to whom the *Porte étroite* was dedicated, and the "indescribable emotion" aroused by rereading was less esthetic than nostalgic—it made him recall the days when he believed and aspired.

Although he was glad enough to have attained success at last, he could not help a feeling of annoyance at the marked preference of the public for this book over all his other work. "If I were to die today," he wrote in 1910, "all my work would disappear behind *La Porte étroite*." What he wanted was for this book to obtain an equal footing with his others and particularly with *L'Immoraliste*, which he considered its counterweight; but admirers of the one could not forgive him the other. "It is hard for them to admit," he wrote in 1909, "that these different books lived, and still live, side by side in my mind. They are successive only on paper and because of the total impossibility of writing them at the same time. Whatever may be the book I am writing I never give myself to it entirely, and the subject that claims me the most insistently immediately afterwards has meanwhile been developing in the opposite side of myself."

It was therefore natural for him to value this "opposite side" more highly in 1909 than the one which *La Porte étroite* represented; but in a more durable way and with the advantage of perspective he came to feel that this book was not to be classed among his most characteristic, his most individual contributions to literature. "Of all my books," he wrote in 1922, "the one which . . . brought me the most substantial, the warmest, the most immediate praise was the one which (not the least effective perhaps) remains the most outside of the body of my work, which *interests* me the least (I am using the word in its subtlest sense) and which, everything considered, I should be the most willing to see disappear."

All that yet remained to be said was so much more important. Repeatedly between 1911 and 1914 he stated that he had not yet even begun to deliver himself of his essential message. "It seems to me," he wrote to Jammes in 1911, "that up to the present I have written merely 'early works,' and that only now I am face to face with the large projects"; and two years later he wrote in his Journal: "Sometimes I think that I have written nothing serious up to now, that I have presented my thought only ironically, and that if I were to disappear today I should leave a picture of myself that even my guardian angel could not recognize."

Directly or indirectly he had allowed religion to shackle him. Racine had been silenced by it in mid-career, not entirely, Gide guessed, because he no longer wanted to write but because of the thinness of the subjects that were in accord with his new piety. Literature presented the paradox that the "new creature" was an old subject; in the hidden mysteries of the "old Adam" lay the true novelty.

"You are at perfect liberty," wrote Gide, "to limit yourself to already cultivated lands if you do not feel equal to coping with the new and reducing them to order; but allow others, to whom robustness, hardiness, *curiosity,* and perhaps a certain ambitious and passionate unrest propose a bolder adventure, to attack these new territories."

Not piety, not the life of reason, least of all calculated self-interest, but behavior unconsciously motivated in the roots of one's being, ardent spontaneity, a passionately curious pushing on to the new: here were the fields he wanted to explore. Nor was this all; there was a personal element in his preoccupations. To explore the roots of one's being meant to bring them into the light of day, and that in turn involved open avowal of one's secret tendencies. Ever since he had discovered and admitted to himself his homosexual tendencies he had felt that sooner or later "everything must be made manifest," and by two steps: first a biological, psychological, and sociological investigation of homosexuality, and second an avowal in the form of an autobiography of his own addiction to it. The projects became respectively *Corydon* and *Si le grain ne meurt;* both were first issued in private printings, and both were openly published in 1924, though *Si le grain ne meurt* was not put on sale until 1926.

His long delay in coming into the open arose partly from a natural irresolution before a fateful and decisive step, but largely because such a revelation would be painful and embarrassing to friends, family, and above all to his wife. Before he could provoke a scandal that would cause suffering to others he had to convince himself that in so doing he would not only serve the law of his own being but do service to persons like himself. That his desires were not unique a little rational reflection showed him at the outset; that homosexuals were more numerous than he had at first supposed was gradually borne in upon him; and he finally became persuaded that these social pariahs were obscurely obeying some law of nature about which the public was in ignorance and that therefore the stigma attached to their anomaly was an injustice. Here, then, was the justification that he needed: self-revelation could become a crusade on behalf of a persecuted minority.

Gide was at work on *Corydon* as early as 1908, before he had finished *La Porte étroite*, and he continued his efforts at intervals for the next two years. But friends whom he took into his confidence (particularly his brother-in-law Marcel Drouin, who was uncompromisingly hostile to the whole project, and Paul Laurens, who objected chiefly to the manner of presentation) persuaded him to lay the work aside. In the spring of 1911, however, he had twelve copies of what he had so far written, secretly and anonymously printed in Belgium; at that time two and a part of the third of the four projected dialogues were completed, and the rest, unprinted, existed as notes and rough draft. The printed copies were not circulated but put away in a drawer. In 1917 and 1918 he took up the project again, and in 1920 published the four dialogues with a preface in an anonymous private edition of ninety-seven copies. For the public edition of 1924 he wrote a second preface.

To arrive at a fair judgment on *Corydon* and on Gide's motives in writing it calls for all the sympathetic understanding we can summon. The book is undisguised special pleading, an attempt to rationalize and justify desires of which, at one time certainly, he would have been glad to be rid; unless the reader is already a partisan of the cause he must divest himself, in order to be just, of the profound indoctrination of the religion, morals, and customs of our current civilization, and of his still more deeply rooted personal sexual preferences—no inconsiderable task.

And it is precisely this heterosexual prejudice that is the topic of the first dialogue between Corydon, a homosexual, and the narrator, a typically prejudiced but not unintelligent heterosexual. Corydon tells his own rather melodramatic story. Before understanding his own nature he was engaged to be married; his fiancée had an adolescent brother by whom he was strongly, if obscurely, attracted and who in turn showed an innocent but caressing affection for Corydon. Feeling that severity, both for himself and for the boy, was in order, Corydon gave him a traditional moral lecture; the youth was reduced to despair and committed suicide, leaving a note in which he confessed an unconquerable love for his future brother-in-law. The affair decided Corydon's vocation; he broke off his engagement, studied medicine, and prepared to devote his life to curing young homosexuals of hypochondria over their abnormality by the means which he had successfully used to cure himself: persuading them that they were not pathological cases.

Corydon addresses himself to the task of convincing his interlocutor that there is such a thing as heterosexual prejudice and that its roots are more in custom than in nature. That there is a conspiracy, general but unconscious, to exalt heterosexuality at the expense of homosexuality, rather than merely a natural expression of a general preference, is shown by the excess of the insistence. Men talk of desire for the opposite sex in a self-congratulatory way, and among themselves with smiles of complicity, as if it were a proof of manliness, strength, naturalness. Everything, they defiantly insist, is right, natural, admirable if it takes place between members of opposite sexes; between members of the same sex everything is wrong, unnatural, base. Against this sweeping judgment Corydon protests; on both sides of the dividing line there are normality and abnormality, and abnormality on the homosexual side is aggravated by the dominant heterosexual prejudice which forces homosexuals into ruses and detours.

At this point it is advisable to take notice of Gide's definitions and the limitation of his subject, which are not wholly clear from the book but which may be supplemented from the Journal. The subject, properly speaking, of *Corydon* is the defense of pederasty ("I call a pederast the man who, as the word indicates, falls in love with young boys"). The case for or against sodomy ("I call a sodomite . . . the man whose desire is addressed to mature men") is not presented, and here Gide shows himself neutral. On the subject of inversion ("I call an invert the man who, in the comedy of love, assumes the role of a woman and desires to be possessed") Gide is not neutral; whereas he considers pederasty "normal," inversion is for him pathological and degenerate, so that theories of the "Urning," the intermediate sex, the female soul in a male body, of such writers as Ulrichs, Krafft-Ebing, Hirschfeld, Edward Carpenter, or, later, of Marcel Proust—are for his purposes basically insufficient.

In order to show that homosexuality (exclusive of inversion) is natural, Gide proceeds in the second dialogue to the natural history of sex in the animal world below man, and makes through Corydon the challenging statement that the "sexual instinct" as an irresistible force precipitating the sexes toward each other does not exist. This apparent flouting of evidence is not so flagrant as it at first appears, for all depends on the meaning one assigns to "instinct," a word so often used to cover ignorance. Corydon, with some reason, claims that precision is an inalienable characteristic of instinct, and precise is exactly what the sexual "instinct" is not. There is an urge to sexual satisfaction and there exists a racial necessity for reproduction; "Nature" (for Gide, like the biologists he quotes and with apologies, finds himself obliged to use this metaphysical entity and to attribute to it purposeful behavior) tries to bring the urge and the necessity together. The animal wants satisfaction and cares nothing for reproduction; Nature wants reproduction and cares nothing for the satisfaction of the animal; she traps him into reproduction with the bait of pleasurable satisfaction.

The male animal cares nothing for the female as such; he is indifferent to her except when she is in heat, and then only as the bearer of an odor which automatically stimulates his desires; for him one female is as good as another, and the odor excites him independently of the presence of the female.

Corydon uses the prodigality of Nature as an argument in proof of the imprecision of the sexual urge: prodigality in the number of males in the insect world, in the amount of seed in animals. The apparent superfluity is in reality a necessity if Nature's end of reproduction is to be served because of the many contingencies to which successful mating is subject. Moreover the female is not indispensable to the satisfaction of the male; to insure the fertilization of all females there must be an excess of the male element, whether as individuals or in seed.

The animal's oversupply of seed and the urge which it

denotes must find an outlet when the female is not in heat or is otherwise unavailable; the excess energy goes into the production of male beauty (conspicuously superior to that of the female among birds and somewhat less so among mammals) and into homosexual activities, which have been observed, in a more or less incomplete form, in a considerable number of species. Male beauty was supposed by Darwin and others to be an element in sexual selection: the female would chose the most beautiful mate she could and the race would thereby be improved. But Corydon is skeptical of this reasoning; if there is competition for a female among males it is the strongest, not the most beautiful, who will win and whom she will be obliged to accept; the "selection" is an impersonal process, and does not involve genuine individual choice. Consequently the beauty of the male is gratuitous. Similarly his homosexual activities serve no utilitarian end and they are not necessitated by a mechanical stimulus like odor; they constitute free play.

The role of the female, then, is conservation; that of the male, variation, experimentation, sport, song.

When in the third dialogue Corydon passes on to a consideration of human sex he points out that in the evolutionary transition from animal to man the mechanical stimulus to reproduction—odor—loses its importance. This fact has immense significance, because the female cannot now depend on the automatic and infallible effect of her periods of heat to attract the male, but must make herself desirable in other ways and at all times. So beauty becomes the appanage of woman, and man, no longer constrained to respond to any female in heat, is free to desire one woman and remain unmoved by another, and the game of love—a human game, quite different from the play of animal mating—begins.

The enormous emphasis laid on female beauty in contemporary society, the proliferation of aids to its achievement such as cosmetics, hairdressing, and clothes, together with the concomitant stiffness and soberness of male attire and the prejudice against aids to masculine beauty, as if there were an intent to make the dull male a foil to the glamorous female—all this suggests how important it is that the female remain attractive, suggests too that she is in serious need of all the support she can get; it is as if society were making a concerted though unconscious effort to second the purpose of Nature. That the female face and figure are inherently more beautiful than the male is (and was still more so at the time of Gide's writing) a canon of popular esthetics which one can call into question only at the risk of being considered a homosexual.

But on this point Gide insists, as artists have often declared, that from the purely esthetic point of view the lines of the youthful male figure are more satisfying than those of the female, and that the popular preference for the female is based on prejudice and disguised desire; and he quotes in support of his belief the reported conversation of Goethe with Chancellor Müller: "Goethe explained to us how this aberration [pederasty] came really from this: that by the pure esthetic rule the male body was much more beautiful and more perfect and more accomplished than the female body. Such a sentiment, once awakened, turns easily to baseness. Pederasty is as old as humanity and one can say therefore that it is natural, that it is based on Nature, although it goes against

Nature. What culture has gained, has won back from Nature, should be firmly held, should on no account be allowed to escape."

Gide was by no means hostile to the idea, used by Goethe as an argument against pederasty, that culture does, and should, inhibit and restrain Nature; it was in fact one of his basic precepts, and he owed it, in considerable measure, to Goethe himself. But at this stage of his argument he is concerned only with showing that admiration for male beauty is esthetically justified and that desire for the male by the male is natural, even though it is not in accordance with Nature's purpose of reproduction.

One further point made in this third dialogue is that the awakening desires of the human adolescent are by nature vague, not specifically and exclusively directed to the opposite sex: "Pleasure is attractive to him, whichever be the sex of the creature that dispenses it . . . he owes his mores rather to a lesson from without than to the decision of his desire; or, if you prefer, I say that it is rare that desire becomes precise by itself and without the support of experience."

The fourth dialogue, not included in the 1911 printing, is extremely important to an understanding of Gide's argument; without it one can readily understand why his friends urged him not to publish at that time. In this concluding section he first takes up the proposal in Léon Blum's book *Du mariage* that the problem posed by excess male energy be solved by relaxation of the social stricture against premarital intercourse by women of good standing. Gide found the idea profoundly shocking, and he said so not only through Corydon but in his Journal. His counterproposal is, of course, the legitimation of pederasty.

The outstanding historical example of pederasty socially accepted and even approved is among the ancient Greeks, whose cultural achievements are universally admired but whose harmonious way of life seems to the modern mind to be vitiated by pederasty. Any student of Greek literature must at some time have been struck by the way this practice is intertwined with the boldest flights of speculation and imagination; Plato's *Symposium*, for example, furnishes inspiring quotations but is disconcerting to read straight through because of its tolerant and even playful allusions to pederasty. Is not this anomaly, Gide asks, in ourselves rather than in the Greeks? Must we not face the possibility that their cultural achievements were accomplished not in spite of but to some degree because of their tolerance of pederasty? It is no historical accident, he continues, that pederasty has been openly, almost officially, recognized, not in times of decadence but in periods of artistic and cultural efflorescence: in Greece at the time of Pericles, in Augustan Rome, in Shakespearean England, in the Italian Renaissance, in France under Francis I and Louis XIII, in Persia at the time of Hafiz.

Pederasty has been associated with martial as well as with artistic qualities: a picked battalion of Thebans, according to Plutarch, was composed of lovers, whose valor and honor were stimulated by their desire to stand well in each other's eyes, and Diodorus of Sicily reports that the warlike Celts were notoriously homosexual.

Moreover, Gide argues, the institution of pederasty in Greece exalted the position of woman by removing her from the arena of competitive desire; the Greek woman was raised for maternity and the home, not to be the instrument of male pleasure. Race suicide is more evident in a country like modern France, where heterosexual pleasure is strongly emphasized, than it was in Greece.

It is important to note that Gide expresses himself as opposed to license and in favor of self-control; he has earlier pointed out the importance of continence for sublimating sexual energy into desirable moral and artistic qualities. He emphatically protests that he has not a word to say against marriage and reproduction; yet he suggests that it would be of benefit to an adolescent, before his desires are fixed, to have a love affair with an older man, instead of with a woman, for educative purposes and as a cure for solitary vice. The proposal disregards the general principle, admitted by Gide elsewhere in his treatise, that sexual practice tends to stabilize in the direction where it has first found satisfaction; to inoculate a youth with homosexual tastes seems an odd way to prepare him for matrimony. A strongly marked homosexual bent is not an absolute bar to reproduction but it would certainly be an obstacle to normal heterosexual relations.

The word "love," freely applied throughout *Corydon* to homosexual relationships, is confusing. These attachments, Gide believes, can be quite as chaste and as idealistic as youthful heterosexual love, and he states that Louise Labé's remark, in *Débat de folie et d'amour*, is equally applicable to them: "Lubricity and ardor of the loins have nothing, or very little, in common with love." The implicit trend of the argument in the fourth dialogue is to reserve marriage for reproduction and to interpret the phrase "normal heterosexual relations" as "intercourse for procreative purposes." Of himself, furthermore, he elsewhere stated that he was capable of the reproductive urge only if no sentiment was involved in the relationship.

Yet in *Si le grain ne meurt*, written in the interval between the inception and the completion of *Corydon*, he
gives us clearly to understand that he felt "love" for
Emmanuèle, that this deep and pure feeling was polluted
if he had physical relations with another woman, but that
in his relations with Arab boys he experienced a natural
"pleasure" uncomplicated by either remorse or love. We
have already noted a progressive intrusion of sentiment
into his homosexual experiences, and might assume that
the feelings described in his memoirs were those of his
youth only, but for the fact that he continued to assert his
distinction between pleasure (or desire) and love. For the
homosexual attachments of his maturity "love" seems the
most accurately descriptive word, but it must have represented something very different from the enduring feeling
he had for his wife.

Perhaps the nearest approach we can make to a reconciliation of inconsistencies is to say that for Gide there is:
first a love that is not directly associated with sex, that
indeed inhibits desire, and that may be addressed to a
man or a woman indifferently; second a love that is associated with sex and that for a homosexual is addressed to
a member of his own sex and for a heterosexual to the
opposite sex; and third a sexual desire that has nothing to
do with love, that may be addressed to either sex, but that
tends to stabilize in one direction or the other.

Despite some confusion and overstatement of the case
it can scarcely be denied that *Corydon* does score a number of valid points: the prejudice of heterosexuality and
the role of custom and convention in its formation; its
invitation to license within its prescribed limits; the illogic
of treating the sexual mores of the Greeks as an embarrass-

ing anomaly instead of as an integral part of their culture. Moreover Gide anticipates (at least so far as his own knowledge and that of the general public are concerned) the findings of psychoanalysis when he describes the sexual urge in terms that suggest the now familiar libido; or when he points out (buttressing himself here on La Bruyère) that the adolescent passes through a homosexual stage, usually unconsciously, before fixing on heterosexuality; Gide does not, however, like the psychoanalysts, consider a physically mature homosexual a case of arrested development.

But with the average reader the general argument can make small headway, not entirely on account of prejudice but because his desires, whether natural or acquired, are fixed in another direction; he likes things well enough as they are. Such initial erotic curiosity as he may have on opening the book finds scant satisfaction, and the idea of pederasty either revolts or bores him. But ostensibly and throughout most of the book Gide asks of the average reader no more than tolerance and understanding; it is to the homosexual like himself that he is chiefly addressing himself, and for the purpose of convincing him that he is not a monster and an outcast but a child of nature as much as is the heterosexual.

Furthermore Gide wanted not only to make a plea for tolerance and to give a message of hope, but to lay bare the truth, to be the first to dare to say what had hitherto been suppressed by hypocrisy and prejudice. He had the feeling in 1910 that what he had to say was indispensable: "I have never had it more strongly, since I wrote *André Walter*, than now for *Corydon*. The fear that another might get ahead of me; it seems to me that the subject is floating in the air; I am amazed that no one makes a move to seize it before me."

As late as 1942, and again in 1946, he insisted that *Corydon* was the most important of his books—not on esthetic grounds (for he admitted imperfections in his presentation and had already declared in the 1924 preface that he intended to disappoint those who might look for "pleasure, art, wit, or anything but the simplest expression of a very serious thought"), but because he believed that his book told the truth, psychologically and sociologically.

But it is significant that Gide does not identify himself with Corydon, whose antecedents, profession, and person are different from his creator's, and who has a serenity and an assurance that Gide would like to have but has not attained. He represents—like Michel in *L'Immoraliste* and the later Edouard of the *Faux-Monnayeurs*—a part of the nature of Gide, who supplies him with arguments but will not personally follow them to their logical conclusion. He represents the pederast at his impossible best, he is what Gide would like—sometimes—to be. But this "sometimes" is important, for the doubt breaks through, and in the words, inconsistently but necessarily, of Corydon. "I do not oppose Uranism to chastity," he says at one point, "but one desire for possession, whether satisfied or not, to another." And again: "I am not opposing debauchery, of whatever sort it may be, to chastity, but one impurity to another." Both homosexual and heterosexual practices, Gide is saying through Corydon, are "impure" by comparison with "pure" chastity. There is here a stubborn remnant of puritanism; his secret ideal is still chastity, and if he is to fall short of it he does not find much moral difference between homosexuality and heterosexuality.

He has a hierarchy of values. At one extreme is desire turned inward on itself, narcissistic; this is the lowest and the worst, it is the experience of hell itself. To attach desire, homosexually or heterosexually, to an object outside of oneself is to escape from hell, but it is an expedient, not a final solution; even if this attachment contains a beginning of love, it is tainted by the desire for individual gratification, in which the sex partners are each other's accomplices in the stimulation of private sensations. "As soon as desire enters into it," he wrote in 1921, "love cannot hope to last." There remains the ultimate ideal, the far end of the road: a totally outgoing unselfregarding love, with its necessary accompaniment of chastity.

Gide recognizes two way stations between narcissism and pure love: homosexuality and heterosexuality; and his principal effort in *Corydon* is to make them appear to occupy the same relative position on the map. He does not seem to recognize that homosexuality is the nearer of the two to narcissism, because in attaching oneself to another of the same sex one is using him as a convenient external projection of oneself. "It is not what resembles me but what differs from me that attracts me," he said in the *Journal des Faux-Monnayeurs,* but however true the statement may have been in some respects it did not apply to his sexual life. He confessed to a lifelong physiological incuriosity about the opposite sex, and in his childhood his physical familiarities with girls had the total indiscretion of indifference, whereas with boys his hands, restrained by shame and a somber attraction, never strayed below the belt.

Corydon states that he was "cured" by convincing himself that he was not sick; in other words he attained peace

of mind not by conquering but by domesticating his inclination. It is quite clear that Gide tried to do the same
thing and sometimes thought he had succeeded. "Ceasing
to call my desires temptations," he wrote in the fall of
1893, "I strove on the contrary to obey them. . . . In so
doing was I not following perfectly natural laws?" And
in a note on *Corydon* written in 1911 he stated: "It is certain that I am writing it out of season and at a time when
I no longer need to do so. . . . I must artificially revive a
problem for which, so far as I am concerned, I have found
a practical solution, so that to tell the truth it no longer
torments me."

That Gide was sometimes able to persuade himself that
his desires were natural and right rather than sinful is no
doubt true, but the rationalization was neither a solution
nor practical. The problem, both inner and outer, remained. If he succeeded in eluding his conscience, he was
still confronted with the difficulty of finding ways to satisfy his desires at a time when he was still keeping them
secret (so he thought) from his wife and from all but a
few very intimate friends; and the difficulty and risk of
finding such ways on his home ground are probably a
partial explanation of his many trips to Italy and North
Africa.

But his stubborn conscience kept tracking him down, as
the periodic recurrence of remorse and self-disgust in the
Journal testifies. On April 24, 1910, for example, he writes,
"The latest adventures I have pursued have left me an
unutterable disgust." On November 14 of the same year
he recalls how at Biskra in 1893 he used to sit quietly in a
native café, attracted by a number of Arab youths but
making no move toward any of them; he goes on, "I well

know that today, more restless, alas, further advanced in debauchery, I could not remain a mere contemplator as I then could." If he was cured, why "alas" and why "debauchery"?

Such reflections cast light on another of his notes on *Corydon,* this one probably written in 1918: "What first made me undertake it, or what gave me the first idea for it, was the disavowal of that false saintliness which my disdain for the ordinary temptation gave me." Such words make the composition of *Corydon* seem like a defiant confession. It is as if he were saying, "You think I am good because I do not seduce young girls or my neighbor's wife? I tell you I am bad; this is what I am." And yet with this motive, or partly with this motive, he writes, not a confession of sin, but an argument to prove that his sin is no sin.

It is this ambivalence that gives Gide's writings their enigmatic quality. "I have never been able to give anything up," he wrote in 1919; "conserving in myself both the best and the worst, I have lived like a man drawn and quartered." He was writing *Corydon* while still at work on *La Porte étroite,* and was engaged in a religious correspondence with Claudel at the time he was preparing an attack on the Church in *Les Caves du Vatican.* Claudel later called it hypocrisy, but he was unjust: it was "sympathy" that was tearing Gide apart—sympathy that had become no more than a name for inner conflict. "I find a great danger in a sympathy that is too accessible. It invites to a succession of different paths, each leading to equally delightful prospects. At one moment the soul becomes infatuated with a soft moist country that contains only what is tender, flexible, voluptuous, and produces it in abundance; at another it is inspired by the arid blaze of sandy dunes."

These words were written in 1911, and by January of 1912 his misgivings seemed to be leading him toward a crisis. "Have I reached the limit of experience?" he wrote in Neuchâtel, "and am I going to be able to get hold of myself again? I must make a wise use of my remaining energy. How easy it would be now to rush to a priest and confess! How hard it is to be for oneself, at the same time the one who commands and the one who obeys! . . . Urgent necessity of getting hold of myself again. But at past forty can one still make resolutions? One lives according to twenty-year-old habits." Without much conviction he proceeded to draw up one of his old sets of rules for conduct: never to go out without a definite aim, to walk without looking in every direction, to take in a train the first compartment that presented itself, to forbid himself every kind of vacillation.

But by that evening, feeling in better physical condition, he was already ashamed of his agitation, and the impending crisis was deferred.

Meanwhile Claudel, in his letters to Gide, had been recurring, more tactfully than at first but still insistently, to the subject of conversion, and he was seconded in his efforts by Jammes whom with small effort he had herded into the fold in 1905. But Gide was more wary now and, beneath a show of emotion, his replies were skillfully evasive. "What shall I say about the close of your letter?" he wrote to Claudel on January 7, 1911. "It stirs me to the depths; but the memory of the ardent piety of my adolescence is sharp enough to make me understand the joy which you describe today— Goodbye dear friend; I leave you on an uncompleted sentence."

In June of the same year he wrote to Jammes, "How many times I have read your letter, dear friend! Ah! what ready access it finds to my heart. How easily your affection persuades me and how beautiful and deep, I feel, is the inspiration that prompts you to write to me in this way. What can I answer? And what answer would not seem to you absurdly inadequate except to fall on my knees as you expect? If a voice as friendly and as gently pressing as yours cannot hasten this result, be assured that no other voice . . . can do anything to retard it."

The following January he wrote in his Journal, "I wish I had never known Claudel. His friendship weighs on my thought, obligates it, impedes it. I still cannot bring myself to cause him pain, but my thinking becomes stronger in opposition to his."

The fact is that by this time Catholicism had almost become a dead issue for him, but because of this "almost" —the faint possibility that submission to the Church in defiance of his reason might prove to be his only escape from a moral dilemma—he kept the door ajar; for this reason and because he did not want to offend his zealous friends. The crux of the matter was that he was unable to accept the principle of authority: the idea that a man, or certain men, or an institution, had the right to make decisions on matters of faith and morals that must be accepted without question. "I do not recognize any authority," he said; "but if I recognized one it would be that of the Church." And in succinct summary of his position he wrote, in February of 1912: "Catholicism is inadmissible.

Protestantism is intolerable. And I feel myself profoundly Christian."

Although Christianity in a broad sense was still a live option for him, there was no major inconsistency in his attacking the Church in *Les Caves du Vatican*. At the most he was pressing on the almost closed door; perhaps he even wanted to slam it shut and thus end once and for all the temptation of Catholicism.

9

Attack on Rome

Between 1909, date of the publication of *La Porte étroite*, and 1914, Gide was occupied with three books: *Corydon, Isabelle*, and *Les Caves du Vatican;* this in addition to critical articles, his Journal (some of which was published at this time), and plans for two treatises never published as such (*Le Christianisme contre le Christ* and *Traité des Dioscures*), for his memoirs (later *Si le grain ne meurt*), and for *L'Aveugle*, which was to become *La Symphonie pastorale*.

Of the three works printed within this interval *Isabelle* gave him the least trouble. It was another of his relatively short tales, limited in scope and polished in execution. Some consider it one of the most perfect of Gide's productions; others find it tenuous, too slight to bear comparison with books of more challenging subject matter. But for once the author had no intention of challenging anyone; in a letter written in 1911, the year of the publication of *Isabelle*, he called it "a semi-playful interlude between two excessively serious works," and to Du Bos he said in 1914: "Only one of my books was written from the outside, so to speak: *Isabelle.* I had seen the story of the book and I wrote it rather like an exercise, for practice, and it shows in the result."

As a matter of fact *Isabelle* is both superlatively well done and relatively unimportant. It comes closer than any of his other works of fiction to being a purely gratuitous work of art; it has no important message to communicate, no utilitarian purpose. But Gide, despite his desire to be judged primarily as an artist, stands thoroughly committed in his works viewed as a whole to the communication of doctrines and ideas; if this were not so he would not have been able to insist that *Corydon* was his most important book. On the same reasoning *Isabelle* could be called his least important production.

Not that it lacks a theme, as is shown by the fact that at one time he planned to entitle, or subtitle, it *The Pathetic Illusion.* But the idea that love is blind, that the realities of living cure a young man of romantic illusions, is so trite a subject that one can only be grateful to the author for having decided not to force it on our attention by the title. The real charm of *Isabelle* is that the whole story seems to emanate by a kind of poetic necessity from the atmosphere of an abandoned manor. It is not an intellectual demonstration but a musical composition. But for these very reasons, and because the story does constitute an exception in Gide's work, it need not detain us here.

"Finished *Les Caves* yesterday . . . ," wrote Gide on June 24, 1913. "It is a curious book; but I am beginning to be thoroughly sick and tired of it."

He did not know how odd it was to seem to his readers, nor what strange belated admirers—Dadaists and other groups of young *avant-garde* intellectuals—were to take it up after the war. In the brief interval between its publication and the fateful August of 1914 it drew considerable abuse and scant praise; it was as much of a failure as *Les Nourritures terrestres* or *L'Immoraliste,* and little more was needed to convince its stubborn author that he had again written a book of unappreciated significance.

No small part of the strangeness of *Les Caves du Vatican* is due to the mutual incompatibility of the ingredients which had accumulated during the long course of its preparation. Gide first told the plot of it to Paul Laurens at Biskra in 1893; probably at that time he had planned no more than the central incident of the supposed abduction of the Pope and the conspiracy to raise money for his deliverance, an idea full of possibilities for satire.

Not until January 1902, however, is there any indication that Gide was thinking along lines that were to lead first to *Les Caves du Vatican* and then to the closely connected *Faux-Monnayeurs.* During a long walk at that time along the outer boulevards of Paris, he tells us, the novel that had long been in the back of his mind began to take shape and its central problem to appear as the relationship between a dozen characters. Hitherto his most natural literary medium had been (and for several more years was to continue to be) the *récit,* the short novel aiming at intensity and perfection of expression rather than breadth of scope.

At about the same time, or a little later, began his deep admiration for Dostoevsky, with whose works he had previously had no more than a casual acquaintance. Typical of his changing attitude toward the great Russian is a Journal entry of May 1903: "We are reading *The Adolescent* [*A Raw Youth*] aloud. At the first reading the book

had not seemed to me so extraordinary, but more complicated than complex, overcrowded rather than substantial,
more curious than interesting. Today I am filled with
astonishment and admiration at every page. I admire
Dostoevsky more than I thought was possible."

From then on he read everything he could find by or
about Dostoevsky, and his interest bore external fruit in
a long article in 1908 entitled "Dostoevsky according to
his Correspondence" (in which he by no means confined
himself to the letters); in a short piece on *The Brothers
Karamazov* intended to arouse interest in the dramatic
adaptation of the novel about to be performed at his
friend Copeau's "Théâtre du Vieux Colombier"; and finally
in six lectures which were published in 1923 with the
earlier material on the same subject and which, whatever
their merits as criticism, constitute an important docu-
ment on Gide's own thought.

The long article of 1908 reveals many of the reasons for
Gide's enthusiasm. At that time the reputation of Dostoevsky was still, as Gide put it, in Purgatory; he had been
presented to French readers in 1886 by Melchior de
Vogüé's *Le Roman russe* with apologies and condescen-
sion as a barbarian quite beyond the sympathetic range
of the cultured French. Gide was moved to assist the rise
of the novelist to the Paradise of literary glory not only by
a readiness to find merit where the general public was too
obtuse to see it but also, one suspects, by a comforting
parallel with his own case: he too was unappreciated, and
his own ideas, like those of his hero, might prove to have
an importance not at first realized. Moreover the letters
showed the deeply human side of Dostoevsky—his weaknesses, his errors, his suffering—whereas the works showed

the godlike aspect of his genius, and his latent capacity for joy through and beyond suffering: all points which awakened a sympathetic response in Gide.

In the doctrine also he found his own ideas mirrored, and above all in Dostoevsky's insistence that individualism and abnegation were not necessarily in conflict. "Must one therefore be impersonal," he quotes Dostoevsky as saying, "in order to be happy? Is salvation in self-effacement? On the contrary, I say, not only should one not efface oneself, but one should become a personality, to an even higher degree than is done in the Occident. Understand me: voluntary sacrifice, in full consciousness and freed of all constraint, the sacrifice of self for the profit of all, is in my view an indication of the greatest development of the personality, of its superiority, of a perfect possession of oneself, of the greatest free will."

As a novelist Dostoevsky seems the opposite of the early Gide, and therein lay a part of his attraction. Where the Russian, pressed for time and money, poured out in rugged abundance, Gide, with ample means and leisure, scrupulously polished his more scanty materials. But beneath the superficial confusion of words and details of his master, Gide learned to discern a real art of character development and relationships; above all he saw what he wanted to develop in his own fictional creations: a structure of unconscious motivation. Dostoevsky's characters so often seem unpredictable because much of their behavior is not dictated by reason or the calculations of self-interest but springs from obscure emotional depths which they do not themselves understand. Here was the treatment called for by Gide's own idea of the gratuitous act.

Slowly the characters of *Les Caves du Vatican* filled out

in his mind, and by 1905 recognizable allusions to them begin to appear in the Journal. Anthime Armand-Dubois makes his first bow with an enormous wen over his right eyebrow which migrates in the finished text to the "southeast of his left ear"; "Barailloul" wears a black wig which he later abandons and he changes the spelling of his name to "Baraglioul." A year later Lafcadio, the central character, makes his entry, and with one of his most characteristic gestures: plunging the point of a penknife into his thigh as self-discipline for a lapse from his plan of deportment.

The title and the names and characteristics of the principal actors of *Les Caves du Vatican,* by contrast with those of Gide's other books, remained remarkably constant throughout the gestation of the novel; on the other hand an important stylistic development took place. The manner which seems most characteristically Gide's own is a musical cadence suggestive of the Bible combined with classical delicacy and restraint. But this style, appropriate enough in *La Porte étroite,* tended to invade other writings to which it was less well suited—*Isabelle,* for example, of which he wrote in April 1910: "The tone does not differ as much as I should like from that of *La Porte étroite;* once more I am indulging in nuances, writing sweetly. I dream of the *Caves,* which I imagine written in a wholly lively style, quite different." The following October he noted: "Last night I read to Em. what I have written of my novel. There are too many nuances, the transitions are too smooth. When I write the *Caves* I shall put one flat tone abruptly beside another flat tone." On finishing *Isabelle* a few weeks later he wrote, "It is probably time now to break with certain habits, certain indulgences in my writing. I want to begin at once. And since this notebook happens to be full, I shall begin another one in which I shall get training, in which I shall cultivate *new relations*. I must not continue on my momentum."

The style of the Journal shows no noteworthy change after this resolution, but the whole tone and manner of *Les Caves du Vatican* are conspicuously different from those of its predecessors; one would almost think it by a different author.

Nor is anything less like Dostoevsky than this new manner of Gide's; if one must find a literary antecedent it is to Villiers de L'Isle-Adam (a writer, incidentally, whom he admired only with reservations) that one must look. The language is elegant, sardonic, distinctly mannered—but quotation of two passages, even in translation, will convey the pervasive tone of the book better than adjectives:

The debonair Julius in spite of himself raised his eyes to the shoulders of his brother-in-law; they were jigging as if activated by deep irresistible laughter; and great was the pity to see this vast half-paralyzed body utilizing in this parody the residue of its muscular resources. Come! Their positions are clearly taken, the eloquence of Baraglioul can effect no change. Time perhaps? the intimate counsel of the holy places. . . .

Soundlessly Véronique pushed open the door, then slipped in furtively, eyes to the ground, like a lay brother passing before obscene graffiti; for she disdained to see, at the end of the room, overflowing the armchair against which leaned a crutch, the enormous back of Anthime arched over some wicked operation. Anthime, on his side, affected not to hear her. But, as soon as she had repassed, he lifted himself heavily from his seat, dragged to the door and, viciously, lips compressed, with an authoritative stroke of the index finger, click! shot home the bolt.

The effect of ironic detachment is accentuated when Gide interrupts his narrative to reprove one of his characters or to address a mock-heroic imploration to his pen; the result is amusing, but detrimental to any sense of reality his fiction may convey: "Halt, O imprudent pen!"— "Lafcadio my friend, you are heading straight for utter banality; if you are to fall in love, do not count upon my pen to depict the disorder of your heart."

A satiric intention is implied by Gide's use of the central episode of the Vatican swindle, which was an early part of the plan as evidenced by the title (he refers, for example, in 1905 to "thinking *again* of the *Caves*") and which may have been the germ idea in 1893. Similarly the inclusion of a critic within the work was an old device, utilized in his first book. But the late adoption of a "lively style" not merely fitted in with these early intentions but accentuated them to the point of compromising his aspiration to write a large scale novel of serious import. The exploration of unconsciously motivated behavior and the criticism of society and the Church can scarcely be taken at their full value when presented in the form of a *sotie*, or farce.

In the course of the long gestation of *Les Caves du Vatican* Gide sometimes thought of his work with hope, amusement, and interest, but toward the end more often with horror. In this change of attitude there seems to be something more than the natural boredom of an author with a book too long in the making. During the year 1912 he was often discouraged and had great difficulty in driving himself to work. On January 30, the day after his return from Switzerland, he was "unable to write anything all day long, from a *total absence of enthusiasm*";

on February 3 his thoughts were "uncertain and painful," and the next day showed "nothing yet"; he was living "in expectation of himself." Throughout the month of February he got no closer to work on his novel than once recording, "I am feeling a little less disavowed by myself. And it even happened that I thought of the *Caves* again without disgust or exasperation."

And when at last the book was finished he regarded the result of his struggles with obvious reservations, and only came to its defense when it was attacked. "All I have written up to now," he wrote on July 6, 1914, "has served only to prepare the ground. My whole work has been merely negative; I have shown only the reverse side of my heart and my mind."

A similar effect is produced by certain sentences of a published letter to Copeau dated August 29, 1913, and serving as a sort of preface to the *Caves:* "Why do I call this book a *sotie?* Why *récits* its three predecessors? It is to show that they are not properly speaking *novels.* . . . *Récits, soties* . . . it seems to me that up to today I have written only *ironic* books (or critical if you prefer), of which this is doubtless the last."

The intentions unfulfilled in the *Caves* were carried over to the *Faux-Monnayeurs,* which began in a "Journal of Lafcadio." Later the role of critical observer was transferred to Edouard, in some respects a double of Gide, and the part of the illegitimate son was given to Bernard. Yet the ingredients of a serious novel are already discernible in the *Caves,* and to their frustrated presence is due a part of the odd savor of the book.

The basic and probably original object of criticism in *Les Caves du Vatican*—the "cellars of the Vatican" or "what lies under the Vatican"—is, as the title suggests, Catholicism, and the attack is made at a critical point in the Church's position. The supreme authority of the Pope derives from the Apostolic succession, supposed to extend back unbroken to Saint Peter, who was designated to head the Church by Christ himself. But what of interruptions in the chain, what of false Popes, what of schisms? Or what if, to suppose a modern case as in the *Caves*, the Pope were abducted and an upstart put in his place? *Ex cathedra* utterances of the Pope are declared by the Church to be infallible, but if the Pope who made them later turns out to be an imposter, what happens to such utterances of his, and the chain of results which they have entailed?

What Gide is suggesting is that the Catholic conception of divine authority vested in human beings is inadmissible; he finds it intolerable that the very salvation of a man's soul should depend on the smooth functioning of a human organization.

Gide's point is emphasized by an epigraph from Claudel's devout *Annonce faite à Marie* (used by permission for the third part of the serialization but withdrawn on the author's demand from the published book): "But of what King are you speaking and of what Pope? For there are two of them, and we do not know which is the right one."

The argument is driven home by a reduction to the absurd. Not only is excommunication in this world of dubious validity if delivered by a fraudulent Pope, but in the life to come may we not discover that the God we have been trying to serve is also an imposter?

Despite his mocking tone Catholicism was no laughing

matter for Gide, not only in the demoralized period that
culminated with the production of *Le Retour de l'enfant
prodigue* but in the recurrence of his religious unrest during 1911 and 1912. In that February of 1912 when he was
having so much trouble working on the *Caves* he made a
significant note in his Journal: "The benefit, the encouragement, that I derive from reading the story of the
condemnation by the Pope of Monseigneur Duchène's
History of the Church enlightens me a little on the secret
cause of my difficulty. Variations on the fear of the *Index.*"

Gide was not the man to have stood in literal fear of the
Index if convinced of the rightness of his cause; his "variations" on this fear were more probably occasioned by a
distrust of the tendencies of his own thought, a dread of
finding an external condemnation reflected in his own
heart; perhaps he also reproached himself for writing
flippantly about serious subjects.

It was in this same February, too, that he summarized
his position as being neither Catholic nor Protestant, but
nevertheless "profoundly Christian."

Les Caves du Vatican, however, can scarcely be called
a "profoundly Christian" book. In it there are no Christians who are neither Catholic nor Protestant, and no
Protestants—only Catholics, and it is they who bear the
brunt of Gide's attack when he passes beyond the doctrinal into the social and moral correlations of religion.
Catholic piety in *Les Caves* centers in the Baraglioul
family and its connections. There is the aged head of the
house, Count Juste-Agénor de Baraglioul, a worldly retired diplomat whose religious practices spring from a
sense of good form and tradition rather than conviction
and who is, as a logical consequence of the book's satiric

premise, neither a knave nor a fool but one of the more sympathetic characters. He is the father, by a high-class courtesan met in his travels, of Lafcadio Wluiki, and by his legitimate spouse of Valentine, Countess Guy de Saint-Prix, and of Julius de Baraglioul. Julius is married to the devout Marguerite and by her is the father of Geneviève (who is sympathetic, clear sighted, and therefore not devout) and of Julie, a precociously pious child of nine.

Julius, the principal target of Gide's satire, is a completely opportunistic hypocrite both as a writer and as a Catholic. His novels are aimed at popular success and admission to the Academy and his piety at preferment and social advantage. The tepid reception of his book *The Air of the Summits* and the temporary check to his aspirations to official literary honors lead him to toy with Lafcadio's ideas for an unconventional novel—assuming, naturally, full credit for them; but better news from the Academy brings him quickly into line with protestations of unswerving constancy to his ideals. He has an eye for the ladies, but with prudence, and when Carola, one-time mistress of Lafcadio, rejects his gallant overtures, his predatory gesture readily becomes paternal, and he contrives to convert the repulse into proof of his moral superiority.

Marguerite, the wife of Julius, is one of three sisters, daughters of the botanist Péterat (a name of absurd implications in French) who, as a result of "conjugal misfortunes," had vowed to give botanical names to all his children; the other two are Véronique (Madame Anthime Armand-Dubois) and Arnica (Madame Amédée Fleurissoire). The latter, although she achieved a much less brilliant marriage than her oldest sister Marguerite, or even than the second Véronique, nevertheless had the choice of two suitors, Amédée Fleurissoire and Gaston Blafaphas, who were already united in the bonds of the tenderest friendship and confirmed in their affection by their common adoration of the pallid Arnica. Compelled to choose between their simultaneous declarations and finding in neither a marked superiority to the other, she finally accepted Fleurissoire because he once accidentally pronounced her given name with the accent on the second syllable, thereby giving it a poetic cadence. But Amédée's success only increased his devotion to Gaston, to whom, in a burst of generosity, he vowed that he would never exercise his conjugal rights on Arnica.

The portrait of Arnica's husband is interesting because in it are caricatured many of Gide's own early, and to some extent still persisting, characteristics and associations: Fleurissoire's flowery name and his marriage into a garden of flowers (symbolically reminiscent of Gide's botanical interests), his timidity and social ineptitude, his vulnerability to insects and vermin, his liability to periodic large pimples or boils, his puritanical morals, his naïve piety, even to the intimate detail of being married to a wife condemned to perpetual virginity. And by another symbolic parallel it is this timid soul who, through high-minded devotion to a false cause, is murdered by Lafcadio, the attractive representative of Gide's Dionysian self.

As for Anthime Armand-Dubois, husband of the second of the flower sisters, one would expect him to be sympathetically presented because, as a scientist and free thinker, he is the declared enemy of Catholicism, and he does indeed come off better at Gide's hands than his brother-in-law Julius de Baraglioul; but he is made amiably absurd, and becomes the means of satirizing the combination of arrogance and naïveté that sometimes appears in the scientific mind.

Armand-Dubois is an experimental psychologist working on rats as a step toward the establishment of a human psychology based on tropisms and having a behavioristic character. "Tropisms!" says Gide ironically. "What a sudden light emanated from these syllables! . . . The cosmos at last became endowed with a reassuring benignity. In the most surprising impulses of the being one could recognize an exclusive perfect obedience to the agent." Meanwhile Armand-Dubois has written a "Note on Conditioned Reflexes" which has created a stir in the academic world.

Evidently such a man is far from the Catholic fold. Only a miracle, his pious wife's confessor tells her, could accomplish his conversion, and destiny, manipulated by Gide, proceeds to turn the figure of speech into a literal fact.

The attitude of Armand-Dubois on miracles is unequivocal. When Marguerite de Baraglioul asks him if he would rather suffer from his sciatica than pray for relief, he furiously replies that if healing were at hand but to get it he had to implore "the honorable Principal" (as he calls God when he is in a bad humor) to upset in his favor the natural order of cause and effect, he would say to the Principal, "Get out with your miracle, I don't want it." And when Julius asks him why, he thumps the table and shouts, "Because that would force me to believe in Him who does not exist."

But that night the Virgin appears to him in the form of the Madonna of a street shrine he has mutilated in a fit of rage, and with her broken arm touches his lame leg.

Instantly he is healed. But the sardonic tone of the narrative emphasizes the author's sense of the incredibility of the reported event: "Still uncertain, one arm extended before, the other behind, he took one step, two steps the length of the bed, three steps, then across the room. . . . Holy Virgin! was he—? Noiselessly he slipped on his trousers, put on his vest, his coat. . . . Halt, O imprudent pen! Where quivers the wing of a soul that is being delivered, what matters the clumsy agitation of a paralyzed body that is being cured?"

Overnight the raging atheist becomes the meekest and humblest of believers, but as a result of his conversion he forfeits the support of his former comrades the Free Masons, and much of his scientific standing, without compensating advantages within the Catholic fold. He bears his misfortunes with such Christian resignation that his devout relatives, who are convinced that if piety doesn't pay there is something wrong with it, are thoroughly exasperated, and his wife Véronique, whose mission in life it has been to suffer and pray for her husband's blasphemies, suddenly finds herself at loose ends, and very much dissatisfied with the situation. At last Julius suggests that Anthime's troubles are due to the fact that the Pope on Saint Peter's throne is an imposter. In that case, decides Anthime, his conversion is invalidated and recantation is called for. And when this has been accomplished, his lameness is restored to the husband and her mission to the wife. The normal domestic equilibrium is back where it was when the inconvenient miracle disturbed it.

The Baraglioul family and their connections represent the established order, based on self-interest inextricably mixed with piety and deeply rooted in long tradition. But the possibilities inherent in a break in this tradition become apparent in the person of Lafcadio, illegitimate son of Juste-Agénor and half-brother of Julius. Just as in the realm of faith a break in the Apostolic succession shakes the Church to its foundations, so in the social sphere the bastard, whose very existence is testimony to a deviation from moral convention, is a threat to the structure of society. He is an outcast, but by compensation he has more liberty than his legitimate relations.

Lafcadio's role in the book is to be the exponent of spontaneous behavior, unadulterated, in contrast to that of his half-brother, by calculations of self-interest. Gide is at great pains to emphasize that this spontaneity is quite distinct from license; hence the rigorous self-discipline of Lafcadio, who punishes himself for lapses into self-indulgence quite as severely as for allowing himself to be duped by others. He is not an ascetic; it is not the joys of the senses that he chastises, but complacency. He will not allow himself to fall into the common human failing of trying to make circumstances redound to his credit. For example, he performs, with great agility and skill, a spectacular rescue of children from a burning building and is in danger of becoming a popular hero. If he had allowed this to happen, he would have had to plunge his penknife many times into his thigh in retribution; but he stands firm in his principles and deprives the crowd of an idol.

If he denies himself complacency or basking in the light of popular favor, he must be equally prepared to flout the laws of society. He helps an old woman with a heavy load and receives her benediction and embraces; he might just as well, he reflects, have strangled her. For spontaneous behavior must be adjusted to circumstances and serve no personal end: she had a load too heavy for her, and so he helped her; she was also ugly and sentimental, so he might have disencumbered the earth of her existence. He is morally prepared for crime but fastidious and scrupulous in his concern for committing just the right one at the right time and place. He must wait for events to ally themselves with his disinterested availability.

An appropriate moment seems to come when he finds himself traveling alone in a compartment with Amédée Fleurissoire, who, though an indirect relation of his, is quite unknown to him. This man is such a wretched specimen of humanity that society would be better off without him. It would be a simple matter to eliminate him, but destiny must coöperate in the act. It is night, and the train is about to cross a viaduct. Lafcadio resolves that if he sees a light outside before he can count to twelve, he will push this miserable little man out the door and over the viaduct. Mentally he starts to count, and before he reaches twelve Amédée's fate is sealed. He falls to his death without a cry and after only a brief struggle.

But Lafcadio has not foreseen the consequences of his experiment in crime. By his act he has set in motion a cause, and he cannot disentangle himself from the effects; detached disinterested behavior has ceased to be possible. Moreover, it is one thing to despise convention and quite another to break an important law; you cannot commit murder without being expelled from normal society and finding yourself automatically in anti-society, the criminal world. The no man's land in which he has aspired to act does not exist.

He is told these things by Protos, a former school companion who has become definitely criminal. In their school

days the two used to divide humanity into *subtils* and
crustacés (roughly the "smart ones" and the "molluscs").
But now Protos has become a professional *subtil*, and
having stumbled upon some clues left by the inexperi-
enced Lafcadio he does a little expert retouching so as
to put the crime beyond the reach of the police—not out of
loyalty to his old companion but because he plans to enroll
the beginner, now in his power, in his organization. For
Protos has become a minor equivalent of the Vautrin of
Balzac (whom Gide greatly admired), the head of an anti-
society; it is he who is the chief architect and organizer
of the swindling "Crusade for the deliverance of the Pope."

But Lafcadio has no more taste for the criminal world
than for normal society, and he is as determined not to be
intimidated as not to be duped; so he dares Protos to do
his worst and calmly disengages himself from his clutches.

Events play into his hand. Carola, the former mistress of
both of them, is convinced that Protos has killed Amédée;
she denounces him to the police and is strangled by him
for her pains. Protos is arrested and convicted, and
Lafcadio, profiting not only by the retouches of Protos
but by the total absence of the sort of motive that could
lead the police to him, finds himself free and unsuspected,
and at the cost of no great injustice to his former comrade,
who, though innocent of the death of Amédée, is still a
murderer. Lafcadio, dissatisfied at the ease of his victory,
tells Julius of his crime, but again his good fortune is too
much for him. It does not suit the prospering Julius to
have his half-brother a murderer, and he ignores the confession. The crowning touch is furnished when the beautiful Geneviève, Lafcadio's niece in a left-handed way but
of about his age, overhears the conversation between her

father and the young man, whom she has secretly loved since she witnessed his heroic saving of children from a burning building; this further revelation of his bold disinterestedness, so different from anything that might be looked for from her father, raises her adoration to such a pitch that she comes to Lafcadio's room in the night and offers herself to him.

Rather indifferently Lafcadio accepts her. But in the morning, and as the book closes, we find him debating with himself whether to accept the fortunate destiny in normal society that is being forced on him or to denounce himself to the police. We are not told what he decides.

The physical depiction of characters, the dialogue, the narrative and descriptive writing, the manipulation of incidents—all this in *Les Caves du Vatican* is masterly, but with a purposeless virtuosity; for the book remains strangely unsatisfying. The abrupt conclusion is partly responsible for this effect. We do not demand at the end of a book explicit explanations and a meticulous tying up of all loose ends, provided that a trend is evident and we are supplied with the material to conclude for ourselves. But Gide does not fulfill this provision. He makes telling, though specious, attacks on Catholicism and on the society of which it is an integral part, but he also ridicules the truculent atheism of Anthime and makes it clear that the criminal anti-society of Protos is not a satisfactory substitute for its respectable counterpart. We are left, then, in a mean ground between the extremes of Catholicism and conventional society on the one hand, and atheism and the criminal world on the other, and are offered for our guidance the doctrine of spontaneous disinterested behavior.

That Gide took this doctrine seriously is implied in this and others of his works of fiction and clearly stated in his Journal. But what does he do with it? Fortunately he does not ask us to approve of the gratuitous murder of Amédée, for Lafcadio himself is disappointed with the results of his experiment and discovers that what Protos says is true: that there is no no man's land, and one must be a member either of society or of anti-society. We are forced to conclude either that Gide abandons his case for disinterested spontaneity, or that the murder is an example of an aberration of the doctrine, or that the really gratuitous act is that of the author in including the incident, just for the malicious delight of drawing a rather nervous laugh from his reader. In any case the serious argument for disinterestedness, given moving expression fifteen years earlier in *Philoctète*, loses rather than gains by its new formulation.

The problems of criminality are even more unceremoniously dismissed, despite the fact that in 1912, just when *Les Caves* was being rounded into final shape, Gide was giving earnest thought, as a result of jury duty in Rouen, to the question of what it is that turns an honest man into a criminal and of what part, if any, is played in the metamorphosis by the gratuitous act. Scarcely a trace of this concern appears in the novel; Protos is fiendish to the point of grotesque humor, and Lafcadio's revulsion from the criminal world is esthetic, not moral.

To such objections Gide could reply—and has in effect replied—that his book is an ironical farce, not a sociological treatise. It is quite true that a work of fiction is under no obligation to be serious; nor do we object to a light, even a flippant, presentation of serious ideas, an effective example of which is Gide's own *Prométhée mal enchaîné*.

The trouble with *Les Caves* is that it is neither one thing nor the other; the early intention of a serious novel is an incubus which the farce cannot quite shake off. Sardonic fantasy neutralizes the social criticism and serious overtones discourage laughter at the wit.

Claudel was violently hostile to the book, as is only to be expected from one of his religious convictions; but one need not share his prejudices in order to admit some truth in his statement to Jacques Rivière that *Les Caves du Vatican* has a sinister, inhuman, nightmare quality about it. The characters, despite the amusing verve with which they are presented, are not human beings but fantastic puppets, and the events in which they are concerned, though frivolously recounted, are of a desperate seriousness.

In an authentically moving passage near the end of the book the author seems to recognize this effect. Geneviève, who has just been thanked and provisionally dismissed by Lafcadio, muses to herself: "How should she tell him that she too, up to now, had been frantically acting in a dream —a dream from which she escaped briefly only at the hospital where, among children of the poor and caring for their genuine suffering, she seemed sometimes to touch at last some reality—a second-rate dream in which her parents frantically participated beside her amidst the absurd conventions of their world, and where she was quite unable to take seriously their gestures, their opinions, their ambitions, their principles, or even their very persons."

Such words make the clever mockery of the book ring a little hollow. They seem to come from a man battling against himself, trying, with his skeptical mind, to laugh down his still half-believing heart.

10

The Rock of Sisyphus

In one of his notes for a novel (undated but belonging to 1921) Gide wrote: "One day X starts reading over some old letters of his . . . and is stupefied to discover that previously he went through a crisis exactly like the present one (a crisis he hadn't remembered) and that then he acted exactly the same, just as stupidly—that is, he realizes that he can't act otherwise; he remembers nevertheless that he had promised himself never to be caught again. . . . Everyone, he muses, always performs the same gesture; or, more exactly, there is in everyone's character a propensity to a particular gesture which determines the conduct of his whole life."

This idea of the fated gesture (used many years later in Gide's *Thésée*) has considerable biographic import, for shortly before writing his note of 1921 he had been reading over all the notebooks of his youth—with exasperation: "Were it not for the salutary *humiliation* I experience in the reading I should tear them all up"; and he had been able to see how closely his moral crisis of 1892 and 1893 paralleled the one which came on him over twenty years

later, how he had made the same mistakes and come out
with the same end result.

On October 15, 1916, for example, he wrote: "Yesterday I had an abominable relapse which leaves my body
and mind in a state close to despair, suicide, madness.
It is the rock of Sisyphus that rolls back to the foot of the
mountain up which he has been trying to push it, that
falls back with him, rolling on him, carrying him down
under its mortal weight and plunging him back into the
mud. What now? Am I going to be obliged all over again
and indefinitely to make this lamentable effort? I think of
the time when, in the plain with no further thought of
climbing, I smiled at each new hour, indolently seated on
this rock which I had no impulse to lift."

His rock of Sisyphus was erotic fantasy and self-abuse.

To contemplate with horror one's unique wickedness;
to struggle, pray, sin, repent, resolve, and then go through
the whole cycle again; to discover that the deeper the
despairing remorse the more certain the next fall; to learn
the perverse frenzy which, once one has slipped, sends
one compulsively down to the very bottom: this dismal
familiar story is that of many an adolescent, particularly
if he is the son of religious and strictly moral parents; and
his salvation comes, not through his self-defeating prayers,
but by a redeeming surge of common sense from his unsuspected psychic reserves; "Lord have mercy" changes to
"Stop being a fool!" and the bedraggled youth emerges
from the swamp to firm ground.

But why should an apparently mature man in his late
forties fall back into adolescence, go through the same
struggles but even more desperately, and come out with
the same result? A part of the answer is that the crisis

of 1916 marked, not the sudden collapse of a successful formula for living, but the climax of a mounting dissatisfaction with it and the emergence, or reëmergence, of a counterformula.

To escape from the burden of guilt one can change either one's conduct or one's attitude toward that conduct. The young Gide did a little of both: he persuaded himself, superficially at least, that his desires were not "temptations" nor their fulfillment "sin," thereby releasing himself from solitary confinement and permitting the joyous discovery of the outside world. The trouble was, as his spokesman André Walter foresaw: if he gave his body what it asked, would he be able to satisfy it? Outside fulfilment of his desires was not always a simple matter, and it did not even wholly deliver him from solitary vice; on the contrary it furnished fresh material for fantasy. But at least his confinement was not now absolute, and it was no longer "sin." He could sit upon his rock and smile at each new hour.

This apparently was the "practical solution" which he said (à propos of Corydon) he had found.

But Gide had not completely uprooted the concept of sin; deep in his heart it still lay, waiting the favorable moment to spring into life and bear once more the bitter fruit of guilt. The moment came, and another and another —moments of fatigue, of decline of fervor, of discouragement over his writing, of renewed obsession, of panic over the failure of attempts at self-discipline. Again and again he had been on the point of return to a religious formulation of his problem. But each time he temporized, and each time a new surge of vitality caught him up again and carried him on.

Meanwhile rumors about his homosexuality were accu-
mulating—and small wonder, considering the hints he had
given in his books, considering too that several of his
friends knew the facts and that from any one of them a
gesture, a word, an expressive silence might start the buzz
of gossip. Moreover *Corydon,* as yet read by very few,
was known to exist: Jammes for instance, not among these
few, referred to it by name in a letter.

And then, quite suddenly and before Gide was ready,
the whole scandal threatened to become public.

In March of 1914, while the *Caves* was in process of
serialization and Gide was staying in Florence with his
friends, the young painter Jacques Raverat and his wife,
he received a letter from Claudel in Hamburg: "In the
name of heaven, Gide, how could you have written the
passage which I find on page 478 of the last number of
the *NRF?* Don't you know that after *Saül* and *L'Immoraliste* you could not afford one more imprudence?
Must I really believe, as up to now I have refused to do,
that you are yourself a participant in this frightful immorality? If you are silent, or if you are not absolutely
forthright, I shall know what to think." And with adjura-
tions to think of his wife, his better nature, and the good
of the young, he signed himself "Your saddened friend,
P. Claudel."

Lafcadio's meditations on the page in question do have
a decidedly pederastic slant, but in the book as a whole
homosexuality has no essential role, and the occasional
allusions to it, like this one, sound rather as if the author
were making it a point of honor, since he had not yet dared
to come into the open, to supply hints to gossipers. Possibly the suggestion that a priest might have lustful de-

signs on a boy (a suspicion, incidentally, of which Lafcadio cleared him) was enough to release the thunderbolt of Claudel's wrath; more probably this last relatively trivial item merely increased the accumulated potential to the point of discharge.

At any rate, Gide now stood directly challenged, and his defiant answer was immediate and equally direct: "By what right is this summons? In the name of what are these questions? If in the name of friendship, can you suppose for a moment that I will evade them? . . . I ask you only to consider this: that I love my wife more than my life, and that I could never forgive you any move, any word, that threatened her happiness." And after urging the secrecy of the confessional he went on to state unequivocally that he had never felt desire for any woman and that it was the sorrow of his life that his constant, prolonged, and fervent love for his wife had never been accompanied by such desire.

To the warning about the bad effect of his writing on the young, Gide replied with a righteous indignation that does not quite ring true: "By what cowardice, since God summons me to speak, should I evade this question in my books? I did not choose to be as I am. I can struggle against my desires, I can triumph over them, I can neither choose the object of these desires nor invent others, on order or by imitation."

He went on, "Is it really possible that you should despise me, repulse me, after reading this letter? . . . However, today I ask for no advice. I expect only your wrath. . . . Goodbye. Now it is for you to extend me your hand, if indeed you still consent to extend it."

The next day, without waiting for an answer, Gide

wrote another letter which betrayed panic and definitely contradicted his earlier claim that homosexuality no longer bothered him: "Since I wrote you two years ago, from these same banks of the Arno, I have had the habit of considering you a little like a priest, and sometimes I have allowed myself to think that God was using you to speak to me. Today I shall know whether this is so, or whether you are only a man like the others. Sometimes I even wish you would betray me, for then I should feel delivered from this esteem for you and for all that you represent in my eyes, which so often checks and encumbers me. . . . And perhaps, after all, this letter of yours, and my answer, will constitute an important event in my life. . . . When I asked you before to tell me of someone to whom I could talk, it was to talk about this—for in truth I *do not see how to solve this problem* that God has written into my flesh. . . . Goodbye [the more definitive *adieu* is used here, by contrast with *au revoir* in the preceding letter]. At present you can do me much harm and I am at your mercy."

Claudel's reply was friendly and compassionate, but he did not attenuate his condemnation of homosexuality, whose sinfulness he proved on the authority both of natural reason and of Revelation. He showed, moreover, an engaging personal humility: "I am too old a trooper to be scandalized by anything, and I don't really know what should give me the right to sit in judgment on anyone. . . . In these grave matters of the flesh we all sin more or less, and I admit to you very sincerely that if I made a comparison between you and me it would be to my detriment. But it is one thing to sin while regretting it, desiring to do better, asking God for the strength to do better, and quite another to believe that one is doing right in doing wrong and to say so and boast of it. For then there is not only perversion of the senses but perversion of conscience and judgment."

In his letter Claudel made two tactical errors in dealing with a man like Gide: he asked him to suppress from the published book the offending passage which had appeared in the *Nouvelle Revue Française*, adding, "Little by little people will forget"; and he said that if Gide would confess to a priest his sins would be exactly as if they had never been—"as is stated in the prophet Joel." Both remarks could be counted on to produce the opposite effect from the one intended.

Gide did not go to a priest and he refused to retract the passage. Instead, and despite the urgency of the situation, he temporized once more and set out on a trip to Turkey. "May I not be forestalled by events!" he wrote on the eve of departure. "Is it really wise to go off on a journey as I plan to do with Mme Mayrisch and Ghéon, when nothing is yet ready, neither *Corydon* nor the rest? But all my life and everywhere I have met again and again this fear of not having time, and of having the ground suddenly give way beneath my feet."

Like many other overcivilized persons, like the Michel of his *Immoraliste*, Gide felt the pull of barbarism. He longed for simple rough peasants, uncomplicated children of nature against an oriental setting, and Anatolia had become associated with this bookish revery. But he was disappointed; what he found was not so much primitiveness as degradation, insensibility, filth. The last straw was to find in the train bearing them to the coast a Turk collapsed on the floor, spouting blood from nose and mouth, apparently dying but not attracting the slightest attention from his compatriots. He was the driver of a carriage bringing Russian passengers to the train; they had been attacked by bandits and he had received a charge of shot in the face. Gide decided that he preferred the Sahara: "The obsession for these lands which has so long tormented me, the agonizing curiosity, is conquered."

At Smyrna he and Ghéon talked to Madame Mayrisch of "the slow decomposition of France, of its virtues lying useless and disintegrating, of the imminence of war"; yet as they sailed westward and Turkey fell behind and the "Greek miracle" approached, he felt that he was coming home. "Now I know that our western (I almost said our French) civilization is not only the best; I believe, I know that it is the *only* one—yes, the civilization of Greece, whose sole heirs we are."

But it is characteristic of him that as their ship entered the harbor of Piraeus he refused, to the astonished indignation of Ghéon, to raise his eyes from his book. He had never seen the Acropolis, but he knew what it would be like and he knew it was there; he did not need to raise his eyes; he preferred to read—of all irrelevant books!— *Wuthering Heights.*

Back at Cuverville he wrote in his Journal on June 11: "I must repeat to myself every morning that the most important part remains to be said, and that it is high time." He well knew what this most important thing was: to finish *Corydon* and to tell his own story in his memoirs. Thus he would both have met Claudel's challenge (though not in the way the Apostle would have wished) and have delivered himself from the self-reproach of hypocrisy. It would take courage, but this he did not lack when he thought he was right. The trouble was that he still was

not sure, and before he could make his public confession
he had to come to terms with the warring elements in his
own heart.

And so he started on a long course of twistings and
evasions. He had been so long away from a piano that
surely he had the right to indulge his thirst for music.
But his wrist became lame and for a day or two he could
neither play nor write. Then letters accumulated and he
had to write answers, making first a rough draft, then
conscientiously polishing and turning his phrases and
spending at the exercise the best part of the working day.
Sometimes he wrote letters which he decided, after all,
not to send; he would file them away, and as often as not
they would turn up in print in the pages of the *Nouvelle
Revue Française* and later in a volume. A sheaf of reviews
(hostile ones) of the *Caves* arrived, and he could scarcely
be blamed for reading them.

What literary work he did manage to do was to toil over
the notes of his Turkish journey, to be published in the
NRF. He was exasperated with them; they were not worth,
he said, four days' work, but they cost him eleven. (After
this it is curious to read, in the dedication to his wife which
heads the published version, that he has transcribed them
"just as they are.") They were only training, he told himself
as he worked over them, for the more important work to
come. "Sometimes," he wrote on June 15, "when I think of
the importance of what I have to say, of my 'Christianity
against Christ,' of *Corydon* . . . I tell myself I am mad
to temporize like this."

But temporize he did, and four days later we find him
blaming the relaxing climate of Cuverville, and longing
for Florence again; "physiological equilibrium" also is

"difficult and dangerous" to find at home. Then he finds a young starling fallen from a nest and gives it the hospitality of the linen room which has been serving as his study. Its antics are distracting and the little fellow insists on hopping up on his shoulder. This is very touching but the corrosive semiliquid droppings on his shoulder and the swarms of tiny itching parasites that desert their normal host in favor of the writer's hand are less so. Finally the bird wins, and Gide has to try to work elsewhere. The saga finally ends with the death of the starling under the claws of the cat. But then the cat shows signs of advanced pregnancy, and another absorbing drama must be watched through.

We know all these details because Gide was clinging desperately to his Journal, forcing himself to write there if he could not do so elsewhere. But even there he found obstacles and excuses when he came to change notebooks: "This notebook inspires me much less than the other; it is absurd and I am ashamed to admit it, but the format of the paper, its quality, its color impede or favor to an extraordinary degree my thought; I would have liked to continue this journal in notebooks of the same format as the last."

The Austrian ultimatum to Serbia, bursting suddenly upon the world in late July, sweeps away such trivialities but without healing Gide's inner conflict. He sends a telegram to a friend in England announcing his arrival in Newhaven, and cancels it with a second, half an hour later. He tries to play the piano for friends, to ease them of anxious thought, but finds another person at the end of his fingers. He speaks roughly to the gentle Madeleine, and apologizes. One day he announces himself galvanized by the approach of tragedy, the looming tunnel full of darkness and blood, but three days later, when the mobilization posters go up and the tocsin sounds, he has "a wet rag in his breast in place of a heart." The next day, August 2, he sets out for Paris with the idea of finding some way to make himself useful; before leaving he kneels down with Madeleine and at his request she recites the Lord's Prayer: "I did this for her and my pride yielded to love without difficulty; besides, my heart associated itself wholly with her prayer."

At the station, crowds shout, "To Berlin!" Trains are late and loaded to overflowing. Paris is almost unrecognizable from its change of atmosphere; its streets are now crowded with tense silent masses, now wholly empty; here and there in front of wine shops men appear and bray the Marseillaise. At night Gide cannot sleep for feeling that the whole city wakes and waits; occasionally the silence is broken by a car dashing at full speed down the street and bleating at the corner. One night a violent thunderstorm breaks out, and to Gide, half dreaming, it seems like a bombardment of the city, or perhaps the end of the world. Either possibility leaves him indifferent.

In the succeeding days people in the street seem different; a frightened woman, evicted from her hotel, dodges along looking for a friendly face in the crowd that has suddenly become the enemy, and when she ventures to address someone she tries in vain to disguise her accent. Strange nocturnal creatures emerge into the daylight, creeping uneasily close to the walls: a broken old man, looking like one who has escaped from premature burial and can no longer find a place in the world, led, shuffling, by a small boy singing a cracked song; someone—a man?

a boy?—is surrounded by hooting children, to whom he offers patient silence; from a little distance he looks like a schoolboy, but closer inspection reveals a worn and wrinkled face.

If war has galvanized and reunited disintegrating France, it has also unleashed the corporate beast. All social levels are united in the denunciation of everything from beyond the Rhine; German music and philosophy are demolished, German stores are sacked. Under the eyes of the uncertain police a Maggi dairy is raided and a young tough, thrown up by the popular wave, leaps into the show window, seizes an earthenware coffee pot, holds it aloft, and dramatically dashes it to the ground, to the insane applause of the crowd. The tattered relics of military glory are exhumed: "Rather death than dishonor!"— "The field of honor"—"To Berlin!" Communiqués tell of valiant fighting, of holding firm, even of gains; but when subsequent news reveals the German army miles and cities nearer Paris, new slogans appear to explain the anomaly: "The German army sucked in by France," "The invasion canalized."

And one who watches, saddened, uninfected by the general delirium, becomes suspect; fingers point, whispers circulate, he is not a "true Frenchman." Everyone is patriotic, everyone is busy, and when Gide is asked ironically if he is continuing his "little literary amusements" the shaft strikes home, for he is not at the front, he is not writing, and his efforts to occupy himself usefully seem futile.

For a few days he worked at the Red Cross, but finding his duties reducing themselves to the discouragement of others also eager to serve he gave it up and looked elsewhere. Finally, as the German armies rolled through

Belgium and refugees were squeezed southward, he founded with some friends—among them Charles Du Bos and the Belgian artist Théodore (Théo) Van Rysselberghe and his wife (Mme Théo)—the Foyer Franco-Belge for the relief of displaced persons; and here regularly for the next year, and periodically thereafter during the war, he occupied himself. At first he and Ghéon boarded with the Van Rysselberghes; later Madeleine came up briefly from Cuverville and they opened the Auteuil villa. But Madeleine felt more in her place and more needed at Cuverville; there she retired and there periodically Gide joined her for, at first, brief relief from his life of "philanthropist and parasite" and later for longer periods of somber meditation and struggle.

Long days at the Foyer brought an exhaustion that was more emotional than physical. Hour after hour Gide and his colleagues received the bewildered, frightened, desperate refugees, assumed their burdens, lived through their horrors in sympathy, and on through the evenings discussed the day's experiences. "How often," Gide mused in his Journal, "at the Foyer, nursing, consoling, supporting these human rags capable only of groaning, broken down, without a smile, without an ideal, without beauty—how often have I felt rising within me the fearful question: Are they worth saving?"

And the people around him, his friends, not only at the Foyer but elsewhere in Paris and at Cuverville, seemed changed. There was Paul Desjardins, with his official connections, his courteous but skeptical "Oh, indeed?" at nonofficial reports, his air of vast reserves of information which, in his position, he was not at liberty to disclose, his newspaper articles on the "lessons to be drawn" from events. The brilliant Jean Cocteau, who always made Gide feel clumsy and slow, appeared in August of 1914 dressed in clothes suggestive of uniform and with his literary petulance turned martial, making witticisms out of tragedy and then, if they turned flat, turning skillfully to the pathetic as he wistfully crumbled cake into his tea.

Gide's visit to his former music master "La Pérouse" (M. de la Nux) revealed the old man hopelessly at odds with his wife, weak, dazed, refusing to eat, sinking slowly into solitary self-pity and paralysis of will. At the other extreme was the wealthy, assured, ever-successful painter Blanche, who, at the approach of war, had cashed in on investments, moved accounts, and in general prepared himself and protected his holdings, but now, reduced and aged by his unwonted discomforts and the impossibility of foreseeing and forestalling everything, was shivering uneasily about his chilly apartment, trying to evade importunate relatives who had descended on him.

Marcel Drouin, Gide's brother-in-law, also looked ill at ease in his unaccustomed uniform, preoccupied, scarcely able to converse. Yet a few days later at a café, when Gide ventured to suggest that if France had any superiority over Germany it was not in force of arms and that the only permanent victory possible was a "mystic" one, he was shouted down in chorus, and it was Marcel who proclaimed that in that case France should die: "We will die if we must, but at least what dies will be wholly France and not a remnant surviving by some shameful compromise." And with a yell of approval the company raised their glasses to France, and to Marcel who had spoken so well on her behalf.

Only Madeleine seemed unchanged—Madeleine, so

weak and so strong, so pliant and so immovable, so gentle and so stubborn. "I think my heart will not be strong enough for either the great joy or the great sorrow," she wrote from Cuverville in the critical August days. But after the battle of the Marne, when the German armies turned toward Normandy and the Channel, it was her calmness and courage that gave heart to her panicky Norman neighbors, one of whom, an old woman who had been sick, tried stumblingly to tell Gide what his wife had meant to her in words "like lumps of rock," but made eloquent by floods of tears. On the other hand a family discussion between Gide, Marcel, and Madeleine's two sisters Jeanne and Valentine, with voices raised in the heat of argument, caused her to flee terrified to remote portions of the house; and when at Auteuil the central heating broke down she was disproportionately downcast, a submissive victim to the expected bronchitis, whereas Gide was amused and interested by the change of routine. "It is because you are strong," said Madeleine, and Gide somberly remembered *L'Immoraliste*, with its brutal Michel and victimized Marceline. Was he really strong, or only cruelly self-centered?

And who were these people around him, what were these strange happenings? "Sometimes it seems to me that I have already finished living and am moving in a sort of posthumous dream, a supplement to life, without importance or meaning."

The electrifying effects of the outbreak once past, the war became a new monotony. Gide could see the comic side of the situation when a lady at the railway station, inconvenienced by the dislocation of service, burst out indignantly, "You know, I've had just about enough of your war!" but he was not far from feeling the same way. As he had read *Wuthering Heights* before the Acropolis, so now, but in a different spirit, he turned to *Sesame and Lilies:* "It seemed to plunge me into a wave of clean water and all the dust and heat of too long a journey on a dry road were washed away."

He found the volume in the collection of Elisabeth Van Rysselberghe, the daughter of his friends Théo and Mme Théo—the little Elisabeth whom he had watched emerge from babyhood, whose bright sayings he had noted in his Journal (her terrified "I'm losing all my sauce!" at the sight of her cut finger), an Elisabeth now decidedly growing up, stimulated to precocity by all the interesting and liberal-minded people surrounding her parents, avid for English literature, determined on unconventionality, humorous, excitedly arched toward the future. In her library too Gide made the important discovery of Blake, in the selected edition of Yeats; with her too he read Browning, and these two were added to the constellation of Nietzsche and Dostoevsky.

The stresses and emotions of war, coming as they did on top of the sense of urgency arising from Claudel's challenging letter, produced in Gide a supersaturated state of mind which needed but one more jar to precipitate a crisis. The latter half of November 1915, gloomy with squalls of wind and rain, was an appropriate setting for a mounting pessimism about society, about France, about himself. A young man befriended by the Foyer wrote that to avoid rejoining his regiment, he was drowning himself in the Seine, and signed as "Jean the Mad, died 12 November at 5 p.m." The war was not going well: "This carelessness, this vague confidence made up of stupidity and presumption . . . will not be in the least amended by the direst events. They blame this little fact, that unfortunate decision. The trouble comes from farther back, alas. One sees in the hour of danger that the whole edifice from top to bottom is rotten, that the whole of society— But where were their eyes not to have seen it at the first?"

The final jar was not long delayed. It came from his old friend Ghéon, the matchless companion of old days in Paris, in North Africa, in Florence, in Anatolia, in Greece, on whose zest for living the more cautious Gide had drawn heavily.

Ghéon was changing. For years past he had been having moments (but so few that, but for the later event, they would have been forgotten) which seemed to foreshadow his conversion, as when in 1905 he had written: "A Catholic cured of writing: every day brings me closer to taking that road. . . . My past life has clearly sunk into the abyss and with it all that is unpredictable and provisional in the adventure of debauchery. I have discovered that I am faithful, viable, only in the atmosphere of certitude and fixity. . . . I say: Down with art and down with life! But where shall I find a refuge?"

Through the fall and early winter of 1914 Ghéon, attached to the army medical service, had been in a base hospital, but in February 1915 he left for the front. At about the time of his departure Gide had a dream—a not uncommon occurrence with him but of this one he wrote afterward, "From the very beginning I felt its importance; one would have said that it was not made of the stuff of other dreams; I was obliged to pay attention to it."

The dream was recorded in the Journal (almost a year after it occurred) as follows: "I was walking or rather

floating beside someone, a companion whom I recognized
as Ghéon. We were proceeding in an unknown country, a
sort of wooded valley; we advanced with delight. The
valley was becoming steadily narrower and more beautiful
and my delight was reaching its peak when my companion
suddenly stopped, and touching my arm cried, 'Stop!
From now on there is *this* between us.' He did not point
to anything, but dropping my eyes I saw, hanging from
his wrist, a rosary, and I awoke in intolerable distress."

In January 1916, almost a year after the dream, Ghéon
wrote that he had "taken the plunge"; the next day Gide
read in the Gospel of John: "If a man abide not in me, he
is cast forth as a branch and is withered; and men gather
them, and cast them into the fire, and they are burned."
The words seemed to have a particular and an urgent
meaning for him: "Was I not truly 'cast into the fire' and
already a prey to the flame of the most abominable
desires?"

Whereupon he sat down and wrote to Ghéon, "I embrace you, you who have preceded me."

The next day (January 19, 1916) he wrote in his Journal,
"Everything in me must be revised, corrected, reëdu-
cated," and set himself to the task. It was formidable,
and of more than merely private significance; for if a
Laforgue could say "My great metaphysical struggles have
passed into the state of domestic sorrows," of Gide's problem the converse was true: starting with the attempt to
set in order his own somewhat special moral house, he
soon found himself at grips with principles of conduct and
belief that have relevance for every man who stands somewhere between the peace of the clod and the peace of God.

He went on to specify just what it was in him, principally, that needed reëducation: "What I have the hardest time fighting against is sensual curiosity. The drunkard's glass of absinthe is not more attractive to him than for me certain faces met by chance—and I would drop everything to follow them. Indeed the propulsion is so imperious, the purpose so insidious, so secret, the habit so inveterate that often I doubt whether I can escape them without help from outside. 'I have no man, when the water is troubled, to put me into the pool.' "

It was this sensual curiosity which periodically throughout his life drove him into those prolonged feverish walks on city streets or country lanes in search of a face or a form with the requisite suggestion. Propulsion from within —physiological pressure and psychological repression— brought craving for incitement from without; occasionally it came, and if the adventure was followed to its conclusion the inevitable result was self-disgust. But the revulsion was short-lived, and Gide found himself with one more indelible recollection added to his gallery of erotic images, one more phantom lover to enlarge the troop that haunted his nights and sent him back to solitary vice; from which, in turn, he sought to escape in a new walk, pursuing the elusive anonymous but substantial form outside.

No wonder he was struck by reading in Pascal, "We are full of things that throw us outward. . . . Our passions push us outward even if external objects do not present themselves to excite them. External objects tempt us of themselves and call to us, even when we do not think of them." And Gide commented, "Really, Pascal, did you have torments and agitations like mine? Surely not! I am turning your words to my own purposes, giving them a precise meaning which they do not have. You are speaking

in an abstract and general way. Or perhaps you are thinking of the days of your youth?"

The Pascal quotation continued, "In vain the philosophers tell us, Withdraw within, there you will find your
treasure; we do not believe them, and *those who do are
the emptiest and stupidest.*" And Gide added, "That is
what the Evil One says to me too."

His italicizing of the Pascal passage indicates his recognition of the danger for him of solitary meditation. It is
strange that he omitted the sentence between the first two
of his quotation, for it is full of significance for his case:
"Our instinct makes us feel that we must seek our happiness outside of ourselves." His whole experience must
have confirmed the truth of this generalization in his particular case, and from the record of his naked reactions
it is abundantly clear to his reader that his private hell
was solitary confinement to self. The true horror of the
year 1916 was to find himself once more in this hell, with
all his prayers and struggles seeming only to speed the
downward spiral to spiritual death. He never seems clearly
to have formulated, though he constantly suggests, the
principle that the essence of evil IS separateness. Instead,
in these years of crisis, he felt that some light was cast on
his problems by the hypothesis that the Evil One, Satan,
really existed as an active entity, outside of as well as
within himself.

The idea of God stretched back as far as he could
remember, but that of the Devil came to him late: to be
precise, on September 24, 1914, just at the time when
active evil seemed to be breaking out all over the continent of Europe. On the next day he wrote in his Journal:
"Yesterday, departure of Jacques Raverat. . . . Talked

interminably about morals and religion. He believes in the devil; he even told me he had believed in the devil before believing in God. I told him that what kept me from believing in the devil was that I was not quite sure I hated him." Two years later Gide said that "at first I only smiled that autumn evening when suddenly Jacques Raverat introduced [the devil] to me." But the seed took root.

Just a month earlier he had discovered Blake and dipped into him with an astonishment chiefly directed, probably, at the "Marriage of Heaven and Hell," of which eight years later he was to publish a translation. The explosive effect of Blake's small package of spiritual dynamite is not hard to imagine. For years Gide had known the pendulum swing between Dionysian energy and Christian abnegation and, impotent to check it, had taken refuge in the words of his Saul: "My value lies in my complexity." What then could be more reassuringly pertinent than to read:

Without contraries there is no progression. Attraction and Repulsion, Reason and Energy, Love and Hate, are necessary to Human existence.

From these contraries spring what the religious call Good & Evil. Good is the passive that obeys Reason. Evil is the active springing from Energy.

Good is Heaven. Evil is Hell.

THE VOICE OF THE DEVIL

ALL Bibles or sacred codes have been the causes of the following Errors:

1. That Man has two real existing principles: Viz: a Body & a Soul.

2. That Energy, call'd Evil, is alone from the Body; & that Reason, call'd Good, is alone from the Soul.

3. That God will torment Man in Eternity for following his Energies.

But the following Contraries to these are True:

1. Man has no Body distinct from his Soul; for that call'd Body is a portion of Soul discern'd by the five Senses, the chief inlets of Soul in this age.

2. Energy is the only life, and is from the Body; and Reason is the bound or outward circumference of Energy.

3. Energy is Eternal Delight.

Moreover Blake reawakened for Gide the old issue between the artist and the saint and swept away the attempted compromise by categorically asserting that the true Poet is of the Devil's party. And the "Marriage" is studded with further and equally apposite apothegms, such as "The road of excess leads to the palace of wisdom," and "He who desires but acts not, breeds pestilence."

The fact that Gide was deeply impressed by "The Marriage of Heaven and Hell" has curious implications. It gave support and justification to his Dionysian self, but at precisely the time when he was preparing to redefine that side of his nature as "evil" and subdue it. In the "Marriage" Blake transposed "God" and the "Devil," he transvalued (as Nietzsche was to do later but in a different spirit) Good and Evil. The God and the Devil he pictured were not his, they were other people's concepts; the truth, Blake's truth, was spoken by the figure he called the Devil, and elsewhere named Los—a flame of energy and love; Blake's Devil (not the one so called in the "Marriage") was Urizen (Your Reason). He was attacking eighteenth-century rationalism—this above all; he was rebelling, as Nietzsche did later, against "sleep and virtue," against churchly disparagement of the body and its desires, against passivity and resignation and abstention and repression.

All this Gide must have understood because it was so
much in accord with his own ideas—or with the ideas
of half of his divided self; but at the time when he first
read Blake it was the other half that was moving into the
dominant position. Consequently he did not follow Blake
in his transpositions; the "Devil" of the "Marriage" (really
God) remained for Gide the true Devil, whose acolyte the
artist was.

One seed of Blake's planting bore almost immediate
fruit: the humanist replacement of God by man. "God
only Acts & Is, in existing beings or men," says Blake in
the "Marriage," and even more strongly in "The Everlasting Gospel," which Gide undoubtedly read as it is in
the Yeats edition and its title would have appealed to him:

> Thou art a Man, God is no more,
> Thy own humanity learn to adore.

The idea was not new to Gide; he had already encountered it, among other places, in Nietzsche. But Gide had
been unwilling to follow Nietzsche this far; he was ready
now to take a further step in this direction, though still
with some holding back. And so on January 30, 1916, he
formulated a credo which, as it turned out, was to last him
with scarcely a variation for the rest of his life—was to
serve, that is, as a formulation satisfactory to his rational
side:

If I were to formulate a creed I should say: God is not behind us. He is to come. It is not at the beginning but at the
end of the evolution of beings that he must be sought. He is
terminal and not initial. He is the supreme and final point
toward which tends all nature in the domain of time. And as
time does not exist for Him, it makes no difference to him
whether this evolution of which he is the crown precedes or

follows, nor whether he determines it by attraction or by propulsion.

Then comes the passage to which Blake appears to have contributed:

It is through man that God takes on form, that is what I feel and believe, and it is what I understand by the saying: "Let us create man in Our image." What can all the doctrines of evolution avail against that thought?

That is the door by which I enter into the holy place, that is the succession of thoughts which brings me back to God, to the Gospel, etc.

Shall I one day be able to explain this clearly?

For a long time now I have believed this without knowing it—little by little it lights up in me in a series of successive illuminations. The reasoning follows.

Once in this passage (in addition to once in a quotation) Gide capitalizes the pronoun referring to God: "And as time does not exist for Him. . . ." Elsewhere he does not, and the inconsistency makes one wonder whether he obscurely realized that in this creed he was really talking about two things: "God" (the idea of God) and the Creator. It is quite understandable that the idea of God should have evolved and may be reasonably expected to continue to do so; but this tells us nothing about the real existence of a Prime Mover. Gide is now prepared to admit that man has made "God" in his own image, but he still wants God to have created man in "Our Image." He reconciles the two ideas by invoking the factor of eternity, in which time does not exist: man makes "God" in time and when the creation is complete this "God" coincides with Eternal God. Whether Gide arrived at this result by theological sleight of hand or by intuition of a paradoxical truth, the formula satisfied his reason.

Evil at this time was desperately real to him, but of the personal existence of the Devil he was less sure. "I am deliberately using here," he said in one place after mention of the Devil, "a vocabulary and images that imply a mythology in which I do not necessarily believe. It is enough for me that it is the most persuasive in explaining my inner drama." And in another note of the same period: "No sooner had I *supposed* the existence of the demon than the whole story of my life was illumined, than I understood suddenly what was the most obscure. . . . What more glorious than a soul when it delivers itself? What more tragic than a soul becoming enslaved when it thinks it is delivering itself?"

The exact degree of the Devil's reality was not wholly clear to Gide, nor is it very important for us to assess it, for his chief function at this time is indisputable: the Devil is the Reasoner—and here Gide drew less on the "Urizen" of Blake than on Dostoevsky's ideas. Whenever he found his good resolutions being sapped by ingenious rationalizations and sometimes by what seemed incontrovertible arguments, he knew that he was listening to the voice of the Evil One.

And so we come to the painful story of the year 1916, as recorded in two journals, the regular one and the *Cahier vert*, the "Green Notebook," or *Numquid et tu . . . ?*, in which he put down his meditations on Christianity alternately with the account of his defeats that appears in the other. He was not a theologian, he was not an impartial critic, he was a desperate man, ready to clutch at any straw. What did he care about sound logic or discovering the exact shade of meaning intended by Blake, or Dostoevsky, or the authors of the Gospels? What he needed was arms against the Enemy, and he took them where he could find them.

On January 17 he received Ghéon's letter telling of his conversion and he set himself to his task. Despite his creed of God at the end of the road it was to the God of the past that he instinctively turned, for "often," he said, "I doubt whether I can escape without help from the outside."

January 20 was a day full of pitfalls, providentially escaped rather than resolutely avoided, but two days later he yielded to his temptation "as one yields to an obstinate child, for the sake of peace. Dismal peace; darkening of the whole sky." January 25: "Detestable night. I have fallen back as low as ever. This morning, up before 7, I go out for a moment and hear the song of a blackbird, strange, so precociously springlike, so pathetic and so pure, that it makes me feel bitterly the withering of my heart. . . . Since Saturday abominable imaginings have been assailing me, against which I am defenseless. Sometimes I wonder if I am not going insane; everything in me gives way to obsession."

He is somewhat encouraged on that day however by a letter from Ghéon, and on January 27 he states that he has got hold of himself again. In succeeding days he admits to difficulty in reinstating the idea of sin, and he finds the pseudo-reasoning of some devotional books revolting: "I can renounce my reason but I cannot distort it."

February 3: " 'Except a man be born again' [quoted in English]. All this morning I repeated this saying to myself and I repeat it this evening, after measuring all day the fearful shadow that my past casts on my future."

He manages to continue morning and evening meditations, despite interruptions, but he is not very sure of himself. "The best way of fighting temptation is not to expose oneself to it," he writes on February 11. And the Evil One whispers in his ear: "All this is a game you are playing with yourself. With the first breath of spring you will go over to the enemy unconditionally. The enemy? Why do you talk of an enemy? Your only enemy is fatigue. If it were more open your sin would be glorious. Be frank, admit that if you talk of sin it is because this theatrical way of speaking is convenient and helps you recover . . . the free disposition of your body and your mind; soon, when you are well, you will blush to have had recourse to such expedients for your cure." And Gide sadly commented, "Meanwhile, I am still sick—and shall remain sick as long as I listen to that voice."

On the fourteenth he had "another fall."

For a time things go better, and he even begins work on his memoirs. On March 19, at Cuverville, he writes: "Insomnia these last nights; rather painful because of the nervous troubles which reappear—as they always do, alas! —as soon as I begin again to work seriously. Yet I am leading the most well-ordered life, with a continence that I think I have not known since childhood, or at only too rare intervals. Yesterday I threw into the fire two packages of cigarettes I had brought back from Le Havre. Smoking makes me dizzy almost at once; I light a cigarette from obsession rather than with pleasure."

Then discouragement comes back. March 22: "One goes on struggling so long as one thinks one ought to; but as soon as the struggle seems useless and one no longer hates the enemy— But I am holding out, more from defiance than conviction." April 4: "Humbly I ask God this morning: My God support me, guide me, protect me during this day." April 19: "I kneel down and cry aloud: My God, my God, let me be able to pray again! Give me simplicity of heart!" May 12, in the *Cahier vert:* "Have written nothing in this notebook for two weeks. Abandoned readings and devout exercises which my heart, completely dry and inattentive, no longer approved. See only acting, and dishonest acting at that, where I thought I recognized the devil's game. And that is what the devil whispers in my heart. Lord, do not let him have the last word. Today I want no other prayer." June 2: "A period of indifference, of dryness and unworthiness; my mind wholly taken up with absurd anxieties which weary and darken it." June 16 (in the *Cahier vert*): "I can no longer either pray or even listen to God. If perhaps he is speaking to me, I don't hear him. . . . Lord, if you are to help me, what are you waiting for? I can't do it alone, I can't."

In this same month of June he tore out twenty or more pages of the Journal that seemed "as if written by a madman." Not until fall did he begin entries again, and then in a new notebook, so as not to be reminded of the past.

September 16: "I shall only succeed by constant effort, an effort of every hour, constantly renewed." September 17: "Abominable torpor."

September 19: "Yesterday an abominable relapse. The storm raged all night. This morning it is hailing heavily. I get up with head and heart heavy and empty, heavy with all the weight of hell. I am the drowning man who is losing courage and holding out only feebly. The three warnings all have the same sound: 'It is time— It is high time— It is too late.' So they cannot be distinguished from each other, and the third is sounding when you think you are still at the first. If only I could reveal this drama—show Satan, after he has taken possession of a person, using him, acting through him on others. This sounds like an empty figure of speech. I myself have only understood it for a short while: you are not only a prisoner; active evil exacts of you a reversed activity; you must fight on the other side."

He goes to Paris, and Mme Théo and Elisabeth get him to accompany them to Versailles. The weather is glorious but awakens no response in his heart. The next day is "empty, wasted. I drag along all through the hours and aspire to nothing but sleep." The day after: "Don't you see that you are talking to a dead man?"

A week later, sitting on a bench in the Cuverville grounds, he writes: "I am lost if I do not succeed in getting hold of myself before winter. Those summer months were abominable, with no work done and profound disintegration. I think I was never farther from happiness. Always with the vague hope that from the bottom of the abyss I could raise that cry of distress of which I am no longer capable. One can, even when very low, look up to the sky; but no, however low I was I looked still lower. I was renouncing heaven. I was no longer defending myself against hell. Obsessions and all the preliminary symptoms of insanity. Really I frightened myself; I was incapable of taking the advice I could so easily have given another.— To speak of it like this, am I already sure of being out of it?"

He was not yet out of it but there were signs of recovery. He began to see more people, thought of spending the winter at St. Clair, probably with or near the Van Rysselberghes, but gave up the idea on seeing the sad resignation in Madeleine's acquiescence; he planned a preface for an edition of the letters of his late friend Dupouey, had ideas for novels, worked again on his memoirs.

But on October 15 came another relapse and despair:

"Lord, you know I give up being right against anyone. What does it matter that it is in order to escape from submission to sin that I submit to the Church? I submit. Ah, loose the bonds that hold me. Deliver me from the fearful weight of this body. Ah, let me live a little, let me breathe! Snatch me from evil. Do not let me stifle."

But this surrender, almost belied by the words in which it was cast, was scarcely made before it was retracted, and the entry of two days later begins: "Age comes on without any hope of understanding my body better. A happy equilibrium almost immediately followed my lapse and my distress. I should like to see in it an answer to my prayer; but I know well enough that at the moment when I uttered that cry the worst of my distress was past. . . . It is unseemly to seek to interest God in physical lapses which a better hygiene could overcome quite as well."

Here, plain to be seen, a new orientation is at work. Desperate petitions to the God of his childhood simply have not, as a practical matter, worked; in fact they seem to have made matters worse, just as they did in his youth. But the old virus is not easily shaken off, and on October 21 he writes, "Worked a little better. Prayer." On the twenty-sixth he notes, "Lapse day before yesterday and yesterday," then significantly adds, "It is best not to worry too much about it. It is not good to keep your nose too close to your fault."

And on the last day of the year he writes: "No desire to continue in this notebook. Oh, not to be able to liquidate all this past, on this last day of the year of disgrace 1916."

11

The Renunciation

THE SYMPTOMS OF THE SPONTANEOUS REACTION AGAINST HIS excesses of piety and debauch, already discernible at the close of 1916, slowly accumulate during 1917. Work on his memoirs continues, at times rather satisfactorily. The idea of death haunts him, but in retrospect it only accentuates, even to some degree explains, the coming and explosive reconversion to life. On March 1 he makes the significant remark: "This pendulum movement to which, despite every resolution, my mind yields would plunge me back into extreme license if only external circumstances and my physical condition permitted greater exaltation."

Follows a desolate period, with war, icy wind, and rain without, and a mournful preoccupation with death within. On March 10 he takes up his long-neglected Bible and reads of the woman "which had a spirit of infirmity eighteen years, and was bowed together, and could in no wise lift herself up"; Gide commented: "How should I not recognize myself in her?"

The very next night, by a now familiar sequence, was

"haunted, desolated, ravaged by the phantom of X., almost palpable, with whom I wander for two hours or in whose arms I roll to the very steps of hell. And this morning I get up with vacant head, scattered mind, raw nerves, a ready prey to evil. Last night I did not wholly give way to pleasure . . . but I wonder whether this semblance of resistance was not worse. It is always a mistake to enter into converse with the devil. Whatever you do he always gets the last word."

But work, some small trips, correspondence, and finally and above all the coming of spring clear the air and prepare the way for the decisive external encounter which revolutionizes his state of mind. On May 5, with his arrival in Paris, we feel that Gide has entered a new zone of experience: "A calm like this I have not known for months, for years. It would take a real process of reasoning not to call it happiness. If only I had not been wakened several times in the night by disturbances in the villa . . . if only I had been able to sleep my fill, I think I should have awakened ten years younger. Even after this mediocre night I felt no particular fatigue and especially not that deep disturbance of mind and body that almost always follows incomplete satisfaction.—Marvelous fulness of joy."

Two weeks later he says, "I hold myself in to keep from talking of the sole preoccupation of my mind and my flesh." As the days succeed one another this preoccupation becomes identified as "M."

On the sixth of the following August he goes to Switzerland to spend some time with M. after the latter gets out of camp. Follows a curious passage of the Journal where Gide the diarist is still "I" but speaks of his acting self, the rejuvenated and infatuated Gide, in the third person, calling him "Fabrice," no doubt in reminiscence of the natural and spontaneous hero of Stendhal's *Chartreuse de Parme;* "M." is called by the pseudonym of "Michel":

Although he is too silent, I like to travel with Fabrice. He says (and I believe him) that he feels infinitely younger at 48 than he did at 20. He enjoys that rare faculty of starting afresh at each turn of his life and of remaining faithful to himself by resembling himself less than anything else.

Today, traveling first class (something he has not done for a long time), in those new clothes with an unaccustomed cut and in a hat which is prodigiously becoming, he confronts himself in the mirror with astonishment and finds himself fascinating. He says to himself: "New creature, today I can refuse you nothing." . . . Heavens! what beautiful weather! He is ready to burst from having been shut in this morning by the rain. Alone in this empty region of the Swiss first class he strides up and down the corridor with a dominating air.

In the next entry he tells of how "the fear of seeing the adolescent grow up too quickly tormented Fabrice incessantly and hurried his love. He loved nothing in Michel so much as the childishness he still retained in the intonation of his voice, in his impetuosity, in his caressing ways."

On another day:

The languor, the grace, the voluptuousness of his glance were inexpressible. Looking at him Fabrice for long moments lost consciousness of time, place, good, evil, the proprieties, and himself. He doubted whether a work of art had ever represented anything so beautiful. He doubted whether the mystic vocation of the one who used to precede and accompany him in pleasure, whether his virtuous resolution, would have held firm before so flagrant an invitation, or whether, to worship such an idol, the other would not have turned pagan again.

In the succeeding months Gide runs through the gamut of love's distractions: physical infatuation, the agony of separation, tender concern for the welfare of the beloved, jealousy—even the recognition in himself of the potentiality for a crime of violence. But through it all is the dominant note of joy; it is as if he were trying to match every page of despair in the 1916 Journal with its opposite in 1917. Dark days, gloomy weather that formerly depressed him seem only to add to his exaltation, as when, on December 15, he writes of a walk to Criquetot, near Cuverville: "The sky was lowering, very dark, heavy with storm; a great wind from the sea disheveled the clouds. The thought of M. kept me in a constant state of lyricism which I had not known since my *Nourritures*. I no longer feel my age, nor the horror of the times, nor the season, or only to find in them a new exaltation; if I were a soldier with a heart like this I should meet death with joy."

Although he was sometimes discouraged with his writing, he kept at it. By January 14, 1918, *Corydon* was practically complete and he would have liked to finish up the memoirs, but after reading some pages of them aloud to a friend he was disappointed in their effect: they were too manifestly inferior to the "marvelous book" of Proust (*Du côté de chez Swann*, once refused for the *NRF* by Gide but now taken over from the original publisher). And he was losing confidence again in his own vitality and youth: "Can the reserves of health and joy accumulated last summer be exhausted? An inner decline makes me fear so. I am thirsty to plunge anew into life."

Shut in again on himself, with vitality draining away, he finds himself again confronted by his religious dilemma, behind which lurks its invariable obverse, sin and despair. February 22: "It is hard, you say, for you to affirm that God is. But isn't it still harder to affirm that he is not?"

March 1: "Very bad nights for the past four days. It is very hard for me to prolong for more than two weeks the benefit of the diversion of Paris." March 3 shows an effort to get a grip on himself: "After a good night (or at least a little better) today I feel much heartened. I set this down to reread in hours of distress and anguish: never have I felt my mind more active and more lucid, my body more supple, my heart more warm. Never have I felt more happy. Never have I breathed more voluptuously. Never has the suffering or the joy of a friend—no, even of the first person I meet—found in me more response, nor the suffering of my country more echo. Never have I felt greater strength or greater desire to embrace, or greater capacity to inspire."

But on the very next day: "Insomnia again; anguish, exasperation and at last surrender—not so much from excess of desire as to get it over with and be able to sleep again. But sleep mocks this mediocre relief which is followed by no relaxation. . . . Ah, how I long for the health, the smiling repose of body, the happy equilibrium which I feel with M. and which make even chastity easy when I am with him."

On March 8 he goes to Paris, then spends a week in Brittany with M., and returns to Paris; it is over a month before he gets back to Cuverville. April 28: "A period of dissolution, haunted by the memory and the need of M. The need of getting beyond, of pushing my demon to the limit, of exhausting my desire." May 4: "To get along without M. no longer seems to me possible. He is all my youth."

By this time it is clear enough what has happened. When in 1917 Gide escaped (relatively and temporarily) from the solitary confinement of the preceding year, it was by an exteriorization of his inner vice: M. banished the phantoms but only on the condition of Gide's total dependence on him. As soon as M. disappeared, even briefly, the phantoms reëmerged, M. became himself a phantom. Gide's overflowing joy in the presence of M. was his gratitude to his equivocal deliverer, the measure of his preference of the outgoing to the ingrowing, his involuntary recognition of the truth of Pascal's neglected sentence: "Our instinct makes us feel that we must seek our happiness outside of ourselves."

Meanwhile time was rushing on and M.'s adolescence—the transitional moment necessary to Gide's desires—would soon be over. And Gide turns to the thought of death, at first with incredulity. "I think of death," he wrote in September 1917, "and am unable to persuade myself that I have only a limited number of summers more to live. Ah, how little my desires have diminished, and what difficulty I have in reducing them! I cannot consent to putting my happiness in the past. And why should I? Never have I felt younger and happier than during the past month." But two months later the idea of death is gaining: "The thought of death pursues me with a singular stubbornness. At every move I calculate: How many times already? How many times more? And in despair I feel as if the cycle of the year were speeding up."

The spring of 1918 was a critical moment both for France and for Gide, and in his Journal his attention was divided between his engrossing personal affairs and his country's danger. On May 10 he wrote a disquisition on the power of Germany and the futile heroism of the Allies, but closed it with, "What is the good of writing all this?"

and the next day his only entry was, "The greatest happiness next to that of loving is confessing one's love." On May 19 he returned "bursting with happiness" from Limoges, where he had spent two days with M. June 2: "The Germans are at Château-Thierry. Days of anguished suspense."

But before the year closed the war was to be won by the Allies and Gide was to reach, and pass, the turning point of his career, a crisis with which his wife was closely associated.

Despite their frequent separations, their mutual devotion seemed unthreatened until 1916. In the spring of that year Gide began writing *Si le grain ne meurt* and in the second paragraph opened the subject of the solitary vice which was causing him such distress at the time of writing. Although Madeleine probably knew that he was writing his memoirs, it is unlikely that he said anything to her about their contents at this time; but she knew her man and she had a way, Gide had discovered, of sensing when he was doing something of which she disapproved.

In June came the episode of the pages "written by a madman" and torn out of his Journal. "They reflected," Gide said, "a terrible crisis in which Em. was involved, or more accurately of which Em. was the cause. I tore them out at her request after she had read them. Or at least if out of discretion she did not ask me to tear them out, I felt too clearly the relief it would give her not to suggest it at once." We cannot tell what the lost pages contained, but we do know that she felt a strong repugnance to appearing in any of her husband's writings, and particularly in a context of which she disapproved. "I have a horror of indiscretion," she said, and Gide replied, "And I have an even greater horror of falsehood."

From this time on she seemed to be trying to detach herself from him, and him from her, not for the specious reasons of Alissa in the *Porte étroite* but as a way of registering her resistance to his tendencies, of which she knew more than he realized at the time. He began to find it difficult to get speech with her, and one day in October 1916 he made an appointment with her for early the next morning, and she said she would be there. Ostensibly it concerned only a letter she was to read to him but Gide attached considerable importance to the meeting. The next morning he hurried his toilet, postponed his private devotions, and hastened down to her room. She was not there, but the letter lay open, inviting him to read for himself. He preferred to await the pleasure of hearing her read it herself, and seating himself at a window he tried to interest himself in a book. But he could not put his mind to it, listening for her step, wondering what could be keeping her, whether she had forgotten. At last he heard her in the hall, still busy about one thing or another. Finally she started to wind the old grandfather clock. He heard two strike, then the half; as it was then past eight o'clock and the clock had the old-fashioned double stroke, he calculated that he had fifty-four more to listen to. Unable to wait he went out into the hall. "I left the letter on the table for you to read," she said as if it were the most natural thing in the world. "You see I had things to do. When this clock isn't on time the whole household is late." She offered no excuse, and Gide thought to himself, "My poor friend you will always meet with clocks to wind whenever it is a question of meeting me."

The following December he worked up his courage to the point of beginning to read his memoirs aloud to her, and though he was still far from the part where he was to make explicit revelation of his homosexuality he was very nervous, and he read "with such palpitations of the heart" that at times he was obliged to stop.

Through the next year and a half there was no overt change in their relations, no sign that Madeleine suspected anything about M.; in March 1918 Gide wrote in his Journal: "Em. cannot know how it tears my heart to leave her and find happiness far from her."

The storm broke the following June when he decided to leave for England with Marc Allégret (whose full name we may use at this point, following Gide's example) and Madeleine resisted his intention with all the force at her command; if she had been silent before it was probably not from ignorance. Gide refused to give up his plan, but he left Cuverville in deep unhappiness. "I leave France," he wrote on June 18, "in a state of unutterable distress. It seems to me that I am saying good-bye to all my past."

Later Madeleine told him how she had felt at his departure: "After you had left, when I found myself all alone in the big house you were abandoning, without anyone to lean on, without knowing what to do any more or what was to become of me, I thought at first that there was nothing left for me but to die. Yes, I really thought that my heart was stopping, that I was dying." And then she thought of the letters Gide had written her from their childhood on, every time they were separated for a few days. She had kept them all, neatly arranged and locked in a secretary in her room. They were, she said, her most precious possession, but now she went and got them, read them all through once more from beginning to end, and as she finished each one she threw it in the fire.

Gide returned in the fall knowing nothing of what had happened. He found it hard to get back to work, puttered around with his bees, read desultorily. Then Browning once more fired his enthusiasm, and he read poem after poem. "Prospice" he found "glorious" and he read it aloud to Madeleine:

> Fear death?—to feel the fog in my throat,
>   The mist in my face,
> When the snows begin, and the blasts denote
>   I am nearing the place . . .

That very day he had recorded an "obsessive fear of death." But the end of the poem was an inspiration:

> For sudden the worst turns the best to the brave,
>   The black minute's at end,
> And the elements' rage, the fiend-voices that rave,
>   Shall dwindle, shall blend,
> Shall change, shall become first a peace out of pain,
>   Then a light, then thy breast,
> O thou soul of my soul! I shall clasp thee again,
>   And with God be the rest!

A few days later he was reading "By the Fireside" and considered using one stanza of it as an epigraph for the second part of *Si le grain ne meurt:*

> My own, confirm me! If I tread
>   This path back, is it not in pride
> To think how little I dreamed it led
>   To an age so blest that, by its side,
> Youth seems the waste instead?

The mood for writing his memoirs returned, and for a
few weeks he wrote no more in the Journal. Then on
November 21, finding himself in need of a detail that he
thought he might find in one of his letters to his wife,
he asked her, as he had often done before, for the key to
her secretary. Madeleine turned very pale, and with an
effort that made her lips tremble she told him that she had
burned all the letters.

Many years later he described his reaction to the discovery:

For a full week I wept from morning to night, seated by the
fire in the room that was the center of our life together, and
still more at night after I had gone to my room, hoping that
some evening she would come to me. I kept on weeping, without trying to say anything to her except by my tears, always
waiting for a word, a gesture, from her. But she continued to
busy herself with little household affairs as if nothing had
happened, passing back and forth near me, indifferently and
as if she did not see me. In vain I hoped that the constancy
of my grief would triumph over her apparent insensibility, but
no; probably she hoped that the despair in which she saw me
sinking would bring me back to God, for she admitted of no
other way out. . . . And the more I wept the more we became
strangers to each other; I felt it bitterly, and soon it was no
longer over the destroyed letters that I was weeping but over
us, over her, over our love. I felt that I had lost her. Everything
was giving way beneath my feet: the past, the present, our
future.

Such a reaction far exceeds what might be expected
from an affront to the vanity of a writer proud of his
letters. Gide did say at the time, "Perhaps there never
was a more beautiful correspondence," but he later was
ashamed of this fatuity and disavowed it. A part of the

deeper explanation appears in suppressed passages of the Journal later published in *Et nunc manet in te:*

It is the best of me which has disappeared and which will no longer counterbalance the worst. . . . I feel myself suddenly ruined. . . . Did she realize that she was destroying the sole ark in which my memory could later hope to find refuge? To these letters I had confided the best of myself, my heart, my joy, my changes of mood, the occupations of my days. I suffer as if she had killed our child. . . . They were not really love letters; I dislike effusions and she would not have permitted praise, so that usually I hid from her the emotion with which my heart was overflowing. But my life was woven there before her eyes from day to day.

Madeleine was intimately and permanently associated with the religiously aspiring side of his nature, on which he set a higher valuation than on the other, the Dionysian, which he accepted because he must, and rationalized and tried to justify. But his God, by and large, was not Madeleine's God; his revolt from the strict Protestantism of his upbringing had been lasting and sincere. There was, it is true, an ineradicable strain of puritanism in his makeup, and he could never quite quench the memory of the particular direction that the religious ardor of his youth had taken, nor rid himself of the impulse, when discouraged or frightened, to pray desperately to the God of the past—as he had through the whole of 1916. But the ground on which he aspired to meet Madeleine was not that of the past but of the future. He had long since abandoned his naïve desire to take her with him on his physical travels, but there still remained the explorations of the spirit. He wanted to take her by the hand and bring her out of her retreat, draw her from her timid clinging to the past, give her the courage to set foot on a new path. "Every time I plunge back into Christianity," he wrote, "it is still she that I am seeking. She feels it perhaps, but what she feels above all is that I am trying to snatch her from Christianity."

It took Gide a long time to clarify in his own mind the nature of this new path. For years he could not see beyond his oscillations between license and discipline, Christianity and Dionysianism. He felt obscurely that there was good in both extremes, that there must be some way in which energy and joy could exist beside self-loss, and *because* of self-loss. Meanwhile there were vague feelings that did not fit into a pattern: the impression that the people and the objects around him were not quite real, that there was behind them a more substantial reality which was always eluding his grasp. There was too his short-lived and incomplete experience of "living in the third person—a blessed state."

Strangely enough 1916, the "year of disgrace," was also the year when he reached the clearest understanding of his objective, and gave to it the name of the "Kingdom of God." Perhaps his very despair of that year, the harrowing of his soul by remorse and fear, helped to open his eyes, or perhaps it was the emotions of the war, or again simply because a slowly ripening fruit had at last reached maturity.

What Gide meant by the Kingdom of God is seen most clearly from *Numquid et tu . . . ?*, the "Green Notebook" written chiefly in 1916. The title is drawn from the Vulgate version of two verses of the Gospel of John: *Numquid et vos seducti estis?*, and *Numquid et tu Gallileus?* ("Are ye also deceived?" and "Art thou also of Galilee?")—the meaning being, for Gide, "With these ideas can I too be called a Christian?"

A very few excerpts from this booklet give us the essence of what he had to say:

"Except a man be born again" [quoted in English]. To see everything new: isn't the Kingdom of God just that? The innocence of the little child:

Except ye become as one of these—of these little ones who *are naked and who are not ashamed.*

For I was alive without the law once. Oh, to attain to this state of second innocence, to this pure and laughing delight! . . .

Eternal life is not only to come. It is even now wholly present in us; we live it from the instant we consent to die to ourselves, to obtain from ourselves that renunciation which permits resurrection into eternity. *He that hateth his life in this world shall keep it unto life eternal* (John xii, 25). . . .

What peace! Here truly time stops. Here breathes the Eternal. We enter into the Kingdom of God.

In other words the eternal order of the Kingdom of God lies everywhere about us always, but we are blind to it because of imprisonment in self. If we could but consent to lay down our personal selves we would see the world transfigured and we could step at once out of time into eternity. Here, in 1916 and approached through the Gospels, is something very close to what he said in 1892 in the *Traité du Narcisse* from the viewpoint of Greek mythology and Neo-Platonism.

And here is his version of the same idea in the *Nouvelles Nourritures* (1935):

I find that every object of this earth that I covet becomes

opaque by the very fact that I covet it, and that the whole world loses is transparency, or else my eye loses its clearness, so that God ceases to be perceptible to my soul, and that, abandoning the Creator for the creature, my soul ceases to live in eternity and loses possession of the Kingdom of God.

In the light of this conception a passage from his Journal for 1916 (January 24), which might have passed for a mere bit of nature description, takes on a new significance:

Yesterday evening there was an ineffably strange and beautiful sunset; the sky was full of pink and orange mists. I wondered at it particularly as I crossed the Grenelle bridge, reflected by the Seine laden with barges; everything melted into a warm and tender harmony. In the Saint-Sulpice tram from which I was contemplating this spectacle with wonder I observed that nobody, absolutely nobody, noticed it. Not one of those faces that did not seem absorbed, full of care.

The next month he was so struck by an article in the *Journal de Genève* about the Serbian retreat that he copied a passage of it into his Journal, underlining the significant words:

There were panics alternating with sudden returns of hope. *There were also hours of a strange sweetness. Past, future, nothing mattered any more, and every minute* one lived with all one's sensitivity.
First it rained. Then it turned fair again, with the fair weather of late autumn and its great veiled skies, its pale sun, its too short twilights. *And the landscape was as if transfigured.*

Gide's celebrated *Symphonie pastorale,* written during 1918, also has pertinence to self-loss and transfiguration. The story, conceived as early as 1893 (he told it to Paul Laurens in Biskra), had been increasingly on his mind since 1910. Probably it was the skeleton of the plot, together with a perception of its possibilities, that he had in mind at Biskra.

A pastor gives the protection of his home and a name, Gertrude, to a blind, speechless, and brutishly ignorant girl of uncertain age but probably in early adolescence. With great care and effort he teaches her to speak and to read books with raised characters, and she develops with phenomenal rapidity into a beautiful and intelligent young woman. Their relations are those of creator and creature, and the reciprocal bond brings love. With the naïveté of his profession the pastor is the last to understand what is going on in his own heart; he awakens to the situation when his son Jacques falls in love with Gertrude and he finds himself opposing the match by various rationalizations. Then Gertrude obtains her sight by an operation and discovers that Jacques has the face which she has imagined for the pastor; it was he, she believes, that she has loved without knowing it. Jacques, instructed by the errors of his father, becomes a Catholic and enters the priesthood. Gertrude too becomes a Catholic, but seeing no solution to her life commits suicide—not merely because she cannot marry Jacques but because she can now see not only the beauty of the world which during her blindness she had to imagine, but the marks of suffering on the faces of those around her, and in particular on the face of Amélie, the pastor's wife. That expression, she feels, is in part her doing, and she blames the pastor for not having prepared her for pain and evil.

Some of the multiple possibilities of this framework Gide exploits by telling his tale through the pastor's journal; in this way the reader can understand what is happening before the pastor does himself. Amélie too is subtly presented by this technique; at first, seeing her only through the exasperated but professionally charitable eyes of her husband, we find her wholly unsympathetic, but gradually and in spite of the pastor her solid virtues appear.

Another aspect of the novel is the contrast Gide saw between the Catholic Church and an evangelical Christianity. For the pastor is not simply a naïve deceiver of himself, he is also the spokesman of his creator's belief that the true Gospel of Christ is a doctrine of joy, freedom, and love; he cannot believe that the love he bears Gertrude is anything but innocent and right, despite laws, rules, and conventions. Jacques on the other hand is a literalist, a formalist, a disciplinarian; in Christ's time he would have been in his place as a Pharisee; in the present Gide sends him to the Catholic Church.

This was the aspect of the novel that concerned him in 1910, and a note in his Journal makes explicit his position between Catholicism and Protestantism: "I shall doubtless feel called upon to write a preface to my *Aveugle* [*Symphonie pastorale*], without which it would be misleading. I would say: If being a Christian without being a Catholic is being a Protestant, then I am a Protestant. . . . But my Christianity stems only from Christ. Between him and me I consider that Calvin and Saint Paul are two equally pernicious screens. Ah, if Protestantism had only been able to throw off Saint Paul at once! But it is to Saint Paul precisely, and not to Christ, that Calvin is related."

At this date, and indeed until the book was well on its way to completion, Gide called it *L'Aveugle* ("The Blind Girl," perhaps, but the indeterminate gender of the French title makes it equally applicable to a man or a woman and it is clear that the physical blindness of Gertrude is not the only blindness of the story). But in June 1918 for the first time he referred to the book by its present title of *La Symphonie pastorale,* and it may well be that the change reflects the insertion of a new aspect, or at any rate a shift of emphasis. A "pastoral symphony" suggests a development of multiple themes in a rustic setting, but Gide is more specific than that. In an incident near the middle of the book he makes the pastor take Gertrude to a concert in Neuchâtel where they hear Beethoven's sixth symphony, the "Pastoral." She knows that one movement is entitled "By a brook," and the pastor by his fumbling but spontaneously poetic attempts to make her understand what the world looks like has helped her to form an inner vision of its beauties:

Long after we had left the concert hall Gertrude was still silent and as if in ecstasy.

"Is what you see really as beautiful as that?" she said at last.

"As beautiful as what, my dear?"

"As that *scene beside a brook.*"

I did not reply at once, for I reflected that these ineffable harmonies depicted, not the world as it was but as it might have been but for evil and sin. And never had I dared to speak to Gertrude of evil, of sin, of death.

"Those who have eyes do not know their good fortune."

Yet when she obtains her sight the world is quite as radiant as she had imagined and she cannot at first understand why others seem indifferent to it. Then she sees the unhappiness, the preoccupation on their faces, and realizes what it is that puts a screen between them and the ever-present paradise. She too will lose her spiritual vision now that she has the eyes of the flesh, she too will know suffering and preoccupation with self. And as a matter of fact in the short time she lives after receiving her sight she shows herself unjust in a way she would never have been in her blindness: by telling the pastor she was mistaken, that it was Jacques she loved all the time. This could not be true, for when she had no sight and could not compare the appearances of the pastor and his son, she loved the father for his voice, his mind, his gentleness to her. When she saw Jacques, youth called to youth, self awoke, and she became unwittingly unjust. But she did know that she, like the others, would lose her vision of paradise, and she could not endure the prospect; she preferred to die.

Self-loss and transfiguration were very much on Gide's mind in 1918 when he was writing *La Symphonie pastorale;* it was not so with the formally religious elements, which, faithful to his earlier intention, he put in. Or it might be more accurate to say that he did not want to have them on his mind; they belonged to a past that was too painful and still too close. "Today," he wrote on October 16, 1918, "I have the greatest difficulty in getting interested again in the state of mind of my pastor . . . and I fear that the end of the book will suffer for it. In the attempt to reanimate his thoughts (the pastor's) I have again taken up the Gospel and Pascal. I both want to get back a state of fervor and don't want to be caught by it; I am reining in and whipping up at the same time; which doesn't give worthwhile results."

But with his Dostoevsky lectures (delivered in 1922 and published the following year with the earlier material on the same subject) he felt free to concern himself with his more recent interests. "Quite as much as a book of criticism," he said as he was preparing the volume for the press, "it will be for the discerning eye a book of confession; or rather a profession of faith."

Gide was quite frank in admitting that he was using Dostoevsky for his own ends: "Dostoevsky is here often merely a means for presenting my own thoughts. I should be more apologetic about it if I thought I had thereby misrepresented the thought of Dostoevsky, but no. At the most I have, like Montaigne's bees, sought by preference in the work what my honey needed. However great the likeness of a portrait, it always resembles the painter, and almost as much as it does the model." This is honest, at least, and on the whole accurate. What Gide saw in Dostoevsky is there, and he backs it up by abundant quotations—although one might well feel that in one instance, the relation of art to the Devil, Gide has read too much of his own idea into the text; but for the most part one can only criticize the distribution of emphasis, an objection which his frank avowal disarms.

In these lectures he announced the discovery of his personal "four-starred constellation": Nietzsche, Dostoevsky, Browning, Blake. All four were concerned with the problems of good and evil, of the existence of God, of the possibilities of man, and of motivation; and in all four Gide saw what is most conspicuous in the case of Browning—a will to optimism. The solutions proposed by the four differ widely, and perhaps the most striking contrast is between Nietzsche's will to power and Dostoevsky's abnegation: "On the one hand we see the renunciation of self, the abandonment of self; on the other the 'will to power,' the exaggeration of nobility, and it is noteworthy that this will to power in the novels of Dostoevsky always leads to disaster."

Yet in their opposite positions on this question each shows a trace of the other's thought: Nietzschean is the idea of the man-god (put by Dostoevsky into the mouth of his mystic Kirillov), instead of the Christian God-man; Dostoevskyan is Nietzsche's "It is not permitted to look toward oneself during the event; then every glance turns into an 'evil eye.'"

The differences in temperament and talent between Gide and Dostoevsky are striking enough but perhaps not as fundamental as they at first appear. Nothing was more foreign to the prudent and abstemious Gide than the gambling fever and periodic alcoholic intemperance of Dostoevsky; yet they shared a tendency to obsession, differing only in its direction. Gide was not epileptic like Dostoevsky, but he could perhaps see in this physiological taint something analogous to his own sexual abnormality: "At the origin of every great moral reform, if we look carefully, we shall always discover a little physiological mystery, a dissatisfaction of the flesh, an unrest, an anomaly. . . . I do not know whether one could find a single reformer, of those who have proposed new evaluations to humanity, in whom one could not discover what M. Binet-Sanglé [author of a book on *The Madness of Jesus Christ*] would call a taint."

The two men are most closely drawn together by their common veneration for the Christ of the Gospels, combined with an anti-Catholic bias; for this latter Gide has by now acquired as a result of venomous attacks by Catholic critics, of seeing what conversion had done to friends, and perhaps by reaction from his own near-surrender.

Examples of the divided self to be found in Dostoevsky were naturally of the greatest interest to Gide, who found three levels within the Russian's characters: first "an intellectual region foreign to the soul and from which, nevertheless, come the worst temptations. It is there that lives, according to Dostoevsky, the perfidious, the demonic element." The second level is that of the passions, "devastated by cyclonic storms; but however tragic the events determined by these storms, the souls of the characters are not definitely affected." Finally there is the deep region unreached by most characters, that of the second birth.

That the Devil should be essentially the Reasoner and his subtlest most perfidious temptations intellectual was an idea congenial to Gide, and his discovery of it in Dostoevsky was justified. But Gide presented the concept of the diabolic element in art largely on his own authority, and fell back on Blake for confirmation; but he ignored Blake's transposition of good and evil, God and the Devil. He found more authentic support in Hale White's *Autobiography of Mark Rutherford,* and quoted a passage about the "bisection" of man, "the distinction within him, vital to the very last degree, between the higher and the lower, heaven and hell."

It is no surprise to find Gide dwelling in these lectures on self-loss in Dostoevsky; he had already done so in his article of 1908. But now, and perhaps as a result of the rereading he did in preparation for the lectures, he found in *The Possessed* still more striking confirmation of the relation of self-loss to the "Kingdom of God."

"You've begun to believe in an eternal life to come?" asks Stavrogin. "No," replies Kirillov, "not in an eternal life to come, but in eternal life here. There are moments, you reach moments, and time suddenly stops, and it becomes eternity." To which Gide was able to add as

commentary almost the exact words he had written in
Numquid et tu . . . P: "Eternal life can be even now wholly
present in us. We live it from the moment we consent to
die to ourselves, to obtain from ourselves that renunciation
which permits immediate resurrection into eternity."

In another passage quoted by Gide, Kirillov continues
his interrupted description:

There are seconds—they come in groups of five or six—when
you suddenly feel the presence of an eternal harmony completely realized. It is not an earthly experience. I'm not saying
that it is heavenly but merely that a man in human form cannot
bear it: he must either change physically or die. This feeling
is clear and undeniable. It is as if you suddenly became aware
of the whole of nature, and you exclaimed, Yes, this is true.
When God was creating the universe he said at the end of each
day of creation, Yes, this is true, this is good. It—it is not profound emotion but only gladness. You don't forgive anything
because there's nothing to be forgiven. You don't love—oh, it's
above love! The most terrible thing is that it is so frighteningly
clear and such joy. If it lasted longer than five seconds the
soul could not bear it and would be severed from the body.
In those five seconds I live a whole life, and I would gladly
give my whole life for them, they would be worth it. To endure
it ten seconds would require a physical transformation.

Here for Gide was a moving description of the Kingdom
of God, the experience of eternity here and now; but when
he quoted the passage he already felt that he was excluded
from the Kingdom, that he had chosen, in spite of himself,
the alternative of hell, for he wrote in 1918:

Every clear-sighted sinner can have now a complete foretaste of hell. And isn't it hell already to know the place of rest,
to know the way there, and the gate, and to remain excluded?
To feel the bright light of love grow dim, the screen of flesh
grow thicker, this flesh grow constantly heavier and oneself

become ever more attached to it? . . . Hell—as well as Heaven—is within us.

And why, knowing the way and the gate, did he feel excluded? The answer is given in *Numquid et tu . . . ?:* "The truth is that I love this flesh that I hate even more than You. I am dying from not being able to exhaust its attraction." To him were denied not only the visions of Blake but the five seconds of Kirillov. All that he had was a glimpse, a moment when the world glowed a little, enough to show him that there was an intolerable brightness hidden from him by the screen of flesh. In order to have seen more he would have had to make a renunciation for which he was not ripe.

Finding himself excluded from the Kingdom of God, Gide's thoughts turned to the idea of destiny, to which he could make a kind of submission: perhaps he was never "meant" to attain this supremely desirable second birth, perhaps the true significance of his life, the Idea he was born to make manifest, was quite other. And in this new direction too he found support in Dostoevsky, who wrote in *The House of the Dead:* "No man lives without an objective of some sort and without an effort to attain it. Once the objective and the hope have disappeared anguish often makes of the man a monster." This was written in 1861, when his objective, like that of his fellow convicts in Siberia, was liberty, escape from prison. But later, in 1877, he said, "One should not spoil one's life for any objective." And Gide concluded: "We each have a reason for living, superior, secret—secret often even for ourselves—and quite different certainly from the exterior objective which most of us assign to our lives."

Unshaken was Gide's conviction of the spiritual truth

of self-loss, but if he could not find it in the Kingdom of
God he might achieve some sort of substitute for it in submission to his destiny. He would follow where the path
led, with all the burden of his habits, his abnormality, his
basic character. If the path led to public abuse, disgrace,
separation from those he loved, he would accept it all in a
spirit of sacrifice. But in accepting the nature of his destiny
he must accept the whole of it, not only its carnal appe-
tites but its doubts, its hesitations, even its reconsiderations. Yet at the same time he must refuse to lean on the
past, he must deny himself the luxury of Christian repentance and prayers, he must move on, he must serve life
without being its slave: "I choose to serve; I do not choose
to be a slave—the slave of my past, the slave of my plans
for the future, the slave of my faith, of my doubt, of my
hate, of my love."

The paradox of Gide's renunciation of 1918 was that it
was a giving up of the desire to give up, a renunciation of
renunciation; and the act of giving up which he found
himself unable to achieve and which he consequently renounced was intimately bound up with Madeleine. Up to
now he had played self-assertion against self-loss, giving
the preference now to one now to the other. In *L'Immoraliste* he had emphasized self-assertion, in *La Porte
étroite* self-loss, but in both critically, with a suggestion of
the opposite. He had reserved the right sometime to take
up his option on what in 1916 he learned to call the Kingdom of God, to pass with Madeleine through the strait
gate. He was a little like Saint Augustine in his youth,
praying, "O Lord give me continence—but not yet." There
was no hurry; the faithful, loving Madeleine was waiting
and the materials for the message he would compose on

passing through the gate were there, in his letters to her.

Then suddenly the situation changed, and he discovered that he had temporized too long. Madeleine became elusive, then suddenly intractable; he pushed against her new resistance and she burned the letters. In his heart he knew that the fault was his, that he had without intending it made a choice, and that he had failed to penetrate her extraordinary reserve and understand her side of the situation. "Alas," he wrote four days after his discovery of the burning, "I realize now that I have warped her life much more than she has mine."

Three years later he was thinking back over that fall of 1918, remembering how, before his discovery of the loss of the letters, Browning had brought him the assurance, when he was thinking of death, of the eternity of his love. Then he had suddenly learned that it was already too late, and since that day: "I have not regained complete awareness of my moral continuity." And once more he had recourse to Browning:

> Since now at length my fate I know,
> Since nothing all my love avails,
> Since all, my life seemed meant for, fails . . .

12

Counterfeit

IN RETROSPECT GIDE REALIZED THAT FROM NOVEMBER 1918 on, from the time he discovered that the letters had been burned, there was something different about him. "After that," he wrote in 1939, "I never again really recovered a taste for life; or at least not until much later, when I found that I had regained her esteem; but even then I did not really get back into the game, I lived always with the indefinable feeling of going through motions in a world of appearances—appearances that are called reality."

And yet, aside from the disembodied mood (an old one but more frequent now), there seems for several years to be no great change. Through the pages of the Journal moves the same Gide with his familiar torpors and bursts of vitality, his despair and his enthusiasm, his "relapses into the worst" and his resumption of devotional reading, with the admission, "Scarcely a day passes but what I reopen the whole question." What is new is at first only a tendency. By his own fault and yet not by his deliberate act a bridge has been burned behind him; he stands on the far side, uneasily shifting his weight from one foot to the other, hesitating, looking back, yet knowing in his heart that he is committed to setting out on a new path. "When the road which opens up before your mind saddens even unto death persons who are infinitely dear, you can both believe that you must follow that road and advance upon it with trembling, a divided heart, hesitations, reconsiderations. . . . What I lack is not constancy but ferocity." These words were written in January of 1921, and six months later he said, "It seems to me that all my desires become less fierce, as the felicity, to which I aspired, of perfect communion with her becomes more remote."

But he had not yet abandoned this dwindling aspiration nor on her side had Madeleine, despite her resistance and her apparent coldness, lost hope for him. The following November, Massis launched in the press another furious attack against Gide, and a few weeks later Madeleine wrote, still using the familiar second person singular, "What greatly disturbs me is the malicious campaign started against you. Of course it is the strength of your thought and its authority which unleash it. Ah, if you were invulnerable I should not tremble. But you are vulnerable and you know it, and I know it." And Gide commented, "Vulnerable I am not, I was not, except through her. Now it is all the same to me and I no longer fear anything. What have I to lose to which I still cling?"

The break with his past was shortly to be still further accentuated by an important event: the birth to Elisabeth Van Rysselberghe of a daughter whose paternity Gide later publicly acknowledged. About this situation it would at present be rash (as well as discourteous to living persons) to speculate; all we can do is to call attention to certain relevant parts of the published record.

In October 1921 Gide left home with a despair almost like that of June 1918 when he "said farewell to all his past." This time he wrote: "I left Cuverville like one who dies." Two weeks later he noted: "Arrived last night at Roquebrune. As the moment for leaving her [Em.] approached I felt more painfully all that attached me to her and I reached the point of doubting whether reason really counseled this departure."

In November he was back at Cuverville, and the journey —to Pisa, Siena, Orvieto, Rome—seemed like a dream. He plunged into work on the Dostoevsky lectures that he had promised to Copeau, but with difficulty and reluctance. On December 12 he wrote: "What am I to do? What is to become of me? Where can I go? I cannot stop loving her [Em.]. Her face on certain days, her angelic smile, still fill my heart with ecstasy, love, and despair—despair at not being able to tell her so. Not one day, not one moment have I been able to summon the courage to speak to her. We are both immured in our silence. . . . I cannot imagine myself without her; it seems to me that without her I should never have been *anything*. Each one of my thoughts has been born in relation to her."

Then he goes to Paris to continue his work on Dostoevsky which, he says on February 8, 1922, goes very well since Elisabeth has left him.

On July 16—the very day, as he learns later and with a sense of its symbolic significance, on which Madeleine gave away the little cross he had given her—Elisabeth joins him at Hyères on the Mediterranean shore. In August he goes to the annual "decade" of Paul Desjardins at Pontigny, accompanied, among others, by Mme Théo and Elisabeth. On September 10 (at Colpach) he records that he has not heard from Madeleine for over a month: "My heart is full of darkness and tears. I am taking a dislike to everyone around me and everything that keeps me from her, that justifies her in breaking away from me. While thinking this morning of my small value without her, of the weakness of my heart, I came to understand better the necessity of intermediaries between man and God. . . . I came also to a better understanding of the complicated game of the devil and of how the noblest feelings are those of which he is the most jealous and which he tries to turn against God. I am not sure whether there is left in me anything that could give grounds for hope."

Then comes the important entry for January 11, 1923: "I say a few words to Em. of the affair that summons me to E. I cannot hope or even wish that Em. should consider what she glimpses of this story as other than a very lamentable catastrophe, and yet I have the greatest difficulty in restraining myself from protesting when she concludes, from the little I dare say to her about it: 'I have always thought that it was unfortunate that El. was raised without religion.' For it goes without saying that El. is not happy, cannot be happy, has not the right to be happy—and here I cannot object without imprudence; but I suffer intolerably from these false ideas, derived, I feel, from false premises."

Three days later he leaves "for Roquebrune, for Genoa, for the unknown," adding that he never leaves Cuverville "without a kind of heartbreak."

But these "heartbreaks," these conflicting emotions, have about them a strange impersonality: "It seems to me that nothing that I do, nothing that I feel, any longer involves my moral responsibility. . . . I am already dead

and the life I am now living is a sort of unimportant supplement which *commits me to nothing*." Under these conditions his mind sometimes acquires an extraordinary
acuity, and during sleepless but no longer distressing hours
of the night it seems to him that if he had a secretary at
hand he could dictate "a quarter of a book." The new path
on which he is about to enter is by a sort of contradiction
an old one, that of his youth, but reëxplored in a new spirit;
he quotes with satisfaction Vigny's saying: "A beautiful
life is one in which a thought of youth is realized in
maturity."

He tries to explain away conflicts and contradictions
within him. Admitting that he has lived "torn apart"
(*écartelé*) he nevertheless insists that the result has been
not so much disquiet and suffering as a pathetic intensi-
fication of the feeling of living: "The most deeply opposed
tendencies have not made of me a tormented but merely a
perplexed being." And then he goes on to say: "Shall I
tell you what keeps me from believing in eternal life?
It is the almost perfect satisfaction I experience in effort
itself and in the immediate realization of happiness and
harmony."

Here he is beginning to compose a new attitude, a new
legend about himself which he is shortly to publicize in
response to attack: that of the man who is infinitely sympathetic, but detached, serene, secure. A typical expression
of this attitude comes in 1928:

For a long time they reproached me for what they called
my disquiet; then, when they began to understand that this
disquiet was not in me but in my characters and that I could
not depict their disquiet without having emerged from it myself, they reproached me for having found the calm and the

serenity which enabled me to produce. They did not imagine or admit that disquiet could reach an end elsewhere than in the port where they were anchored.

This "serenity," obviously slanted toward publicity, is belied by the continuing distress revealed in the Journal; and yet it is not wholly insincere. We get a little better idea of what Gide really felt by a phrase or two in a letter to Charles Du Bos, written from the Congo in 1925: "This 'state of security'—which on dull days becomes apathy—is my constant state. It results no doubt from my total renunciation as a result of the terrible crisis that I have talked to you about; so that I wonder sometimes whether one should not see in it a form of despair; the happy form."

It was from the ground of these complex thoughts and emotions that grew Gide's *Faux-Monnayeurs,* his chief bid to be considered a serious novelist. And his new orientation was signalized by the fact that it was written for Marc: "It was for him," he said in 1928, "that I wrote the *Faux-Monnayeurs,* to capture his attention, his esteem, just as I wrote all my preceding books under the influence of Em., or in the vain hope of convincing her."

He began serious work on the book in June of 1919. No fictional work of his contains less directly autobiographical material, but none is so sinuously and intimately intertwined with the very roots of his character and thought. "Everything I have been seeing and learning," he admitted early in the *Journal des Faux-Monnayeurs,* "and all that has been happening to me in the last several months I want to put into this novel." As we follow its elaboration during the six years of its composition—in the *Journal des Faux-Monnayeurs* (the subsequently published record he kept of his thoughts while writing the novel), in the regular Journal, and in the book itself—we can see it as the transposition into literary terms of the problems he is facing and the attitude he is trying to assume toward them: sympathy, self-assertion and self-loss, loss of a sense of continuity and of moral responsibility, the duty of manifestation and its opposite vice of hypocrisy, homosexuality, reason and mysticism, disinterestedness—all of these, directly or indirectly, find their way into the novel.

There is little doubt that the *Faux-Monnayeurs* is descended from the project of January 1902 when Gide wrote, "I think out, or at least imagine and feel take form at last, the vague novel of which I have been dreaming: that is, the *relations* between a dozen characters." It is clear too that the *Caves* was an intermediate step, a first attempt which was deflected from the goal in part at least by the intrusion of the ironic manner. But by now it must also be evident that the *Faux-Monnayeurs* could not have been written in 1914; certain essential experiences were still lacking, and above all the break from his wife. *Les Caves du Vatican* was scarcely a book of which Madeleine would have approved and yet it did not directly attack the principles for which she stood and the reader is not invited to admire the extremes to which Lafcadio's principles led him. But the *Faux-Monnayeurs* was a serious defense of the duty of self-manifestation and a frontal attack on the hypocrisy which impeded it. "I brood ecstatically over the possibilities of each being," said Gide through Edouard, "and lament all that is atrophied by the lid of convention."

Gide had expressed himself as dissatisfied not only with the ironic but with the critical tendencies of his previous books. Nevertheless in the *Faux-Monnayeurs* he set himself (among other self-imposed obstacles) the task of "developing at the same time the critical spirit and energy, those two contraries." The problems in which this effort involved him were apparent early. In August 1921 he wrote: "Perhaps the extreme difficulty I find in making my novel progress is only the natural result of an initial defect. At times I am convinced that the very idea of the book is absurd and I get to the point of no longer understanding at all what I am after. Properly speaking there is not one center for my efforts, they polarize around two foci, as in an ellipse. On the one hand the event, the fact, the external datum; on the other, the effort of the novelist to make a novel out of this. And that is the principal subject, the new center which throws the story off its axis and lures it into the imaginative. And in the end I see this notebook in which I write the history of the book wholly incorporated in the novel, for the greater irritation of the reader."

The prediction was very nearly fulfilled, for the slim volume of the *Journal des Faux-Monnayeurs*, overlapping, small as it is, with the novel, would certainly have been much more substantial had the *Faux-Monnayeurs* itself not been provided with a journal of the same sort, kept by the novelist Edouard, who is writing a novel called *Les Faux-Monnayeurs*. The result is that Gide's novel, although less ironic than the *Caves*, is even more critical, and more so than any book he ever wrote: critical in the sense of a consciousness of consciousness, and then a further awareness behind that, in a continuing regress. It was impossible for Gide to escape from the acute self-awareness which was one of his outstanding characteristics.

The relationship of Edouard to Gide is complex. We

are permitted to make a superficial identification of him
with the author first because he is writing a book called
Les Faux-Monnayeurs and second because in his character and ideas he resembles his creator. "A character
all the more difficult to establish," wrote Gide, "in that
I attribute to him much of myself. I have to draw
back and push him away from me in order to see him
well." But he insisted (outside of the book) that the
reader should distinguish, and was annoyed with critics
who failed to do so. Even Martin-Chauffier, the editor
of the *Œuvres complètes*, implicitly incurs this blame for
quoting Edouard's statement, "I have never been able to
invent anything," and adding, "Let us without scruple
attribute to Gide this confession of Edouard's." With considerable annoyance Gide objected: "'I have never been
able to invent anything.' It was by this sentence in the
Journal of Edouard that I thought to separate myself most
clearly from Edouard, to distinguish him. And it is this
sentence on the contrary that is used to prove that,
'incapable of invention,' it was myself that I depicted in
Edouard and that I am not a novelist."

But Martin-Chauffier admits, and the reader can realize
for himself, that a real distinction between Edouard and
Gide is both intended and achieved. More than an *alter
ego* Edouard is a combination of stalking horse and scape-
goat. After making some observations in the *Journal des
Faux-Monnayeurs* on the "pure novel" Gide adds, "I think
all this should be put into the mouth of Edouard—which
would permit me to add that I do not concede him all
these points, however judicious." Gide liked to play with
the idea of the pure novel, but recognized its impossibility.
It was Edouard who was to be saddled with the attempt

to write one and its failure, for his *Faux-Monnayeurs* unlike Gide's was never to be finished. "I must carefully respect in Edouard," said Gide, "all that makes him unable to write his book. He understands many things, but he pursues himself in everyone and everything. True devotion is practically impossible for him. He is an amateur, a failure."

But to write a book which was at once a novel and a novel about a novel was a wager that Gide had vowed to win, and the second part of this program was implemented by a number of suggestions. One of these occurs in the first chapter, and is put into the mouth of a schoolboy in the Luxembourg Gardens:

What I would like is to tell the story not of a character but of a place—here for example, a lane in a park like this one—tell what happens there from morning to night. First there would come the nursemaids, nurses with ribbons—no, first the gray characters, ageless and sexless, to sweep the lane, water the grass, change the flowers—the stage and the setting before the opening of the gates, you understand? Then the entry of the nursemaids. Urchins make mud pies, squabble; the nurses slap them. Then the exit of the little ones, and next the working women. There are the poor ones who come to eat on a bench. Then the young men looking for each other, others who avoid each other, still others who are isolated, the dreamers. And then the crowd, at the time of the band concert and the closing of the stores. Students, as now. In the evening lovers who kiss; others who part in tears. Finally, at nightfall, an old couple. And then suddenly the roll of a drum: closing time. Exit everyone. The play is over. You understand: something that would give the impression of the end of everything, of death—but without talking about death, naturally.

A diversity of characters can also be drawn together by a community of time, as Gide suggests when he pictures

Edouard on the deck of his channel boat at the moment when Laura, the abandoned mistress of Vincent, finally drops asleep in her dismal hotel room, Bernard awakes in the bed of Olivier, and a hot day is about to dawn in Paris.

Slightly more importance is given to the saying, which would have been forgotten if Stendhal had not brought it up in *Le Rouge et le Noir,* that "A novel is a mirror which you carry along a road": for Edouard his journal is the mirror and it is there that he looks for his image of reality and for the material of his novel. And then there is the idea—the statement of a problem rather than its solution— of the art of the fugue transposed into literature. Edouard (and Gide) have a multiplicity of characters and of themes; in some way they must be blended into an orderly development.

But we get close to Gide's final way of grappling with his problem when Edouard starts discoursing on the pure novel and talks of "stripping the novel of all the elements that do not specifically belong to it." Physical description, even of characters, belongs properly to photography, dialogues to the phonograph, exterior action to the cinema. Naturalistic novelists are on the wrong track when they try to present "a slice of life"; the fault of this school is "cutting its slice always in the same dimension—length, time. Why not in width? Or depth?" The naturalists are right in not imposing a dramatic and foreseen end on their material; they err in enslaving themselves to time and space. A slice of life "in depth" could be the presentation of a single event from several points of view, as Browning did in *The Ring and the Book*—and as Gide for a time thought of doing in the *Faux-Monnayeurs,* leaving, in the final version, some traces of the abandoned method.

The novelist should not concern himself with things as they directly seem nor with events as they occur in the everyday world; he should create his own reality, the reality of art. And how? Edouard comes up with an answer about which he declines to generalize dogmatically but which will serve for himself and Gide: "I begin to glimpse what I would call the 'deep subject' of my book. It is, it will be without doubt, the opposition between the real world and the representation we make of it to ourselves. The manner in which the world of appearances imposes itself on us and in which we attempt to impose on the outside world our private interpretations, makes the drama of our lives."

And for unifying the novel's multiplicity what was more useful than the idea of counterfeit, which means trying to impose on someone else one's own valuation?

Counterfeit appears in Gide's novel on several levels. There is first of all literal counterfeit: the passing off by a gang of schoolboys of gilded glass counters as gold coin. This is but the symbolic representation of the moral counterfeit of their elders, the hypocrisy which the boys are unconsciously imitating in their illegal traffic. Then there is the literary counterfeit of the novelist Passavant, whose opportunism and worldly success are the antiphon to Edouard's ineffectual sincerity. And finally we have the counterfeit of ideas: the passing off, and the acceptance as ultimate truth, of intellectual stylizations of reality. Like the thin coating of gold that covers the glass counters, ideas have a certain value, but in time it wears off; they have a temporary utility, but if they serve too long they lose their gold and become worthless.

GIDE AT MID-CAREER

By this device of counterfeit Gide was able, not only to make his book a "crossroads of ideas" and coördinate in his ellipse the two axes of his material—the critical and the creative, the novel and the novel about the novel—but to give expression to some of his most cherished convictions. But however satisfactory the unifying principle of counterfeit might be in theory, there yet remained serious practical problems in its application, and to solve them Gide used considerable ingenuity and had recourse occasionally to not wholly plausible coincidence. There are in the book some half-dozen major groups of characters, any one of which would offer the material for a full novel, and they overflow and overlap into still other groupings; between them Edouard, collecting material for his novel, acts as liaison agent.

Of basic importance both as a breeding ground for moral counterfeit and as a center of radiating relations is the Azaïs-Vedel boarding school. Both the aged Azaïs (the founder and titular head of the school but at the time of the story an upstairs oracle, invisible but spiritually omnipresent) and his son-in-law Vedel are profoundly corrupted by their Protestant ministry. They are moral by profession, and since their faith is their livelihood the luxury of doubt is denied them; all situations, events, characters, must be met and interpreted in accordance with irrevocable principles and attitudes, and an insidious hypocrisy is the inevitable result. The effect upon Vedel's children is either vitiating or frustrating. One son, Alexandre, escapes from the stifling atmosphere by going to the colonies, where he makes more debts than money. Rachel, the eldest daughter, "prefers to stay at home,"

that is, she has sacrificially dedicated herself to the imple-
mentation of the Divine Providence in which her father,
mother, and grandfather profess complete trust, preferring
not to see the sacrifices, humiliations, and expedients by
which their daughter contrives, not only to make household ends meet, but to send money to her shiftless brother
abroad. Sarah, under the necessary mask of hypocrisy, is
wholeheartedly pursuing the delights of the sin denounced
by her parents and is in a fair way to becoming wholly
vicious. Armand, the unhappy offshoot of a part of Gide's
nature, is the most clear-sighted of the family, despises
the hypocrites, and respects only Rachel. But he is paralyzed by his intelligence and a victim to obsessive fantasy;
he finds it impossible to break out and act. "Whatever I
say or do," he says, "a part of me remains behind, watching
the other part compromise himself, observing him, mocking him, hissing or applauding him. Divided like this, who
can be sincere?"

Through Laura, the remaining Vedel daughter, contacts
are established with other groups of the novel. Laura is
attractive and honest but she is weak, sentimental, and
something of a defeatist. She falls deeply in love with
Edouard, who spent two years in the *pension,* and he returns her affection—with reservations. His own analysis of
his attitude toward her is so reminiscent of Gide's toward
Madeleine that parts of it are worth quoting:

Laura does not seem to suspect her power; as for me, who
can penetrate to the secret places of my own heart, I well
know that up to this day I have not written a line that she did
not directly inspire. When she is with me I feel her to be a
child still, and all the skill of my talk I owe to the constant
desire to instruct her, convince her, fascinate her. I see noth-

ing, hear nothing, without at once thinking: What would she say? . . . By a strange crossing of loving influences our two natures have distorted each other. Involuntarily, unconsciously each of the two beings who love fashions himself on the image in the heart of the other. . . . A day comes when the true nature reappears, slowly stripped by time of its borrowed vestments; and if it is these ornaments that the other loves, he will press to his heart only deserted finery, only a memory, only mourning and despair.

Ah, with what virtues, what perfections, I have adorned her!

How irritating is this matter of sincerity. *Sincerity!* When I speak of it I think only of her sincerity. If I turn back toward myself I no longer know what the word means. I am never anything but what I think I am—and that changes ceaselessly, so that often if I were not there to fit them together my morning self would not recognize the evening one. Nothing could be more different from me than myself. It is only in solitude that the substratum sometimes appears and that I attain to a certain fundamental continuity; but then it seems to me that my life slows down, stops, and that I am really about to cease to be. My heart beats only by sympathy; I live only through others; by proxy I might say, by wedding myself to another, and I never feel myself more intensely alive than when I escape from myself to become anyone at all.

This force which decentralizes the ego is such that it volatilizes the sense of property and therefore of responsibility. Such a person is not of those one marries. How can I make Laura understand this?

All of the sense and several of the sentences of this piece of introspection are lifted straight from Gide's *Journal*. It is extraordinarily true and penetrating (at least so far as Gide is concerned, for one can never quite persuade oneself of Edouard's existence); yet one can sympathize with Edouard's difficulty in presenting such subtleties to Laura as an explanation of why he will not marry her. She is a simple soul and she loves him; perhaps she would have better understood the reason which he did not tell her: that he, like his creator, finds boys more sexually attractive than her.

Another group is the Molinier family: Oscar Molinier, who "deceives" (but only technically) his wife Pauline, Edouard's sister; and their three sons Vincent, Olivier, Georges. Olivier is an aspiring writer, and his uncle Edouard takes in him a tender interest which is, to a certain extent, reciprocated. Their relations are lover-like, with advances, withdrawals, blushing confusion, occasional jealousy. After a lamentable literary dinner at which Olivier gets very drunk and makes a fool of himself, his uncle takes him home to his own apartment. The next day Olivier attempts suicide, on the theory that once one has known perfect joy there is nothing left to live for. His mother is an intelligent woman and not blind to what is going on, but with exceptional broadmindedness she is willing to admit that in the long run it may all be for the best, and she does not interfere.

Through Vincent Molinier, contact is established with the Azaïs-Vedel center. He acquires tuberculosis; so does Laura, who, unable to marry Edouard and on his advice, marries Douviers, a good-natured but not very intelligent Cambridge professor. Laura and Vincent meet in a sanitorium and, both thinking they are going to die, do not scruple to become lovers. Laura becomes pregnant and then both uncomfortably recover. Vincent has from his parents a sum of money destined to meet the expenses of his medical education; he plans to use this money for Laura, but finds that it is insufficient for all that is now demanded of it. He gambles with it, makes startling gains, and by a series of steps in which the Devil (in his capacity of rationalizer) plays a large part he arrives at the point of abandoning Laura and eloping with a Lady Griffith, a charming but basically evil character.

Parallel to the Molinier ménage is the Profitendieu family. Albéric Profitendieu, an examining magistrate, is younger, richer, and healthier, but less advanced in career, than his colleague Molinier, and he has been (technically) deceived by his wife. Of the children, Charles (a lawyer), Cécile, and the youngest, Caloub, are his own; the next to the youngest, Bernard, is illegitimate. The wife's fault is known to the husband and has been forgiven and ostensibly forgotten. There are, however, letters, and it is the discovery of these by Bernard that causes him to leave home and take temporary refuge with his friend Olivier. Albéric Profitendieu develops into a somewhat sympathetic character in that he feels a marked preference for the son who is not his own; he has a disinterested affection and a sort of admiration for this product of a break from moral tradition.

The old music teacher La Pérouse, whom we have met in the Journal and *Si le grain ne meurt,* is another center, and his domestic misfortunes are used to draw various elements of the plot together. It is to bring La Pérouse's grandson Boris to Paris that Edouard, accompanied by Bernard and Laura (who in her pregnancy has turned to Edouard for support), goes to Saas-Fée in the Pennine Alps. Little Boris suffers from a nervous complaint and is under the care of a Polish woman psychiatrist; probably the most beneficial part of her therapy is furnished by her small daughter Bronja, who plays lovingly and happily with Boris. Advantage of the Saas-Fée episode is taken for some exposition of psychoanalysis by Sophroniska, the psychiatrist, and of the art of the novel by Edouard. Boris is taken back to Paris and put in the worst possible place for him: the pension-school of Azaïs and Vedel. In putting him there Edouard thinks he is indulging a curiosity for experiment but is really yielding to a prompting of the Devil. Then old La Pérouse, sinking slowly into senility, persecution complex, and paralysis of the will, attempts to commit suicide, lacks the courage, and thereafter announces that he is dead; he is rescued by Edouard, who gets him a position in the school. Boris falls into the clutches of a cruel band of schoolboys, the same who have been concerned with the passing of counterfeit coins. When the counterfeit scheme becomes too dangerous they invent a "Brotherhood of Strong Men," whose first purpose is the exclusion of Boris. Later they invent the further refinement of admitting him just to make him do their will in payment: first he must resume the practice of "magic" (self-abuse) from which he is in the process of being weaned, and then he must do nothing less than commit suicide to prove that he is a genuine "strong man." The plot is actually accomplished in a classroom supervised by La Pérouse; his grandson shoots himself before his eyes with the very pistol which he had loaded for his own abortive suicide.

At Saas-Fée somewhat implausibly one of the false coins turns up, and it is discovered that Strouvilhou has been there. Strouvilhou, a former inmate of the Azaïs-Vedel *pension*, is the leader of the boys who circulated the false coins. He is cynical, lawless, and callous, but his depravity springs from a frustrated idealism. There is a little of Nietzsche in him, and a little of the anarchistic Souvarine of *Germinal* (Gide's favorite among the novels of Zola):

Philanthropy [he says to Passavant] has never been my strong point . . . nor egoism either. They would like to have us believe that there is no other escape from egoism than a still more hideous altruism! As for me, I claim that if there is anything more despicable than man it is many men. Nothing can persuade me that the addition of sordid units can give an exquisite total. I never get into a tram or a train without wishing for a fine accident to reduce to pulp this living garbage— myself included, you understand; I never enter a theatre without hoping for the fall of the chandelier or the explosion of a bomb; and even if I were to be blown up with it, I would gladly carry one under my coat, if I weren't reserving myself for something better. . . . I don't know whether I have what is called a hard heart; I have too much imagination, too much disgust, to think so, and it doesn't matter. It is true that I have long since repressed in this organ everything that threatened to soften it. But I am not incapable of admiration and of a sort of absurd devotion; for, being a man, I despise and hate myself as much as another. . . . And if I can't endure the thought of a Christ sacrificing himself for the thankless salvation of all these horrible people with whom I brush elbows, I find some satisfaction and even a sort of serenity in imagining this rabble rotting to produce a Christ—although I should prefer something else, for all his teaching has served only to sink humanity a little deeper in the muck. Misfortune comes from selfish ferocity. A consecrated ferocity: that is what would produce great things. In protecting the unfortunate, the weak, the rachitic, the wounded, we are on the wrong track; and that is why I hate the religion that teaches us to do so.

The novel contains two supernatural personages of great but not immediately obvious importance to an understanding of the whole. Particularly deceptive is the first of these, the Devil, whose name and legend are so much a commonplace of everyday conversation that they are scarcely noticed. When Gide speaks of some sophistry of Edouard's as a "prompting of the Devil," or when the Devil rubs his hands with glee at some act of Vincent, it seems metaphoric in the familiar tradition. But we know that Gide, without quite believing in the literal existence of the Devil, attached great importance to him as a symbol of purposeful evil. As far back as September 1914, after his conversation with Jacques Raverat, he wrote, "Certainly there will be someone in my novel who believes in the devil." And the promise was fulfilled in Vincent Molinier.

At first, as a prospective medical student and then as an amateur naturalist, he does not believe in the Devil, and it is then that the principle of evil gets hold of him. His first clear step on the Devil's path is acceptance of the sophistry, "We are going to die, consequently nothing that we do has moral consequence," and using it to seduce Laura. His next diabolically inspired rationalization is over the money he first intended to use for Laura's confinement, then recognized as insufficient and risked in gambling; there followed the intoxication of success, accompanied by the tossing, too late, of a part of his gains to Laura, and her indignant rejection—her pride now being buttressed by Edouard's money—of any support from her faithless lover. At this point Vincent, discovering how successful are his rationalizations and his gestures of pure egoism, begins to suspect that the Devil is on his side, that he has won the world at the price of his soul. Lady Griffith is a powerful adjunct of the Devil; her philosophy of life is based on the recollection of seeing, during the shipwreck of the *Bourgogne,* two sailors in a lifeboat chopping off the fingers of drowning swimmers trying to get into the overcrowded boat. "I understood," she tells Vincent, "that I had left a part of myself to sink with the *Bourgogne,* and that from then on I would cut off the fingers of a mass of delicate sentiments to prevent them from climbing in and sinking my heart."

Vincent elopes with Lady Griffith, and all her projects of getting him started as a naturalist and oceanographer are fantastically successful. But they come to hate each other with a fierceness that does not interfere with bodily embraces but does in the long run lead to the murder of Lady Griffith by Vincent. The last we hear of him, in a letter of Alexandre Vedel, is that he is a madman who thinks that he is the Devil.

This Devil, it is quite clear, is the principle of self-assertion. To save oneself is to lose one's soul.

The other supernatural personage is an angel, who is presented in a much more flagrantly unusual way. Bernard meets him as the result of an unspoken offer of himself. Already he has disinterestedly and without carnal desire loved Laura; now, having just passed his baccalaureate with distinction, he feels the need to love and to serve. "He had been meditating for a few moments when he saw approaching, gliding so lightly that one felt he could have walked on water, an angel. Bernard had never seen any angels, but he was not in a moment's doubt and when the angel said, 'Come,' he rose docilely and followed." They went into the church of the Sorbonne, where there were a number of other angels, but "Bernard did not have the sort of eyes to see them." Bernard did not believe precisely in any God, but he offered himself with a deep emotion, and tears ran down his cheeks. "You offered yourself in the same way to Laura," said the angel. "Come with me."

On the way out they meet one of Bernard's schoolmates whom he does not like, who has also passed his examinations and now gives the beadle money to pay for a candle. Bernard shrugs his shoulders; when he emerges from the church the angel has disappeared. In the early afternoon he appears again, urges Bernard to make up his mind as to what he is to do with himself, and leads him into a public meeting where a series of orators urge the advantages of joining a particular party and backing its line. Young men circulate in the hall and pass out forms to sign. "Do you think I should sign?" Bernard asks the angel. "Yes, surely," answers the angel, "if you doubt yourself." Bernard says, "I no longer doubt myself," and throws away the form.

Then the angel, behaving a little like the Ghost of Christmas yet to come with Scrooge, conducts Bernard to the Boulevards, where everyone seems sure of himself, indifferent to others, yet full of anxiety. "Is this the picture of happiness?" asks Bernard, his heart full of tears. "Then the angel led Bernard into the poor quarters whose wretchedness he had not previously suspected. Night was falling. They wandered long between tall sordid houses inhabited by disease, prostitution, shame, crime, and hunger. It was then for the first time that Bernard took the hand of the angel, who turned aside to weep."

That night Bernard, like Jacob in the Bible, wrestles with the angel all night, and in the morning they separate without a clear advantage to either.

The next day Bernard consults Edouard about his problems, and in telling of his experience with the angel he says, curiously enough, "Yesterday, urged on by some demon or other, I went into a public meeting." At the time of meeting the angel he had no doubt whatever of his identity; now he feels vaguely that he was a demon. The meaning of this confusion becames apparent when he continues, "If I were certain of preferring the best side of myself I would give it the advantage over the rest. But I can't even know what the best side of me is. I debated all night, I tell you. Toward morning I was so tired that I thought of enlisting before my class was called up."

Here we have the symbolic significance of the angel: it is devotion to something outside, the loving gift of one-self—in other words self-loss at its best, as opposed to the demon of self-assertion. At the same time the individual cannot know for certain what is the true path of self-loss, nor even, except in moments of exaltation, whether self-loss is the right policy after all. Edouard's solution, which is also Gide's and the sum total of his morality so far as it can be gleaned from the *Faux-Monnayeurs,* is: "It is good to follow one's inclination provided that it leads uphill."

The multiplicity of situations and characters in the novel are matched, and more than matched, by its profusion of ideas. The theme of counterfeit ties together the novel and the novel about the novel, for not only do the situations of the creative aspect of the book constantly illustrate the passing off of the spurious for the genuine, but in the critical part we have the false, the insincere, literary production of Passavant (whose name, suggestive of "Get ahead of others," is symbolic of his opportunism) at one extreme and the honest but impractical and frustrated effort of Edouard at the other. The counterfeit idea also entails subordinate themes: illegitimacy, the conflict of youth and age, the tyranny of convention. Beyond these themes there is a further proliferation of suggestions: mysticism, classicism, puritanism, the incompatibility of individual sexual desire and true love, the necessity of detachment, the duty to pursue the new and dangerous instead of contenting oneself with the old and secure, the problem of the reality of the self, the possibility of impersonal emotion— all ideas which our knowledge of Gide makes familiar but none of which is pursued to any kind of conclusion.

There are those—critics for the most part—who see in the *Faux-Monnayeurs* a truly great and significant novel, but the reaction of the average reader is more apt to be an uneasy dissatisfaction. A part of this may be due to the pervasive atmosphere of homosexuality. There is only one explicitly homosexual incident and it is handled with great discretion, but one has the constant feeling that these characters, even an ostensibly heterosexual one like Bernard, see with different eyes from one's own. A part of the dissatisfaction may come from Gide's deliberate dropping of ideas which one would like to see carried further; a part also to the scenario-like presentation of situations, with its concurrent obligation upon the reader to fill in details for himself; most of all perhaps to the insubstantial delineation of character, which is perhaps the one characteristic, if any, that is widely expected of the novel.

The question of whether the *Faux-Monnayeurs* is a novel would scarcely need to come up if Gide himself had not insisted that this indeed was a novel, and his first one. That it is not a "pure" novel in the sense of his own theories he would have been the first to admit. Is he then, as some have suggested, writing a novel to end novels, making a deliberate attempt to sabotage the *genre*? But what, after all, do these considerations matter to the ordinary intelligent reader? It is a book of fiction at any rate, and in many respects a brilliant performance.

It is quite clear from the record that some of the characteristics striking the reader as defects are there with the deliberate intent of the author, or at least with his full knowledge and claimed intent. For example:

"The difficulty comes from this, that for every chapter I have to start afresh. *Never take advantage of impetus acquired:* that is the rule of my game."

"Constantly reviving difficulties of a book which is fed by *invention* alone, which will not take advantage of any impetus."

"Not to establish the continuation of my novel in the prolongation of lines already traced: there is the difficulty. A continuous upsurging; every new chapter must set a new problem, be an opening, a direction, an impulsion, a cast ahead, for the mind of the reader. But he must leave me, like the stone out of a sling. I am even willing that he should come back and hit me like a boomerang."

At one point Gide thought he had found in Stendhal one who also refused to take advantage of impetus, at least stylistically: "In Stendhal a sentence never either necessitates its successor nor springs from its predecessor. Each remains perpendicular to a fact or idea." But six years later when his novel was almost finished he seems to have changed his mind: "Every sentence [in *Le Rouge et le Noir*] is stretched like a bowstring; but the sentence always flies in the same direction and toward a target always visible—which permits one readily to see that it reaches the mark." For himself, however, he declined to allow the target to be seen, he forbade his sentences even the flight of the rocket toward the open sky with a long trail of fire behind; he preferred the random and ephemeral but continually renewed flash of the roman candle; his characters must not build up a cumulative effect; of his story it must remain true that "it could be continued indefinitely."

And why should he have set himself rules which precluded the very virtues which we are accustomed to think of as essential to the novel?

Looking back on the *Faux-Monnayeurs* in 1930 and contrasting himself with Bourget, he wrote:

I think that Bourget will be obsolete in twenty years—or say fifty. But he makes me realize what success I could have had with my *Faux-Monnayeurs* if I had consented to develop my picture a little. The extreme concision of my notations does not give the superficial reader time to get into the swing of it. This book requires a slowness of reading and a meditativeness that are not ordinarily given at once. . . . I was careful to indicate only the significant, the decisive, the indispensable; to avoid all that "goes without saying," where the intelligent reader could fill in by himself (that is what I call the *collaboration of the reader*). Bourget spares you nothing. But the reader is grateful to him for it.

Yes, the average reader, the lazy reader.

But I recognize that this thinning of the story permits a large surface of contact between the reader and the characters. The atmosphere, if not too abstract, is filled in. Sometimes I tell myself that a too constant concern for art, a rather empty (but spontaneous, irresistible) concern, made me fail in the *Faux-Monnayeurs;* that if I had consented to a more conventional and banal way of writing, one which permitted a more ready acceptance by readers, I should greatly have increased their number; in short, that I "cast my net too high," as Stendhal put it; much too high. But flying fish are the only ones that interest me. . . . I write only for those who understand at a hint.

"Verisimilitude" (I think that is his word) in Bourget is perfect. A disciple of Balzac, he is deeply plunged in reality.

He never gets bogged down in it as I would surely do if I tried to succeed in that field.

My *reality* is always a little fantastic. At bottom I can never quite believe in it (any more than I can in life) and have never been able to subscribe to Gautier's saying, "The artist is a man for whom the external world exists." Much more often the artist, who is always something of a mystic, is the one who does not believe, or does not wholly believe, in the reality (in the *exclusive* reality at any rate) of the external world.

Penetrating as is this piece of self-criticism, it needs both discount and emendation: discount because of Gide's tendency to exaggerate the merits of his most sharply criticized books (just as he deprecated the more successful ones) and perhaps because he makes a virtue of abstaining from what the limitations of his talent preclude; emendation because he makes it appear as if esthetic considerations alone determined his choice of procedures in the *Faux-Monnayeurs*, whereas moral and temperamental factors were also involved.

Clearly, declining to take advantage of impetus is the literary equivalent of nonattachment, disinterestedness, pushing always on; and losing himself in a character is religious self-loss transposed into art, as is apparent from these words in the *Journal des Faux-Monnayeurs:* "It is certainly easier for me to make a character speak than to express myself under my own name, and the more the character differs from me the easier it is. . . . While doing so I forget who I am, if indeed I ever knew. I become the other. . . . I am no longer someone but several people. . . . To push abnegation to the point of total forgetfulness of self. . . . My heart beats only through sympathy."

As this passage indicates, his "total forgetfulness of self" is both artistic and moral, and in both aspects there is more than a touch of complacency and some wishful thinking.

To take first the artistic side, there is another passage of the *Journal des Faux-Monnayeurs* where Gide says:

> The poor novelist constructs his characters; he directs them and makes them talk. The true novelist listens to them and watches them act; he hears them speak before knowing them, and it is in accordance with what he hears them say that he understands little by little *who* they are.
>
> I added "watches them act" because for me it is rather the language than the gesture that instructs me, and I think that I should lose less from the loss of sight than from the loss of hearing. Yet I *see* my characters, but not so much in their detail as in their mass, and still more in their gestures, their bearing, the rhythm of their movements. . . .
>
> I wrote the first dialogue between Olivier and Bernard and the scenes between Passavant and Vincent without knowing at all what I would make of these characters, nor who they were. They imposed themselves on me in spite of myself.

One hears stories showing how great novelists like Dickens or Balzac came to believe in the real existence of their creations, and the anecdotes have point only because for their readers too the characters live. But even his most enthusiastic admirers can scarcely make the same claim for Gide's characters; they are rather pretexts, functions of a situation, mouthpieces of ideas. Perhaps the basic difference is that for Dickens and Balzac the world of ordinary human experience was intensely living and real, they projected their mental creations into this seen and felt environment, and the characters came to life in it. Gide, on the other hand, more complex, more dissociated than either of his great predecessors, lacked on his own admission a sense of the reality of the external world; consequently, in his own mind his imaginative creations had to compete with a not very real reality. But for his reader they simply partake of the unreality of the world as Gide presents it.

Something of all this appears at the end of a long and interesting passage of the Journal where he sets down for the benefit of Roger Martin du Gard an exposition of his sense of unreality: "I do not worry about knowing whether or not I believe in the external world; it is not a question of intelligence either: it is the *feeling of reality* that I lack. It seems to me that we are all excitedly moving about in a fantastic show and that what others call reality, their external world, has not much more existence than the world of the *Faux-Monnayeurs* or of the *Thibault*."

The moral implications of "total forgetfulness of self" in the creation of a character are underlined by the phrase, "My heart beats only through sympathy." Although the complacent ring of these words is modified by our realization that he uses "sympathy" not in the sense of "compassion" but more technically, we do know that Gide earnestly desired self-loss and perhaps found solace in the hope that his type of sympathy was an approximation of it. But he knew too that it was partly a confession of a lack. He makes Lafcadio say (the Lafcadio of the early *Journal des Faux-Monnayeurs*, before he was superseded by Bernard), "This need I have for movement, for rendering service, which is the clearest source of my happiness and which makes me constantly prefer others to myself, is perhaps after all only the need to escape myself, to lose myself." To a similar effect are the already noted words of Edouard: "I am never anything but what I think I am—and that changes constantly. . . . Nothing could be more different

from me than myself. It is only in solitude that the substratum sometimes appears and that I attain to a certain
fundamental continuity; but then it seems to me that my
life slows down, stops, and that I am really about to
cease to be."

Gide's self-loss, whether as an artist in the *Faux-
Monnayeurs* or as a man in life, is a counterfeit of the
spiritual act; it is a disguise for the horrified flight from
self-confrontation, the foredoomed effort of a supremely
self-conscious man to achieve the spontaneous adaptation
to environment of his less complex fellows. The higher
self-loss can only be achieved by passing through the
extreme limit of self-consciousness. Failing that, there is
no retreat to lower experience; one must make oneself as
comfortable as possible on the horns of one's dilemma.
And that, essentially, was what Gide was doing.

And lest we prematurely assume that we have caught
him in self-deception let us note one more passage of the
Journal des Faux-Monnayeurs: "I must . . . let the reader
have an advantage over me, I must go about it in such a
way that he may think he is more intelligent than the
author, more moral, more clear-sighted, and that he discovers in the characters and in the story many truths in
spite of the author and as it were without the author's
knowing it." Moreover we must remember that self-loss,
in whatever context, is one of those intellectual construc-
tions all of which, on Gide's own showing, are more or
less counterfeit, and of temporary value at the most.

During this period when he was writing the *Faux-
Monnayeurs* nothing is less like true self-loss than his
voluble explanations of how he has attained it; nor is
anything less detached than his self-defense against the

furious attacks of his Catholic critics. But Gide was not
deceiving himself: joy, he said, was the hallmark of the
"Kingdom of God" and enduring joy he did not have—at
the best he had resignation lightened by an occasional flash
of physical vitality. Throughout the composition of his
book he was haunted by the thought of imminent death,
by the suspicion that this was to be his last work. He was
obsessed by the feeling that he must shortly meet a rendez-
vous with destiny, some desperate adventure calling for
self-immolation, from which he would not return.

13

A Humanist in Utopia

•

On June 8, 1925, Gide finished the *Faux-Monnayeurs* and on the following fourteenth of July he and Marc Allégret left for the Congo.

He had made a general clearing up of back business. Not only was the *Faux-Monnayeurs* (six years in the writing and much longer in mind) ready for the printer, but his general confession was complete. *Corydon,* privately and anonymously printed in 1920 in a very small edition, was offered to the public in May 1924, in a new edition bearing the name of the author, and this despite a personal call the previous December from Jacques Maritain, who long and earnestly besought Gide to withhold it; even his request that the author should pray to Christ for guidance before the release was refused. *Si le grain ne meurt,* which contained the full history of his homosexuality, had also been printed in a very limited edition; by 1924 the first complete public edition was ready, although it was not actually put on sale until October of 1926. Moreover, for the time being Gide was written out, intellectually emptied by all that he had poured into the *Faux-Mon-*

296

nayeurs. He was ready for something new, and preferably something drastic.

He hurled himself into the Congo adventure "as into an abyss," and as his ship the *Asie* bore him southward off the west coast of Africa he wrote, "Already it has stopped seeming to me that I have wanted it exactly (although for months my will has strained toward it); but rather that it has imposed itself on me by a sort of ineluctable fatality—like all the important events of my life. And I even get the point of forgetting that it is just 'a plan of youth carried out in maturity'; before I was twenty I promised myself this trip to the Congo; that is thirty-six years ago."

Something of the importance which Gide attached to this journey appears from the record of his interview with Claudel not long before his departure. The war and the remoteness of Claudel's diplomatic posts had, since 1912, prevented their meeting, but from time to time Gide had sent Claudel one of his books or asked for his collaboration for the *NRF;* and his *Dostoevsky* and *Numquid et tu . . . ?* were of a sort to raise Claudel's hopes for the ultimate conversion of his friend.

In May 1925 Claudel, after his ambassadorial post in Tokyo and before going to Washington, was in Paris and a meeting was arranged for the twenty-fifth. After it Claudel jotted down on Gide's latest letter:

Saw Gide the 14th in the evening.

Long and solemn conversation. He tells me that his religious unrest is over, that he enjoys a kind of *felicity,* based on work and sympathy. The Goethe side of his character has won out over the Christian. I speak to him of my Carmelites, of all union, of the prayer of annihilation. He seems deeply interested and shaken. He is leaving for French Equatorial

Africa with the idea that perhaps he will not return. His wife.

The last words were apparently a note for action, for in August, after Gide's departure, he wrote to Madeleine:

Madame,
I am obsessed by the impression that perhaps you would like to talk to me about a soul that is dear to you, the thought of whom has preoccupied me for twenty-five years and the key to whom God has placed in your hands. If I am mistaken, forgive me. If not, I should be happy to meet you when and where you choose, whether in Paris or at Cuverville.
Please accept my respectful homage.
Paul Claudel.

To which Madeleine replied from Cuverville:

Dear Monsieur Claudel,
Your letter is for me new evidence of the faithful friendship in God which you bear to my husband; this friendship has always deeply touched me.
I have indeed felt much distress at this long and remote sojourn in darkest Africa which he has desired—but if I had more faith I would not be so anxious. All those who love André Gide, as this very noble soul deserves to be loved, should pray for him. I do so every day—and you too, do you not?—It is in this way, I believe, that we may meet the best.
Dear Monsieur Claudel, may I express to the friend you are all my gratitude, and all my admiration to the great writer.
Madeleine André Gide.

On board the *Asie* Gide and Marc were the only ones traveling "for pleasure"; the others were in business or administration. "What are you going down there for?" they asked, and Gide replied, "I am waiting till I get there to know."

As a matter of fact he had been given a "mission" by the colonial ministry, some sort of vague inspection tour, to be followed by a report; and he bore as a consequence letters of introduction from the directors of the *Compagnie Forestière Sangha-Oubangui*, the company that had the rubber concession for that province of French Equatorial Africa. Although he did not at the start take his duties very seriously, he confessed to a curiosity about what went on behind the scenes. He had read Conrad's *Heart of Darkness* and *The End of the Tether*, and he was suspicious of imperialistic exploitation. Perhaps there were abuses to uncover?—but meanwhile his credentials offered him facilities for travel, and the urge to see new lands, to incur fatigue and danger, was strong upon him.

Dakar, as seen on the night of July 25, was not encouraging. There was a little animation in front of the hotels and on the violently illuminated terraces of the cafés, and Gide was pleased to see Negroes again. But the total effect was dismal: "Nothing could be less exotic, more ugly."

And so on down the coast: Konakri in French Guinea, Tabu on the Ivory Coast just past Cape Palmas and the corner of the continent, Grand Bassam crushed between a lagoon and the ocean, and finally French Equatorial Africa, "the enchanting country where they die of hunger," with a first stop at Libreville. From the talk of his fellow travelers and from his own subsequent observations he was to learn more and more that French Equatorial Africa was "the Cinderella of the French colonies," and that the adjoining Belgian Congo—so much more alive, with better salaries for officials, better sanitation, better administration—owed its superiority to the fact that it was the sole recipient of its government's colonial efforts.

At Mayumba, a little farther down the coast, Gide was delighted with the trip ashore: the rhythmic chanting of the paddlers, the exciting moment of crossing the bar, the liberal packets of water that drenched the passengers and dried almost at once in the sun and wind. Then there were the first penetration into the equatorial forest, the meeting with the administrator in a chair with carriers, the shouts and leaps of the Negroes, the wild flight of crabs on the beach, high-stepping and looking like monstrous spiders.

By August 9 the *Asie* was shouldering its way slowly up the current of the Congo. "Ah," wrote Gide, "if I could only not know that life's promise is shrinking before me! My heart beats no less strongly than at twenty."

The next day they reached Matadi and left the *Asie*, for above that point and until Stanley Pool, rapids prevented navigation of the river; they took the Belgian train through Thysville to Kinshassa, and on August 14 they crossed to Pool to Brazzaville, the capital of the French colony.

Here they made a number of excursions, and Gide was in ecstasies over the strange and enormous butterflies; the best of them escaped him because he had lost the handle of his net. And there were the blazing flowers, the maggots, the swarming termites!—"If I had a second life to live it would make me happy only to study termites." And at night, in the pleasant guest cottage set aside for their use by the governor, the mild but breathless air was enlivened by a concert of crickets and frogs.

During their stay in Brazzaville, Gide took occasion to attend the prosecution of Sambry, "an unfortunate administrator sent out too young and with insufficient instructions, to a too remote post." Not knowing how to get on with the natives he tried to rule by terror, lost his hold, and committed cruelties for which he was called to account. Gide listened, somewhat saddened but not deeply concerned; he was more interested in a large butterfly which flew in the window of the courtroom, settled on his hand, and allowed itself to be captured.

Governor Engels of the Belgian Congo, when they visited him at Léopoldville across the Pool, advised them to visit Coquillatville (otherwise known as Equateurville from its position on the equator) and to meet their river boat the *Largeau* farther upstream. Accordingly on September 5 they boarded another boat, in company with the Duchesse de Trévise, who had been sent out by the Pasteur Institute in connection with the study of sleeping sickness. Before leaving Brazzaville, Gide wrote to Charles Du Bos:

I had the greatest pleasure in meeting again here the Duchesse de Trévise, whose simplicity, authenticity, and frankness stand out agreeably against the colonial background. With her one can either talk or keep silent, and that is extraordinarily restful.—We are agreed that your presence here would be out of place. Yes, I imagine you among the colonials with as much difficulty as among the negroes, and that is why everything in me that eludes this country speeds to you.

And as if in justification of the opinion of Gide and the Duchess, Du Bos was so completely bored by Gide's subsequent *Voyage au Congo* that he could not finish reading it.

Gide continued to find the Duchess charming and the flora and fauna absorbing. He had brought along a number of books, all old friends that could give him an assurance of satisfaction: La Fontaine, Corneille, Molière, Racine, Bossuet, Goethe's *Elective Affinities*, Stevenson's *Master of Ballantrae*, White's *Autobiography of Mark*

Rutherford (which he considered translating but decided that his own specialized interest in it did not justify the project); and to rest himself from continuous observation he turned to these. It is curious to read, written from the heart of equatorial Africa, reflections on Bossuet's *Traité de la concupiscence* or attempts to decide which of his famous funeral orations is the most eloquent.

Having joined the *Largeau* near the confluence of the Congo and the Ubangi, they proceeded up the latter to Bangui. Here the Duchesse de Trévise was assigned a "charming" guest house and Gide and Marc one which was "very agreeable, vast and well ventilated." They took all their meals with Governor Lamblin (a delightful and modest man and an excellent administrator) and made excursions to points of interest. The inhabitants of the villages turned out to receive them, first with the military salute and then, at their acknowledgment, with screams of laughter and stampings of joy. And on return it was pleasant to stretch out in a comfortable rattan chair by the window of the guest house, and alternately read *The Master of Ballantrae* and watch the downpouring rain.

Their last and most considerable excursion, made after the Duchess had departed in pursuit of her duties, lasted three weeks and took them beyond Rafai, near the border of the Anglo-Egyptian Sudan. It turned out to be their farthest penetration eastward. Their plan was to spend Christmas with Gide's friend the administrator Marcel de Coppet at Fort Archambault, some four hundred miles northward from Bangui, and then to turn back, pass through the country of the great lakes, and emerge on the eastern coast of the continent. But Coppet's appointment as governor of the Lake Chad region necessitated his proceeding to

Fort Lamy, north of Fort Archambault, and they decided to accompany him and then return southwestward, emerging at Douala in Cameroon. Gide always regretted having missed the eastward journey and a sight of the lakes and the sources of the Nile. But this change of plans still lay in the future.

Back at Bangui by October 17, they had a few days in which to prepare for the really arduous part of the journey, and during them Gide had occasion to meet a representative of the *Compagnie Forestière*, which he was later to attack. "How agreeable these agents of the great companies know how to make themselves!" he wrote. "How could the administrator who does not protect himself against their extreme amiability take sides against them afterwards? How avoid lending a hand, or at least shutting one's eyes to the little irregularities they commit? And then to their serious exactions?"

It would have been easy to reach Fort Archambault by a quicker route than the one they chose: people in a hurry went north two days by automobile and then, leaving the waters that drained south and west to the Congo, took a boat for four or five days of easy downstream travel on rivers flowing north toward Lake Chad. "But this is not what tempts me," said Gide, "and we are not in a hurry. What we want is to leave the usual routes, see what is ordinarily not seen, penetrate deeply and intimately into the country. My reason tells me sometimes that I am perhaps a little old to rush adventurously into the bush, but I don't believe it."

On October 26 they left Bangui; the next day they lunched with Pacha, the "sinister" administrator of Boda, and by nightfall had arrived at N'Goto, where occurred the most significant event of their trip. Having retired early they were both sleeping deeply when, at about two o'clock in the morning, they were awakened by the arrival of an important native chief, Samba N'Goto, who had wanted to see them during their dinner that evening but had refrained out of politeness. Now he had received a summons from Pacha to return at once to his village and, fearing to delay, he had ventured to wake the travelers in order to tell them his message. Since he had no interpreter it was impossible to comprehend what he had to say, but Gide managed to make him understand that if he would return later he need not fear the consequences of delay in obeying Pacha's summons.

What they learned the next day was summarized by Gide in a letter to Governor-General Lamblin written a few days later:

On the 21st of last October Sergeant Yemba was sent by the administrator of Boda to impose sanctions on the inhabitants of this village (Bossué, between Boda and N'Goto). They had refused to comply with the order to transport their residence to the Carnot road, as they were anxious not to abandon their crops. They argued further that the people living on the Carnot road were Baya, whereas they were Bofi.

Sergeant Yemba consequently left Boda with three guards (Bondjo, N'Dinga, and N'Gafio). This little detachment was accompanied by Baoué, a head man, and three men under his orders. On the way Sergeant Yemba requisitioned two or three men in each village they passed through and took them along in chains. When they reached Bodembéré the sanctions began. Twelve men were attached to trees, while Kobélé the head man of the village took flight. Sergeant Yemba and the guard Bondjio fired on the bound men and killed them. Then there was a great massacre of women whom Yemba struck with a machete. Then, having seized five young children, he shut them in a cabin to which he set fire. There were in all thirty-two victims.

Let me add to this number the head man M'Biri, who had fled from his village (Boubakara, near N'Goto). Yemba found him at Bossué, first village to the northeast of N'Goto, and killed him on about the 22nd of October; I have not been able to assure myself of the date.

Please believe, sir, that it was by no means my intention on coming to this country to conduct an investigation. . . . It was to you that Samba N'Goto intended to speak, thought at first he was speaking [he first saw Gide traveling in the Governor-General's automobile], for needless to say I quickly undeceived him, promising however to cause the account of these facts to reach you, as otherwise they might never do. They seem to me grave and I am sure they will not fail to alarm you.

Please consider, sir, that an imprudently conducted investigation might result in the ruin of Sambo N'Goto whom Monsieur Pacha will not forgive for having talked. If you question Monsieur Pacha, in all probability he will make the responsibility for these abominable acts fall on Sergeant Yemba, saying that he misunderstood or wrongly executed his orders. It seems to me however that Yemba was merely inspired by the spirit of his master who, when I saw him in passing, seemed to me a somber and a sick man, who does not conceal that he "hates the negro" and who proves it.

At Bambio on the 8th of September, a market day, ten collectors of rubber working for the C.F.S.O. [*Compagnie Forestière Sangha-Oubangui*]—for not having brought in any rubber the preceding month (but this month they brought in a double amount)—were condemned to circle around the company office under a burning sun carrying very heavy beams. If they fell guards flogged them to their feet. The "dance" began at eight o'clock and lasted all day under the eyes of Messers Pacha and Maudurier, seated at the C.F.S.O. post. At about eleven o'clock a man named Malongué, of Bagouma, fell to rise no more. They carried his body to Monsieur Pacha, who said simply, "*Je m'en f . . . ,*" and had the dance continue. All this took place in the presence of the collected inhabitants of Bambio and of all the chiefs of the neighboring villages who had come for the market. I have the account from several sources.

Gide went on to say that he was not including the names of witnesses to the "Bambio dance" at their request and that if they were questioned they would probably, from fear of Pacha, deny having seen anything. When the governor made tours of inspection he was permitted to see only what would redound to the credit of his subordinates. "Traveling as a simple tourist," added Gide, "I can sometimes see and hear what is too far down to reach you. When I accepted the mission which was entrusted to me I had no very clear idea of what my role might be and in what way I could be useful. If this letter can be of any service to you I shall not have come in vain."

Then he summarized a number of other abuses which merited investigation, notably prison conditions in Boda, forced labor on the roads, porterage by women, and procedures whereby the C.F.S.O. evaded paying the natives for rubber at the contracted price. He added that these abuses, so far as his observation went, were limited to the administrative division of Boda.

Gide's accusations in this letter were the basis of his attack on the C.F.S.O. and of the official investigations which followed. He wrote also to the head of the C.F.S.O. at Brazzaville enclosing and requesting forwarding of a letter to Monsieur Weber, a director of the company in Paris, regarding accusations against the company of a certain Monsieur Blaud whom Gide had met in the forest. The official in Brazzaville acknowledged receipt and forwarded the enclosure, but Weber did not reply directly.

After Gide's return to France and the publication of his *Voyage au Congo,* Léon Blum, at that time a member of the Chamber of Deputies and director of the newspaper *Le Populaire,* took up Gide's accusations in an article in his paper; this time Weber felt obliged to reply with a long letter which was published in *Le Populaire,* and made further statements at a meeting of the stockholders of the company. Weber's general line was to discredit the witnesses, chiefly Samba N'Goto; he did not make the mistake of fulminating against Gide but instead accused him, with an air of courteous tolerance, of hastiness, inaccuracy, and imagination. Gide answered point by point, and the official investigation demolished the smooth arguments of the director and supported Gide. The final upshot was that the Minister of Colonies announced in the Chamber that "All the great concessions expire in 1929. I assure the Chamber that none of them will be renewed or prolonged." The statement was not entirely accurate, for the concession of the C.F.S.O., the company chiefly incriminated, did not expire until 1935. Nevertheless the scandal undoubtedly had a moderating effect on its policies of exploitation and alerted officials of the administration.

Gide had had earlier contacts with social injustice but without a sense of personal responsibility. The case of Samba N'Goto, however, caught him, not only when he had made a provisional settlement of personal problems and when his literary work was at a standstill, but during a journey in which he was actually, though vaguely, charged with an official mission. He could not therefore without loss of integrity shirk the duty, but it was for him a painful one. He worked for several nights on his letter to the Governor-General, and during the days it was the human fauna rather than the butterflies that drew his eyes: the women toiling in the rain at the repair of the road over which his car was to pass, and after the end of the motor road the bearers of his chair, to spare whom he often preferred to walk, sometimes covering thirty kilometers on foot in a day. "Impossible to sleep," he noted on October 30. "The 'Bambio dance' haunts my night. It does not satisfy me to say, as is often said, that the natives were more unfortunate before the French occupation. We have assumed responsibilities toward them which we have not the right to evade. From now on there is a deep grief within me; I know things which I cannot bring myself to accept. What demon drove me into Africa? What did I want in this country? I was at peace. Now, I know, I must speak."

But this opening of his eyes to the previously concealed horrors of human exploitation, if it distracted him from entomological pursuits and poisoned his leisurely enjoyment of favorite books, did not prevent fruitful meditation; perhaps it even stimulated it. After his return to France he wrote of "the charm of those long days of travel through the bush in the Congo; I could cultivate for hours a single quiet thought, let it develop all its ramifications within me; I doubt if even the stove of Descartes was more propitious than litter travel and walking."

Walking was better than riding, and better than both were the occasional moments of stillness and solitude in the deep forest. "I have an increasing horror of the litter," he wrote on November 10, "in which I am uncomfortably jolted and can never for an instant lose the feeling of the bearers' effort. Every day we plunge deeper into the unfamiliar. All today I have lived in a state of torpor and semiconsciousness, 'as though of hemlock I had drunk,' losing all notion of time, space, myself." Later there were the moments in the forest near Lake Chad: "Surely if I remained motionless for a few minutes nature would close in again around me. Everything would be as if I did not exist, and I myself would forget my presence to become simply the power of sight. Oh, the ineffable rapture! There are few minutes that I would have a greater desire to live through again. And as I advance in this unknown vibration, I forget the shadow pressing close behind and whispering, 'All this you are still doing, but for the last time.'"

Despite unforeseen delays they were very nearly punctual for their Christmas appointment at Fort Archambault, arriving at midnight of December 25. After accompanying Coppet to Fort Lamy and then continuing still farther northward to Lake Chad, they set their faces toward home on February 20; on May 7 they were in the port of Douala, back in "civilization" and finding it an unpleasant contrast to the wilds: "What a hotel! The most forbidding way-station lodging is preferable. And the white men! Ugliness, stupidity, vulgarity." A week later they were back on board the *Asie,* and by early June, Gide was at home in Cuverville.

One of his first concerns after his return was to arrange to attend the "decade" at Pontigny. But Paul Desjardins, the sponsor, had already and prematurely decided that Gide's place was now outside of literature; he telephoned, "You are now assuming a very important task. With all my heart I associate myself with it. Count on me—but it is also necessary that for a time you should break with literature. The best way to prove it—in case you are thinking of Pontigny—is *not to come* to the literary decade but to the political one." This did not suit Gide at all; he still felt incompetent in politics and was engaged in the Congo investigation from a sense of duty rather than inclination. Accordingly with the aid of Du Bos he got himself invited to the literary decade, and attended.

He had not always been so eager for these sessions, but this time the topic was particularly close to his heart: "The debate between Humanism and Christianity." It was, as he wrote to Du Bos, precisely the one then taking place within him. For the past ten years, ever since writing the credo about God at the end of the road, he had been tending toward a humanist conception of God; at the same time he was unwilling to let go of Christianity—or of his own interpretation of Christianity. Now he was confronted with the task of reconciling two opposing ideals; or perhaps, since his trend was definitely toward humanism, it would be better to call it a salvage operation, an attempt to recover from the wreck of his faith such bits as might still serve his needs.

The decade turned out to be something of a disappointment. "The conversations," he noted on August 29, "are becoming more and more specialized. Only professional philosophers can take part. I am amazed at the subtlety of mind of those who, without any creative power, consume the restlessness of their strong intelligence in the examination and critical analysis of the works of others. When I tried in a few words to bring Montaigne back a little closer to reality, to *his* reality, when I tried to come down a little from those abstract regions where the air was become unbreathable for a number of us, I was taken for the enemy of philosophy."

Gide could interest himself in philosophic abstractions only for so long as they palpably represented the realities of human experience. A humanist, in the loose sense of one interested in human nature, institutions, and arts, he had always been; in the sense also of esteeming and cultivating the virtues called humanistic: justice, liberty, knowledge, tolerance, amenity, doubt as an instrument in the search for truth. His concern with such matters in 1926 represents, not something new, but a reformulation of old problems, a maturation of slowly developing issues. What is new is his realization that contrary ideas cannot be maintained indefinitely in balance but eventually do become issues; one must take either the one or the other. And so in a series of writings that were to occupy him, off and on, for the rest of his life, he made public his inner debates and their outcome. To mention only the most outstandingly relevant of these, there were in 1929 his two essays on Montaigne and *Un Esprit non prévenu,* in 1931 a miscellany entitled *Divers* (which included a reissue of *Un Esprit non prévenu*), in 1935 *Les Nouvelles Nourritures,* in 1943 *Interviews imaginaires,* and in 1949 various pieces of *Feuillets d'automne.* And of course back of all this there is the rich confusion of the Journal. Although with his usual distrust of an imposed consistency he has presented us in these writings with many contradictions and unresolved dilemmas, it is not very hard to discover the constants behind them.

The issues involved are: the relationship of God, man, and nature; of the past (or tradition) and the future (or progress); of liberty and authority (civil or religious); of the individual and society.

To a certain extent the debate between humanism and Christianity served as a focus for these issues. As he wrote in June of 1926:

The difficulty comes from this, that Christianity (Christian orthodoxy) is exclusive and that belief in *its* truth excludes belief in any other. It does not absorb, it repels.

And humanism, on the contrary, or by whatever other name you call it, tends to include and to absorb all forms of life, to explain if not to assimilate all beliefs, even those which reject it, even those which deny it, even Christian belief.

Culture must understand that in seeking to absorb Christianity it is absorbing something deadly to itself. It seeks to admit something which will not admit it, something which denies it.

As we watch the varying fortunes of his inner battle we can see the recurrence, in moments of fatigue and discouragement particularly, of his sentimental attachment to his Christian past, as for example when he says in the *Nouvelles Nourritures:* "I return to you, Lord Christ, as to God whose living form you are. I am tired of lying to my heart. It is you whom I find everywhere when I thought to flee you, divine friend of my youth. I believe that there is no other who can give contentment to my exacting heart. It is only the devil in my heart who denies that your teaching is perfect and that I can renounce all except you, because in renouncing all I find you."

There is some justification for seeing in this publicizing of repentance a return not merely to the qualified contrition of *Le Retour de l'enfant prodigue* but to its literary opportunism, for we read in the Journal for May 7, 1927: "Believers, I have known your state. *Et ego.* I know that this monstrous idea, planted deep in our minds, brings us to that pathetic state from which the work of art can profit."

But Christianity had on him a hold deeper than could be accounted for either by nostalgic sentiment or literary opportunism. As we thread the maze of his self-communings we discover that, as foreshadowed in *Numquid et tu . . . ?,* Christianity— what it meant to him as distinct from what it meant to others or in the world—was the core of his positive doctrine. It might have been called by another name, but Christian he was brought up and Christian he chose to name it. It is a formulation of experience rather than an intellectual concept; at no time, not when he is bitterly attacking the Church, not when he asserts the diabolic origin of his art, not even when he denies the transcendent existence of God and the immortality of the soul, does he venture to doubt this central "Christianity" of his own. "Sometimes," he wrote to François Mauriac in 1927, "I diverge from Christ, sometimes I doubt—*never certainly the truth of his words nor the secret of superhuman happiness they contain*—but rather the obligation to listen to them and to follow Him."

Gide's ideas on Montaigne are a convenient index both of his increasingly humanistic attitude after the First World War and of his individual divergences from the great figures of historical humanism and their successors.

After his *Dostoevsky* it is no surprise to find that, in his essays on Montaigne, Gide finds in him what will give support to his own thought, even if he has to put a little discreet pressure on the text to find it: the ambition of Montaigne to "remove the mask" from men and things, his admission of contradictions and inconsistencies, his individualism, internationalism, and sympathetic attention to the opposing viewpoint. In Montaigne's "There is no one who, if he listens to himself, will not discover a form that is his own, a master form, which struggles against upbringing and the tempest of the passions contrary to it," he could see a similarity to his own concept (in the *Narcisse* and *Dostoevsky*) of the Idea a man is born to make manifest.

Certain of Montaigne's common-sense maxims, corresponding as they did to only a part of Gide's nature, met with but a dubious and partial assent. Of these is his condemnation of "transcendent humors" which make men want to escape from the human condition: "This is folly," declares Montaigne; "they transform themselves into beasts rather than angels." But for Gide one of the values of the great essayist was just this conflict in him between the beast and the angel, or—and here Gide uses an analogy that did not exist in the sixteenth century—between Don Quixote and Sancho Panza, with the squire growing, toward the end, at the expense of the master. In this conflict Gide's sympathies were with Don Quixote; "I do not love man," he had written, "I love what devours him," and in Cervantes' novel the mad knight corresponds to Gide's devouring eagle of aspiration and Sancho Panza to the sluggishness of the ordinary mortal.

Of Gide's differences from Montaigne one of the most striking is revealed by his attitude toward the famous "Que sçais-je?" of which he said, "I have the temerity to assert that this skepticism is not what pleases me in the Essays nor is it the teaching I find there. If perchance I interpret them to suit myself it is in order to obtain from them something better than doubts and questions." Nor did he relish the religion of expediency expressed in the saying, "It is not my reason that is called upon to bow but my knees"; personally he would have been glad to suffer for a belief, and for him doubt was not a privilege but a regrettable handicap. Moreover he saw in Montaigne the first of a line of Catholics who were not Christians, a type which he well recognized but whose position was the reverse of his own.

"Skepticism has had its day," he wrote in 1924; "nothing more is to be expected from it." Hence the earnestness of his desire to formulate his faith; hence too the hesitations and confusions of his thought, for to say that a belief is necessary does not make it any easier to find.

"When I consider and weigh this word GOD," he wrote in the *Nouvelles Nourritures*, "I am forced to observe that it is practically empty of substance; and that is just what permits me to use it so readily. It is a shapeless vase with indefinitely extensible sides, containing what each chooses to put in it, but only that." And again: "What I used to call God, that confused mass of notions, feelings, appeals and answers to appeals . . . existed, as I know today, only by me and through me."

Here we have the subjective God, made in man's own image; viewed historically as a composite of subjectivisms he is the theological God of the churches. This is the God that Gide would like to abolish: "This idea of God serves perhaps to establish the edifice, but in the manner of the support which at first upholds the arch; once the arch is complete it no longer needs the support." Again, "Wisdom begins where the fear of God ends," and "Humanity cherishes its swaddling clothes, but it cannot grow without discarding them."

On the other hand Gide recognized that the question of the objective existence of God remained unsettled. Should he discard the possible reality with the subjective idea?

"It is much more difficult than one thinks," he said, "not to believe in God. One would have to have never really looked at nature. The slightest agitation of matter—why should it rise? And toward what?" There was in nature a creative spiritual energy, but that was no proof of the existence of some recommended God: "Not only am I unable to see your God in all this, but on the contrary I discover everywhere that he could not be there, that he is not there."

There is then on the one hand the illusory subjective God and on the other the objective God, possibly existent and, if existent, wholly real. Between these positions there is a third: a subjective God that does have some correspondence with the objective God, that begins as a child-like notion largely illusory but grows closer and closer to the objective reality. This position, too, Gide seemed to recognize when he said that the confused mass of notions that he used to call God nevertheless "seems to me today, when I think of it, much more worthy of interest than the rest of the world, than myself, than the whole of humanity." These confused yearnings were God in the making.

On the whole, however, the objective existence of God was one of those abstractions of theology that he was, if not content, then at least resigned to leaving unsolved. For him experience was of more value than abstraction, and in a striking passage of the *Nouvelles Nourritures* he leads us up to the intellectual impasse and then falls back on an intuition of experience:

Prudence, conscience, goodness—nothing of all this could possibly be imagined were it not for man. It is possible for man, detaching all this from himself, to imagine it vaguely in the pure state, that is in the abstract, and make from it God;

he can even imagine that God is the beginning, that absolute being precedes, and that reality is caused by him and in its turn causes him; in short that the Creator has need of the creature; for if he created nothing he would no longer be a creator at all. So that the one and the other remain in a relation and mutual dependence so perfect that you can say that the one would not exist without the other, the creator without the thing created, and that man could not have greater need of God than God of him, and that one could more easily imagine nothing at all than one without the other.

God holds me; I hold him; we are. But in so thinking I am at one with the whole creation; I melt and am absorbed in prolix humanity.

It is interesting to compare these words with those of the mystic Angelus Silesius, who wrote: "Naught is but I and Thou; and if we twain were not, then God is no more God and heaven falleth asunder"; and "I know that without me God can no moment live: If I come to nought, He needs must give up the ghost."

Gide seemed to understand well enough that the antithesis between subjective and objective could not be synthesized on the purely rational level; it could only be transcended. "Some of the 'problems' which disturb us are, not insignificant certainly, but completely insoluble, and to make our decision await their solution is folly. Consequently let us pass beyond them." Again: "The fear of stumbling makes our minds cling to the handrail of logic. There is logic and there is what escapes logic. (Illogic irritates me, but an excess of logic exhausts me.) . . . It is in the absence of logic that I achieve consciousness of myself."

Although Gide rejects the conception of God as a superperson who stands above the machine he has created and is prepared, when suitably implored, to intervene in its functioning, he yet feels that nature, the visible world, is not the whole of God but merely an expression of him, for God is after all spirit: "I have understood at present that, permanent in relation to everything that passes, God does not live in the object but in love." The energy of love creates.

All this is, if not simple, at least relatively familiar from the teachings of various philosophers; moreover it rejoins Christianity through the Platonism of the Prologue to the Gospel of John: "The Word became flesh and dwelt among us." But in the Journal we find Gide struggling with another idea which, if not contradictory to the rest, at least introduces further complexities. On shipboard, January 13, 1929, he writes:

If I were not at the dinner table, a little constrained under the eyes of my neighbors, I would set down at once the major lines, outlining themselves more clearly and vigorously than ever before, of the antagonism between Christ and God—of the *mistake* (it would be fine to explain why this mistake was deliberate and necessary) of Christ in claiming that he and God were on the same side, ending in the ultimately revealing cry, "My God, why hast thou forsaken me?"
God = nature; Christ = supernature.

He returned to the same subject in an "imaginary interview" of 1943, and in the interval his ideas had become both clearer and harder:

There can be no question [he said] of two Gods. But under this name of God I am careful not to confuse two very different things, different to the point of being opposite. On the one hand there is the sum total of the Cosmos and of the laws that rule it; that is the Zeus side, and you can call it God but only by taking away from the word all personal and moral

significance. On the other hand there is the combination of all
human efforts toward the good and the beautiful, the slow
mastering of brutal forces and their utilization for achieving
the good and the beautiful on earth; that is the Promethean
side and it is also the Christ side; it is the full flowering of
man, and all virtues contribute to it. But this God does not
live in nature; he exists only in and through man, or if you
prefer, it is through man that he creates himself, and all effort
to exteriorize him by prayer is vain. It is on His side that
Christ is, but it is the Other that he addresses when, dying,
he utters his cry of despair, "My God, why hast thou forsaken
me?" . . . The God whom Christ represents and incarnates,
the Virtue-God, must fight at the same time against the Zeus
of natural forces and against the malignity of men. . . . The
One whom he called "Father" had never recognized him for
Son. . . . Christ himself was only, as he sometimes said, the
"Son of Man." It is that God only that I am able and willing
to worship.

In a way these words are the logical outcome of the
earlier shipboard meditation, but in 1929 he was not quite
ready to say them. He was still capable of occasionally
supplicating the "Divine friend of his youth." The 1943
formulation is a genuinely humanistic credo. Man must
raise himself by his own bootstraps or not at all; no help
is to be expected from the other side because there is no
other side, there is no one to pray to, no loving Father,
nothing but laws, and laws cannot be supplicated.

But dropping this overloaded and confusing word
"God" we can see the main lines of Gide's thought as a
battle in man between the opposing forces of self-assertion
and self-transcendence. On the one hand are the ingrowing selfish forces both positive and negative: positive desire for domination, possession, enjoyment; negative fear
and indolence. On the other are the outgoing self-tran-

scending forces: love, sympathy, preference of the general to the individual good, nonattachment, total self-dedication in disdain of comfort and security. Self-assertion looks to the past history of natural man and tries to preserve it; self-transcendence looks to what man may become. It is the law of evolution that man should move from self-assertion to self-transcendence, and once an individual has become aware of this law, self-assertion becomes for him "wrong" and self-transcendence "right," and natural sanctions automatically come into play to punish transgression: "It is told that Lot's wife, for having chosen to look back, was changed into a pillar of salt, that is, of congealed tears. Turned toward the future Lot slept with his daughters. So be it."

Gide's insistence on individualism rests on his conviction that self-transcendence is only possible when free, only valid when undertaken voluntarily and in full awareness; that it is in fact the highest expression of individualism. As he never tired of repeating, "It is in the negation of self that the highest affirmation of self springs up and finds refuge."

Christianity for Gide meant conscious alignment with the forces leading to self-transcendence. Christ was the great symbol of self-loss; logically he also represented progress, nonattachment to the past, freedom from authority and tradition, and the churches which took their stand on the backward look traduced him. Worst of all was the unholy alliance between religion and capitalistic greed, or attachment to comfort and possessions. Traditionalists, conservatives, clingers to the past of whatever sort, clerical or lay, were anti-Christian by his terms and became his opponents: "It is the great living hope in me that keeps me from clinging to the past. For I love the past, but I prefer the future. I am interested in what has been and in what is, but still more in what may be and what I should like to have come to pass."—"No progress of humanity is possible unless it shakes off the yoke of authority and tradition."—"You would seek the salvation of humanity in attachment to the past, and it is only by rejecting the past, by rejecting in the past what has ceased to be of use, that progress becomes possible."

It was sentiments like these that in the late twenties and early thirties were leading idealists into the camp of communism. With the cynical unadventurous wisdom of hindsight it is easy to point out how mistaken they were, how "utopian." But to demonstrate the obvious fact that their aspirations did not fit into the hard realities of Soviet policies does not prove the falsity of their ideals. Gide took up the challenge of utopianism in the *Nouvelles Nourritures:*

> The fear of ridicule extorts from us our worst acts of cowardice. How many youthful, self-confident, half-formed aspirations are suddenly deflated by the mere application to them of the word "Utopia," and the fear of seeming chimerical in the eyes of people of sense! As if every great progress of humanity were not due to the realization of a Utopia! As if the reality of tomorrow were not to be made from yesterday's and today's Utopia!

Communism in its literal sense of abolition of private property had an inevitable appeal to a man of means like Gide precisely because it was a threat to his security and comfort; to champion communism was a proof of disinterestedness. It is strange therefore to observe how slow to appear in his writings is any application to his own economic status of his doctrine of nonattachment, stripping oneself for all. Here, for example, is a note of 1923 which brings him to the threshold of the economic question, only to turn aside:

It was total impoverishment that I coveted as being the truest possession. Resolved therefore to give up all personal possession and convinced that I could not aspire to the disposition of anything except by possessing nothing of my own, I repudiated every personal opinion, every habit, every shame, even my virtue, as one throws off a tunic so as to offer an unshielded body to the contact of the wave, of the passing winds, of the sun. Strong in these self-denials I soon felt that my soul was no more than a will to love.

He announces his intention of stripping himself of every personal possession—opinions, habits, virtue—but neglects to add money and lands to the list.

The fact is that Gide, like his mother and other members of her family, had a deeply ingrained streak of canny thrift. Luxurious surroundings intimidated him, he ate in cheap restaurants, in a group at a café his was not the hand that reached for the bill, and sometimes when he had actually paid the reckoning he uncomfortably suspected an indulgent friend of slipping back to add to his insufficient tip. Many were the stories, largely legendary, that circulated about his stinginess: for example that he was seen to give a beggar half a franc and then whisper to him, "When can you pay me back?"

Although this incident is patently manufactured, in others there was a basis of truth. Gide admitted his tendency but tried to put it in a good light, as when he said, "I know that I am close and parsimonious, and to excess. But it is because I wholeheartedly prefer to be able to give away what those who call me miserly so readily spend on themselves."

That this was not an idle boast is shown by a note in the Journal for 1918 stating that he and his wife were giving away one quarter of their combined income. It was Madeleine who did the giving, but with his complete approval. Although he instinctively and uncontrollably clung to money in hand, he believed in generosity.

So long as he could feel that the fact of his fortune did not increase—and perhaps could even decrease—the sum total of human misery, his conscience was at rest. The important thing, he believed, was not the accident of possession, but attachment to possession; meanwhile his money permitted him to write and thereby work upon the moral nature of man, for "It is not the system so much as man himself that must be reformed." Moreover it is not inconsistent to desire the abolition of private property and at the same time realize that giving away all your money under the old system will not bring about the new. "What seems to me an error," he wrote in the *Nouvelles Nourritures,* "is to require of him who possesses the distribution of his wealth; but what a delusion to expect of him a voluntary renunciation of goods to which his soul remains attached."

His preference for moral questions over social questions, and for both over political, and his acceptance of a literary and theoretical instead of a practical role, were eventually shaken; and it was the Congo adventure—seeing men and women as victims of injustice, toiling and suffering in a direct relationship to his own comfort—that opened his eyes. "Have I for a long time, without suspecting it," he asked in 1931, "profited from poverty? Has it not been

what others lacked that permitted me to lack for nothing?
I reject the advantages that permitted my nonchalance.
I can no longer reconcile myself to being fortunate."

By this time he was well on his way to political communism and overt support of the Russian régime.

"In my heart, my temperament, my thought I have always been a communist," he wrote. This natural bent was
with him more a matter of sympathy than of economic
theory, of religion rather than of politics. "What draws me
to the communists is not theories, which I ill understand
and cannot use, it is only knowing that among them there
are some for whom the present state of things is intolerable."—"What brings me to communism is not Marx but
the Gospel."

But it was this same religious spirit, this veneration for
the Gospel, that set him against the defenders of organized
religion and made him approve the anticlericalism of the
Soviet régime. "I am not indifferent, not tepid, and all my
former fervor turns now against them [the Catholics].
The conviction which I feel, which they force me to feel,
that their doctrine is false and their influence pernicious,
no longer permits me to have that accommodating tolerance which is too often considered the accompaniment
of liberty of thought." And when he read of the "deter-
mination to destroy all religion" in the Soviet Union, it
was with pain, because of Madeleine and because of his
own past, but he approved the declaration.

By May 13, 1931, he has progressed to the point of
writing, "I should like to live long enough to see the Russian plan succeed and the states of Europe forced to bow
before what they obstinately refuse to understand." And
two months later, "I should like to cry aloud my sympathy

for Russia and to have my cry heard, be important. I should like . . . to see what can develop in a state without religion, a society without the family. Religion and the family are the two worst enemies of progress."

Yet he still hesitated to commit himself to the cause either publicly or privately, and one of his reasons was his repugnance to ruthless methods: "I can wish for communism while still disapproving the fearful means proposed for obtaining it. A change of sides does not make the saying 'He who desires the end must desire the means' any less disquieting to me. I do not like to feel that hatred, injustice, arbitrariness are on my side. . . . It is a bad moment to live through. I am happy that in Russia at least this wretched task is accomplished. Let us hope that at least *that much* is gained and that there will be no occasion to do it again."

The most fundamental as well as one of the most vexatious of his problems was how to conciliate individualism and communism, liberty and party discipline. "It is only with great difficulty that I clarify my thought. The notion of liberty as it is taught us seems to me false and pernicious. And if I approve of Soviet restraint I must approve also of Fascist discipline. More and more I believe that the idea of liberty is only a bait." As a solution of the difficulty he fell back on his belief that the sacrifice of liberty must be voluntary and that, in accordance with the Gospel precept "Render unto Caesar the things that are Caesar's and unto God the things that are God's," the sacrifice must be of action only, not of thought: "On the side of God, liberty, that of the mind; on the side of Caesar, submission, that of acts." Moreover it was still the individual, more than the mass, that interested him; but he now recognized that sacrifices of liberty were necessary in order to obtain individual rights for the masses.

But even with these guiding rules, so hardly won, he still hesitated. Could his adhesion to communism, with his reservations on freedom of thought and with his incompetence in economic and political matters, do any good? But what a relief it would be to close the inner debate: "To stop simply following one's nose and to move toward something—what an indescribable satisfaction!"

Some needling from without was perhaps a factor in bringing these hesitations to a close. Jean Guéhenno, an able and highly educated writer of working-class origin, published on November 15, 1930, an article in *Europe* in which he cleverly and tellingly caricatured Gide (and incidentally Du Bos) and of which he considerately sent advance proof to the chief victim. It was called "My Beautiful Soul," and among the shafts were the following:

They are furious at being only authors, they would like to be men. . . . Monsieur Gide dreams himself a devil. Monsieur Du Bos sees himself as an angel. And these beautiful souls question and consult themselves, wonder with rapture whether or not they are sinful. Elegant society is invited to these self-communings. Only elegant society. . . . And when fortune has treated you too well, when it has refused you the true drama to which you aspire, what other resource is there but to imitate the drama of others, or else to invent one? . . . In all these conversions, these illusory dramas, these commentaries on pious fables, I see nothing but a cowardly disregard of the present, a refusal of life, a fear of truth. These "beautiful souls" seem to me to constitute a brotherhood of the absent.

Gide acknowledged the proofs courteously and without protest, though pleading not guilty to the charges. Two years later, after Gide had made up his mind about communism but before he had given much public support to the cause, Guéhenno followed up his first attack with another still more damaging, again with the polite attention of advance notice. In his article entitled "Monsieur Gide" we read:

Condemned to being merely a good workman with language, when what tempted him was to be a man rather than an author . . . he reached the point of playing with his soul. . . . He has perhaps a means of imposing himself on the public as a great figure. If drama refuses to come to him, why should he not try serenity? . . . His renunciation of the world is like a final pose which gives him a new publicity. . . . The thoughts of Monsieur Gide too often seem to cost him nothing. This amounts to saying that Monsieur Gide has not suffered enough. . . . His history seems to be that of a slow and difficult conversion to the human. . . . A man of a dying world, a prewar world, everything brought him back to himself, to his monsters, his devils, to all those fables that moved him by their greatness and beauty. . . . But now he has come to the religion of humanity.

Again Gide thanked the author and pleaded not guilty.

On March 8, 1932, Gide decided to make an end of his hestitations and devote himself to the cause. "I know that in wanting to take sides I have everything to lose and the others, those whom I would serve, little to gain." Psychologically his decision acted almost like a religious conversion:

Just as in my youth [he wrote on April 23] I am experiencing a state of devotion in which feelings, thoughts, my whole being, become oriented and subordinate themselves. Moreover is not my present conviction comparable to *faith?* For a long time I deliberately *unconvinced* myself of every creed that could be overthrown by free inquiry. But of this very free inquiry is born my creed of today. . . . In the abominable distress of the world today the plan of the new Russia seems to me the way of salvation. . . . And if my life were necessary for the success of the USSR I would give it at once.

This offer of his life, however, was strictly hypothetical; what he was immediately prepared to risk was rather his reputation, which could be sacrificed as readily from his writer's study as in the arena: "Certainly I do not insist that the tower in which I take refuge should be of ivory. But I am good for nothing if I come out of it. A glass tower, an observatory in which to receive all rays, all waves; a fragile tower where I feel myself ill protected and do not wish to feel protected; vulnerable on all sides; but confident in spite of all and with my eyes fixed on the east."

What he wanted was to remain in a field of action in which he felt competent, and within it to preserve his freedom of thought and judgment. Shortly after making this note about the tower, he had an opportunity to make a stand against an action which would have compromised his freedom. Late in 1932 there was organized in France, parallel to the Russian Association of Soviet Writers, the *Association des Écrivains et Artistes Révolutionnaires,* and Gide was asked to join. On December 13 he declined in these terms:

No, dear comrades. The clearest result of such an engagement would be to keep me from writing anything at all. I have declared as strongly and as clearly as I can my sympathy for the USSR and for all it represents in our eyes and to our hearts, in spite of all the imperfections which opponents bring up. I believe that my coöperation (and in my case particularly) can be of most profit to your (our) cause if I make it freely and if I am known to be *not* a member. . . . Do not see in what I say any desire for self-protection, any safeguard.

You have already seen that I have done my best to compromise myself.

Yet he insisted that "He who is content to remain a contemplator today gives evidence of an inhuman philosophy
or of a monstrous blindness." What then was he to do?
What else but to compromise himself as best he could by
signing manifestoes, writing open letters for or against
something, attending meetings (even presiding over one)
and reading a prepared statement: in favor of conscientious objection to war and of disarmament, in favor of the
USSR, against fascism, against the Italian adventure in
Ethiopia (aligning himself here with a group of Catholics); and always and everywhere reserving his right to
examine and to criticize the cause he was supporting.

Very soon he began to have misgivings about the possibility of serving communism without sacrifice of principle. On March 21, 1933, he delivered a speech against
fascism in the course of which he made a declaration in
favor of the USSR and followed it up with a "Letter to
the Youth of the USSR," where he said, "Some of us, many
of us even in France, look to you young people of the
USSR with admiration and envy; yes, envy for your very
sufferings, for your heroic courage, for your endurance."
In reply Vsevolod Ivanov published in a Moscow journal
a "Letter to André Gide," and it was republished in France;
a phrase in it disquieted Gide and some time later in a
public meeting he referred to it. "I received," he said,
"in November 1933 a long letter from V. Ivanov in which
certain sentences did more to disquiet than to reassure me.
'With us,' he said, speaking so far as I understand him of
the USSR, 'people do not have at all the spirit of sacri-

fice. . . . Men work for themselves for today and for to-morrow.'"

Still more disquieting was the case of Vladimir Kibalt-chich, a writer of Belgian origin living in Russia and writing (in French) under the name of Victor Serge. Like Gide he was a communist who believed in freedom of thought, and he had ventured to write (among other sentiments unpalatable to the régime): "A revolution does not constitute a single homogeneous process . . . it is rather the sum of a multitude of different movements, fortunate and disastrous, truly revolutionary and reaction-ary, healthy and unhealthy. Hence the impossibility of a revolutionary conformism." And in another place: "Prole-tarian literature will not make a notable contribution to the spiritual life of the working class . . . unless . . . it imposes on the writer a single rule of absolute sincerity to his comrades and to himself."

Understandably enough he became suspect to the au-thorities and when he applied for a passport to France it was refused; his writings were boycotted, his son was excluded from school, he was unable to care for his sick wife, and finally he was arrested without a clear charge, severely questioned, and deported to Orenburg.

On June 25, 1935, at the last session of the International Congress for the Defense of Culture, Gide helped, despite the opposition of the Soviet writers, to bring Serge's case before the assembly. Four days later he wrote to the Soviet Ambassador to France, carefully refraining from expressing a judgment on the case but requesting him and his supe-riors to remember that if it were not handled with an appearance of justice the propaganda effect in western Europe would be bad.

When, on June 17, 1936, Gide arrived by plane in Moscow to begin his long-projected tour of the Soviet Union he was full of suppressed doubts and still more burdened with illusions. He thought that "there cannot be a Soviet philosophy, any more than a Soviet mathematics or astronomy, which would be different from philosophy or mathematics or astronomy here in France." He had declared that "Communism will be able to impose itself only by taking account of the characteristics of each individual. . . . Every artist is necessarily an individualist, however strong his communist convictions," and he repeated the sentiment in Red Square itself, adding, "Up to now, in all countries of the world, the writer of worth has almost always been more or less of a revolutionary. . . . Today in the USSR for the first time the question is set in a very different way: the writer, while still a revolutionary, is no longer in opposition."

But these and many other illusions were rapidly swept away. One of the first rude awakenings for this man to whom communism was a sacrificial adventure was to observe the flagrant appeal to his self-interest and comfort in the way he was officially received. Everywhere he was set apart from the herd, installed and entertained in a luxury which contrasted painfully with the living conditions of the majority. He became an official writer: his works were translated and published in enormous editions, bringing in no less staggering royalties—and, had he wished, the usual rule that he could not spend them outside of the Soviet Union would have been relaxed in his favor. He found also that in this state born of revolution the revolutionary spirit was no longer tolerated and that conformity was the only possible way to live in safety;

only one opinion was allowed, and *Pravda* told the people what it was proper for them to know, think, and believe. (And incidentally homosexuality, being an aspect of nonconformism, was condemned.) Everywhere there was gross insularity and prejudice and ignorance of the outside world; disinterestedness and the critical spirit were totally absent from instruction; merit was rewarded only in those who followed the party line. He noted also the evils of deportation, the poverty of the workers and the flagrant inequalities of salaries, the reëmergence of class distinctions, rule by the bureaucracy rather than by the people, the progressive loss of what 1917 had won.

On his return to France, he was quick to announce his disappointment, first in *Retour de l'URSS* and then, when it was criticized for superficiality, with the supplementary, more factual, and better documented *Retouches à mon Retour de l'URSS.*

He professed to believe that Russia would eventually triumph over the errors he signalized and that the fact that one country had gone astray need not compromise an international cause. For a time he strove to maintain the position of a pure revolutionary, independent of Moscow and Stalin, and he made it clear that when he attacked the USSR he meant "he who is at its head"; for the Russian people he expressed great admiration and sympathy.

But the fervor was gone and the strain of maintaining its semblance was too great. He had always believed that moral questions took precedence over political, though for a time he "allowed himself to be persuaded" that man could not grow unless social conditions permitted him to do so. Yet he was always out of his element in political action and he quickly tired of writing about social problems. He was disappointed also in the motivation of communists:

I tried at first to believe that what motivated them was a suffering love for our brothers; I was not long deceived. I tried then to believe that these dry insensitive abstract creatures were bad communists, ill serving a noble cause which I declined to judge by them. But no, I was mistaken all along the line and from top to bottom. The true communists, people told me and proved to me, were indeed these. They were precisely in line and it was I who was the traitor in introducing an unwanted emotion. . . . Slowly I came to the conviction that when I thought myself a communist I was a Christian—if one can be a Christian without "believing."

This valedictory to social action was but an elaboration of what he had written in 1910, before there was any communist state: "Dangerous is every mind that is sure there is a solution to be found in this world, sure that his own is that solution, and ready to impose it on others."

14

OEdipus and Theseus

GIDE'S BRIEF VENTURE INTO A FIELD ALIEN TO HIS TASTES and inclinations had not been without cost to his literary work. "When social preoccupations began to encumber my head and my heart," he admitted on his return from Russia, "I wrote nothing more of value," and even more strongly in 1940 he stated: "The social question! If I had met this great snare at the beginning of my career I should never have written anything of worth." And the record of his publications between 1931 and 1936 bears him out: in those five years he produced nothing worthy to stand with the rest of his work, with the single exception of the *Nouvelles Nourritures*, published in 1935 but chiefly written many years earlier; and even of this book, in which readers have found some of his most significant utterances, he said in 1943, "Of all my books it is the most uneven, the least good. . . . If I had not signed it I should doubt if it were really mine. . . . I do not feel in it that accent of sincerity which is no doubt the clearest value of my best writings."

This sterility was not wholly due to the heavy consumption of his time and energy in political activities; it resulted in part from the fact that when he did find time for writing with a literary intention his social preoccupations deprived his art of its indispensable characteristic of indirectness. The great body of his work was, it is true, committed to the communication of ideas, but normally he presented them with at least an appearance of detachment rather than as a partisan; he spoke through his characters, he presented both sides, and he declined to draw conclusions. But during his communist period his literature was *engagée,* committed to a cause; the "Nathanael" of the *Nourritures terrestres* becomes "comrade" at the end of the *Nouvelles Nourritures.*

At a public meeting in January of 1935 Gide made it quite clear that he considered himself to have made a deliberate and conscientious "sacrifice" of his art for the sake of his social activities; but in the temporary privacy of his Journal he had already admitted that the sacrifice was not wholly voluntary: "If social questions occupy my mind today it is in part because the creative demon is withdrawing. These questions are only occupying the place given up by him. Why should I try to overrate myself, why refuse to recognize in myself, as in Tolstoy, an undeniable decline?" He did not believe, as Madeleine suggested, that his "poetic power" was directly related to his Christian sentiments and declined with them; but he admitted that each of his previous books had been "the exploitation of an uncertainty," and that commitment diminished his inspiration.

Perséphone, a short opera in three tableaux written in 1933 and presented at the state Opera House in 1934 with music composed and conducted by Stravinsky and chore-

ography by Kurt Jooss, offers a good example of Gide's
decline of poetic power. Here, if anywhere, he had an
opportunity for a work of art: a poetic subject drawn from
the Greek mythology which had so often inspired him
and a fine backing of music, dance, and setting. But all
he could produce was labored verses less effective than
those of his youth, and a transparent, almost a naked,
appeal, through Perséphone, for sympathy for the masses.
In the first tableau, she says:

> Nymphs, my sisters, my charming companions,
> How could I continue
> To laugh and sing heedlessly,
> Now that I have seen, now that I know
> That an unsatisfied people suffers and waits.
> O unhappy people of the shadows, you draw me.
> Toward you I shall go.

In the third tableau, she continues:

> I shall go
> To the world of shadows where I know that they suffer.
> Think you that one can with impunity lean over the gulf
> Of suffering Hades with a heart intoxicated by love?
> I have seen what is hidden from day
> And cannot forget the desolating truth.
> Mercury will take me with my full consent.
> I have no need of an order, I go of my own will
> Where not so much the law compels as my love leads,
> And pace by pace, step by step,
> I shall descend to the bottom of human distress.

The opera closes on a paraphrase of the biblical "Except
a corn of wheat fall into the ground and die . . ." which
is surely no improvement on the original:

> It needs must be, for spring to be reborn,
> That the grain consent to die

Beneath the earth, so that it may reappear
In golden harvest for the future.

After his return from the Congo, Gide went through a period of reorientation during which he wrote little more than a record of his perplexities, but 1929 saw the publication, not only of the two essays on Montaigne and *Un Esprit non prévenu*, but of *L'École des femmes;* the latter and *Robert* (1930) were the first two panels of a triptych that was later to include *Geneviève*. The central feature of the series is the portrait of a man who is above all "interested"—that is, at the farthest remove from Gide's cherished ideal of disinterestedness—and who lacks integrity of thought as a consequence. Gide holds the Church guilty of at least complicity in the formation of Robert's character, quoting in support of his charge the statement of Monseigneur de La Serre that "obedience of mind" is indispensable to true Christianity. In a minor way the series follows the technique of Browning's *The Ring and the Book* (considered for the *Faux-Monnayeurs* but abandoned) in that it tells the same story from three points of view: that of the wife, that of the man himself (whose self-defense is more damaging than his wife's indictment), and that of their daughter. The family is neatly divided into two camps, the good and the bad, the disinterested and the interested; the wife Éveline and her daughter have integrity, the husband Robert and his son Gustave do not.

It took Gide two years to complete *L'École des femmes;* for the second part, *Robert,* he was obliged from the nature of the project to abandon his rule of not taking advantage of impetus and as a result he finished the little book in a week. Over *Geneviève,* however, he toiled, off and on, for several years and was never satisfied with it; it finally appeared in 1936. The delay was caused not only by the intervention of his communist interests but by the nature of the subject, for in this part he wanted, not merely to complete the portrait of Robert, but to add that of a modern young woman, and the undertaking proved uncongenial. It may be noted in passing that in this part of the story Geneviève asks Dr. Marchant, a contemporary and close friend of her mother, to give her a child by him.

In 1930 Gide said that if he tried to deal with everyday reality in the manner of Balzac and Bourget he would probably get bogged down in it, and five years later he fulfilled the prediction with his play *Robert ou l'intérêt général;* and this in spite of trying to take advantage of the momentum acquired in a previous effort. The story of the play has no resemblance to that of *L'École des femmes,* but the character of Robert is a carry-over, accentuated by his having a son named Gustave standing in the same relation to himself as the earlier Gustave to his father.

In the preface to his play Gide wrote:

L'Intérêt général was, in a first version which has not been preserved, a play of distinctly partisan tendency, conceived and written at the time of my "honeymoon" with the communist party. In this early partisan form it was translated into Russian by Elsa Triolet and was on the point of being performed in Moscow. The publication of my *Retour de l'U.R.S.S.* straightened that out and probably spared me a success, for at a time when Moscow considered me a genius it was about to be called a masterpiece. The truth was that it was not good for much, and I soon realized it. I would have been wise to abandon it, but I liked certain scenes that I thought well turned, and the character of Robert existed. Was there

not some way of turning this social conflict into a comedy
of character? For a long time I struggled with it. . . . I was
obsessed with it. I give here the product of my efforts. My
best friends (I mean those in whose judgment I have the
most confidence) are agreed that it is very bad. I realize that
if I had always listened to their advice I should have published
practically nothing. . . . But so far as this play is concerned
I am afraid my friends are right.

The reader will be inclined to agree with Gide and his
friends. Although the play is readable enough, it is clear
that Gide, even with the aid of a love interest and his
favorite character of an illegitimate son, is not at home
in the atmosphere of a factory in the midst of a labor-
management dispute, and the theme of the dishonest
thinker and rationalizer has worn thin. The play was
finally completed in its present form in 1944 and was performed in Tunis in 1946.

It is a far cry from these struggles and half-failures to
the important *Œdipe*, written in 1930 on the threshold of
Gide's communist adventure, published in 1931, and performed in 1932. Its purely literary merits are not beyond
dispute; it has been criticized, for example, for excessive
bareness of style and for an occasionally discordant facetiousness. But there can be no doubt that it represents an
extraordinarily adroit exploitation of the materials handed
down from antiquity and utilized without major change
for the presentation of Gide's most cherished convictions,
and that it has considerable biographical significance.

Gide regretted that some people took the central conflict of his play to be the one between free will and deter-
minism instead of the more timely one he intended,
between individualism and religious authority. Œdipus

the King, before he discovers that he is a parricide incestuously married to his mother, represents individualism. He knows that he is not the son of Polybus, who brought him up, but does not know who his real father is. "It does not displease me to know that I am a bastard. At the time when I thought I was the son of Polybus I busily tried to ape his virtues. What did I have, I said to myself, that was not first in my fathers? Heedful of the lesson of the past I looked to yesterday alone for my sanction, my orders. Then suddenly the thread snapped. I had sprung from the unknown, I had no more past, no model, nothing on which to lean . . . no one to resemble but myself."

The result of this break with the past was to awaken his dormant powers and turn him into a self-made man: "I have a horror of special privilege, I do not want to profit from anything that my worth has not merited." Recognizing the danger of excessive pride in his own accomplishments he has exteriorized the power that led to them and given it the name of God. "Who would not be glad to submit to a sacred power if it leads to the position I occupy?" In accordance with this humanist conception of God he has tried to put down superstition in his kingdom by authorizing the killing of the birds formerly used for auguries.

The chorus does not approve of the self-confidence of Œdipus: "We the Chorus, who have the special mission in this place of representing the opinion of the majority, pronounce ourselves surprised and pained at the declaration of so fierce an individualism. The sentiments expressed by Œdipus are tolerable only when disguised. Surely it is a good thing to put the gods on one's side, but the safest way to do it is to be on the side of the priest."

Religious authority is represented by Tiresias the soothsayer who, as a necessary condition for believing in his own mysteries, is blind. "In the fear of God lies my power," he says, but the children of Œdipus, with the single exception of the devout Antigone, are encouraged by the example of their father to cast off the religious yoke. The humanistic serenity of Œdipus is a threat to the power of the priest, who encourages the people to believe that the plague ravaging the city is due to the impiety of the king, and who excites in the mind of Œdipus suspicions about the past that lead eventually to his discovery of the truth and the destruction of his happiness.

Long before Œdipus, Jocasta has known the truth, but she manages to preserve her happiness by refusing to think about its foundation and she tries to quiet his suspicions about certain significant details of the past by assuring him that "no historian has noticed them." But Œdipus will not be deflected: "I want no part in a happiness based on error and ignorance. That is good enough for the people. As for me, I do not need to be happy." And he pushes on to the discovery of the facts.

While Œdipus is in the process of being enlightened we discover that the origin of his humanistic faith is not as simple as it seemed. "I felt myself to be the reply to an as yet unknown question," he said, and to find out what this question was and how he was the answer to it he was on his way to consult the oracle of the God. But blocking the way was the chariot of an unknown, later discovered to be his father, and in the ensuing fight Œdipus killed him. Thereafter he could not continue on his way to the oracle, for "God refuses to reply to a man whose hands are unclean"; he took instead the road leading to the Sphinx, which he conquered by solving its riddle:

For you must know, my children [says Œdipus], that each of us in adolescence, at the outset of his career, meets with a monster who bars his path with a riddle. And although of each of us, my children, a particular sphinx asks a different question, be assured that the answer remains the same; yes, there is one and the same reply to all these different questions, and this single reply is: Man.

At the time of speaking these confident words Œdipus did not yet know the truth about himself; when he discovered it his way of life collapsed. Tiresias urged him to repent of his crime, but Œdipus replied: "A crime imposed by God, placed by Him like a trap on my way. Before I was born it was set, so that I should fall into it. . . . I was hounded." And Tiresias replies, "Hounded by God alone."

Œdipus rejects reconciliation with religious authority and instead puts out his own eyes. "Like you," he says to Tiresias, "I now contemplate the divine darkness. . . . You can no longer vaunt to me your superiority of blindness."

It is at this point that the role of Antigone becomes significant, for to her, the one "who has never lied," Œdipus now instinctively turns. Although she has been vowed to the religious life, she prepares to follow, and lead, her blind father into exile; when reproached by Tiresias for breaking her vow she replies:

No, I shall not be breaking my promise. In escaping from you, Tiresias, I shall remain faithful to God. It even seems to me that I shall be serving him better following my father than I did with you. Up to now I have listened to your teachings about God, but still more devoutly I shall listen now only to the teachings of my reason and my heart.

The play closes with Œdipus saying, "Come, my daughter. You, the only one of my children in whom I am willing to recognize myself and whom I trust, you, most pure Antigone: by you alone shall I henceforth allow myself to be guided."

It is clear that Gide saw in the story of Œdipus a parable of his own life: he too had felt himself to be the answer to an unknown question, had thought first to have recourse to God but had found himself debarred because his hands were not clean. "Who shall ascend into the hill of the Lord? or who shall stand in his holy place? He that hath clean hands and a pure heart." And then Gide, like Œdipus, confronted the Sphinx and solved the riddle by his answer, "Man."

His self-identification with Œdipus is further accentuated by a note of 1939 in *Et nunc manet in te*. Of his distress on learning in 1918 of the destruction by Madeleine of his letters to her he wrote:

Today, feeling myself at the end of my life. . . . I reread without indulgence the journal pages that I then wrote. The despair into which I thought I was sinking probably came chiefly from a feeling of failure; I compared myself to Œdipus when he suddenly discovers the lie on which his happiness is built; I suddenly became aware of the distress in which my personal happiness kept her whom, in spite of all, I loved more than myself; but also, and in a way less easy to admit, I suffered from knowing that she had destroyed that part of me which I thought the most worthy of survival. That correspondence, kept up since our childhood, belonged to us both, seemed to me born of her as well as of me; it was the fruit of my love for her.

After Œdipus and Gide discover the truth their ways part, for Gide keeps his sight and is not led off by Antigone. And who is this "most pure" Antigone, who has never lied, in whom, of all his children, her father best recognizes himself, who serves God better by accompanying her father than by remaining under the yoke of religious authority? A reasonable answer seems to be that she represents Gide's private Christianity, his "Kingdom of God." And if this is so, is it too fanciful to suppose a further symbolic relationship between Antigone and Gide's letters to his wife? We have seen how Gide connected these letters with that "best part" of himself which he associated with the "Kingdom of God," how he thought of them as born of her and of him equally, and how in destroying them Madeleine seemed to have "killed their child." Consequently, if Gide did not follow the example of Œdipus at the end, it was because he had no Antigone to guide his steps; she had been killed by her mother.

Gide and his wife were bound together by their love and their common past, torn apart by their temperaments and beliefs. To his variability she presented constancy, to his self-manifestation reticence, to his future-seeking a clinging to the past. He had no reason to believe that she was acquainted with any more of his memoirs than the early part which he had read to her; like Jocasta she preferred to avert her eyes from what in her heart she knew only too well. On the other hand, she did read at least a part of the *Faux-Monnayeurs*, and her disapproval, as might be expected, was uncompromising: "The approval of a single honorable person," she said, "is all that matters to me, and that your book will not obtain." And

Gide commented, "Anyone who does approve of my book will cease to be honorable in her eyes."

On his return from the Congo, Gide believed that he observed in her a trend toward Catholicism, and he wrote on July 1, 1926:

The slow progress of Catholicism in her soul: it is as if I were watching the advance of gangrene.

At each return after leaving her for a time I discover new regions affected, deeper ones, more secret, forever incurable. And even if I could, should I try to *cure* her? Would not the *health* I should offer her be fatal? Every effort exhausts her.

What convenience, what ease, what lessening of fatigue she would find in this piety by regular doses, this fixed price menu for souls that cannot afford much expenditure!

Who would have believed it? Could God himself have expected it? What! was all that attached me to her—the disposition to wander, the fervor, the curiosity—was all this not her true self? Did she only assume it for the love of me? All this is disintegrating, falling away, nakedly revealing the emaciated unrecognizable soul.

And everything that constitutes my reason for existence, my life, is becoming to her foreign, hostile.

He had been trying, not merely to lure her from retreat, but to make her over. She who in some ways had been to him a mother and a guardian angel seemed to him at times a child unfit to cope with the world. Her clumsiness with instruments kept him in continual anxiety that she would hurt herself, and when he tried to explain to her the use of some unfamiliar tool she would listen with downcast resignation and at the end of the lecture abandon the innovation. When she wound the tall clock in the hall she would climb up on a rickety structure of superimposed chairs; Gide found her a firm stool that would be safer, but at the next winding of the clock the stool would be back where it came from and the shaky chairs would go up again. She bent like a reed before the wind, but when the gust had passed she moved gently back to her original position.

At last Gide gave up. In Heidelberg on May 12, 1927, he wrote:

> The game that I could win only with her is lost. Lack of confidence on her part, presumption on mine. Recrimination and regret are useless. What is not, is what could not be. He who moves toward the unknown must consent to travel alone. Creusa, Eurydice, Ariadne—it is always a woman who holds back, worries, fears to let go or break the thread that attaches her to her past. She pulls Theseus back, she makes Orpheus turn around. She is afraid.

But this abandonment of his efforts to change her was apparently all she had been waiting for to come back to him, and slowly, day by day, a new harmony was built on the ruins of the old.

For some years past she had been failing in health. A puffiness of her features began to veil the expression of her face, her beautiful hands became shapeless appendages, her voice became husky, cataracts began to encroach on her pupils, a retinian embolism threatened the sight first of one then of both eyes, her heart grew steadily weaker. But at the end she was willing with a gradually returning confidence to lean on him; she let him kneel at her feet and dress the wounds of her varicose veins. "Of what is our love made," Gide wondered, "if it persists in spite of the wearing away of all the elements that compose it? What is hidden, behind the deceptive appearance, that I can still find and recognize, that indescribable something

that is immaterial, harmonious, radiant, that one is obliged
to call soul—and what matter the word?"

"My greatest joys I owe to you," she said to him, then
added, "and also my greatest sorrows: the sweetest and
the bitterest."

The end came suddenly in the summer of 1938 when
Gide was away from home. Hurrying back to Cuverville
in response to a telegram, he saw her once more, on her
deathbed; stripped of its smiling gentleness her face looked
severe, so that Gide's last view of her recalled not her
compassion but her condemnation of his life.

I left the lifeless remains [he wrote years later], repeating
to myself *Et nunc manet in te*— "And now she abides in thee."
. . . And if I recur here to the image of phosphorus and its
glow, it is to say that it is because of and in proportion to its
glow that phosphorus matters to me; only the glow matters.
Perhaps I should not speak like this if I had loved her carnally.
How can I explain it: it was her soul I loved, and this soul
I did not believe in. I do not believe in the soul separated
from the body. I believe that body and soul are the same
thing and that when the life of the body ceases both go.

For several years he had foreseen this death, fortified
himself against it, even imagined it as serene and triumphant. But during that time he was still taking her for
granted; she was always there at Cuverville, waiting for
him to come back, and sometimes he chafed a little at
this tie which bound him to the past. Madeleine was
Ariadne holding Theseus at the end of a string as he
adventured into the Labyrinth, she was Eurydice tempt-
ing Orpheus to look back as he emerged from Hades. But
now he realized that the tie had been a stabilizer; now
he was like a kite whose string has suddenly been cut,

pitching crazily in the insubstantial air before plunging
to earth. Or else he was a man sinking in a bottomless
bog, with nothing firm within reach. He had been in such
states before, and his cry "Save us Lord, for we perish,"
even in the original Greek learned from the Testament,
had been of no avail; help had come merely from waiting
and allowing a mysterious psychological adjustment to
take place. Meanwhile it was a relief just to set down his
thoughts in the Journal and to feel a link of sympathy with
some future reader in like case.

He knew well enough, and admitted, that his bereavement was not wholly responsible for his dejection, which
had, as a matter of fact, preceded her death in premoni-
tory attacks of the year before. He had handed to the
printer his *Retouches,* his last word on communism, and
was thoroughly sick of the whole subject. The ominously
entitled "Complete Works" were approaching completion,
the collected Journal was being prepared for publication,
and all he could find in his head were scattered bits and
confusion. "What else was I going to say? Everything
now seems to me repetitious. . . . I should like to call
quits and leave the game. . . . We are entering a new
era, the age of confusion." That day he had hurried to the
Gare Saint-Lazare to meet Elisabeth Van Rysselberghe
(now the wife of Pierre Herbart, one of the young friends
who had accompanied him to Russia) on her return from
London; with his chronic difficulty in recognizing people
all he succeeded in doing was to dash feverishly about the
station bumping into everyone and to end by missing
her completely.

The whole world seemed to him as confused as himself

—or perhaps it was the other way around; at any rate he wrote:

Everywhere I see only distress, disorder, madness, lying, frustrated justice, the right betrayed. I wonder what more life could bring me which I should care for. What does it all mean? Where will it all lead? Into what an absurd mess all humanity is sinking! How and where can one escape?

But how beautiful were the last rays of the sun this evening, gilding the beeches! Alas, for the first time I have nothing in common with the spring. And now those pathetic bird songs in the night.

He told himself that this was old age, this was the end of life, the time when one sought to make one's peace with God. But as his senses dulled, a tide of indifference was engulfing him; he was like a tree no longer stirring with sap, speculatively eyed by the woodcutter.

Every evening [he wrote in Cuverville on July 6, 1937], after the goodnight, I withdraw to my big room and sit a long time in my armchair, doing nothing. I used to read far into the night, but my eyes are tired and the light is not bright enough. So I let my thoughts drift, and I call it meditating. I haven't a single project left in my head, and this idleness of mind is painful. I have always liked work and found excitement in effort. Perhaps (but not here where nothing stimulates my will) I shall still experience an urge to some objective, some book to write, but I tell myself sometimes—often—that I have already said what I had to say and that my cycle is complete. That is why I shall not greatly mind taking my leave.

He had a number of flickers of reviving interest in books and affairs, but on the whole his apathy merged naturally into the deeper despair following the death of Madeleine in 1938. But he was not yet at the end of his resources; again and again in the years following he was to rouse from his stupor and look about him with renewed interest; then the apathy would return. On October 18, 1938, for example, he writes: "I have decidedly made up my mind to be well. In addition to one's actual condition there is a certain consent that one gives which assures and intensifies this condition. . . . For several days now I am delighted to find myself full of courage again." But on the twenty-first of the next month he confesses: "I have taken my leave. However robust I may feel everything seems remote; every awakening (especially after my siesta) brings me back with more difficulty from farther away, and I have to make a greater effort to shake off a sleep that seems increasingly delightful."

Although the approach of war and its outbreak stirred his torpor, they did not encourage to optimism. He detested of course the truculent barbarism of the Third Reich and was glad that the Church seemed to have recovered the courage to resist, but what struck him most forcibly was the slackness, the venality, the disintegration at home. Once more a weary France was confronted by a vigorous and united nation in arms, and once more he wondered whether nonresistance were not the best way to meet the recurrent threat.

After the fall of Poland he was asked to speak on the radio, but refused: "Decidedly I shall not speak on the radio, I shall not collaborate in these 'emissions of oxygen.' The papers are already full enough of patriotic yelpings. The more French I feel the greater is my repugnance for letting my thought be influenced. If it were regimented it would lose all its value." He claimed that he was often in agreement with the majority, but then he saw no advantage in speaking out; only in opposition could his contribution be significant. And he was too un-certain in his own mind to be in opposition.

In May of 1940 he was in Vence in the south of France and about to return to Paris when the news from the north made him delay his departure. As the bulletins of defeat piled up he was in a fever of anxiety and uncertainty, feeling that there was something he should be doing, yet lacking the heart for anything: "Although the days are so short how tediously long is this insipid prolongation of my life!"

Three days later, events have bestirred him to life: "No, after all! The events are too serious, they take up all my attention"; and he goes on with reflections on the causes of the German victories. His emotions are stirred, and the world around him seems to come to life:

Wonderful night [he writes on May 18]. Everything seems to faint in ecstasy in the light of an almost full moon. The roses and the acacias blend their perfumes, the underbrush is starred with fireflies. I think of all those for whom this beau-tiful night is the last and I should like to pray for them. But I no longer even understand what the words "pray for some one" mean, or rather I know that they can no longer have any meaning for me. They are words which I have diligently emptied of all significance. But my heart swells with love.

Gide highly approved Pétain's first speech after the surrender, and it did indeed agree with much that Gide had been saying and thinking: "Since the victory [of 1918] the spirit of enjoyment has carried the day over the spirit of sacrifice. There has been more claiming of rights than offers of service. We have tried to spare ourselves effort, and today we meet disaster." And Gide commented, "It could not be better put."

But the speech of ten days later brought consternation:

Is it possible? Was it Pétain himself speaking? With his free consent? . . . How can one reconcile these words with the noble ones he spoke three days ago? How can one help agreeing with Churchill and giving full support to the declaration of General de Gaulle? Is it not enough for France to be beaten? Must she also dishonor herself?

This indignation was confided to the Journal; not until the following spring did he gird himself for battle against collaboration. The occasion was a book entitled *Chronique privée de l'an 1940,* published early in 1941 by Jacques Chardonne, a contributor to the *Nouvelle Revue Française,* which at that time was being edited by Drieu La Rochelle. On March 30 and in the same mail Gide received the book, which he read with "stupor and consternation," and a letter from Drieu La Rochelle urging him to make an appearance in Paris. Gide wrote out a telegram in reply to the letter:

Appreciate your cordial letter and deeply regret, after reading last pages of Chardonne's book clarifying your positions, being obliged to request you to remove my name from cover and announcements of our review.

He was unable to send this telegram because he discovered that Drieu La Rochelle, who was temporarily in Lyon, had given no address, but he put his resolution into effect as quickly as possible. Six days later he sent a review of the Chardonne book to the Paris *Figaro.* "It would have been much better," he said, "if I had been able to speak freely; such as it is it does not satisfy me. At least it will serve to reassure some friends."

Chardonne's chronicle was a tissue of cynical relativisms. "With him," said Gide in his review, "every *yes* conceals a *no*, and vice versa. Let us mistrust A, for it is B. Chardonne mistrusts everything, even his own mistrust (and there certainly he is not wrong)." Of the accused in the Riom trial Chardonne said outright, "They are innocent," but immediately added, "like all criminals."

Gide's objections, necessarily cautious, were concentrated on the quality of thinking revealed by Chardonne; nevertheless, at one point, after quoting a passage, he did venture to say: "That means, if I understand him correctly, *vive le fait accompli!*" In his Journal he was more outspoken:

I am, however, grateful to Chardonne for having written this book, which casts doubt on everything except himself and the position he has assumed, in harmony with (or in the company of) A. de Chateaubriant and Drieu La Rochelle. This book reacts upon me because I feel clearly as I read it that this position is the opposite of the one I must and want to take, and it is important for me to say so at once. My mind is naturally only too inclined to acceptance; but as soon as acceptance becomes advantageous and profitable I am on my guard; an instinct warns me: I cannot accept being on "the right side"; I am on the other.

Through the summer and fall he worked on a series of "imaginary interviews" for the *Figaro*, in which, although he still could not be too explicit, he was able to defend what he considered the enduring values of French civilization. And he found that he was happier back again at his writing table; he did not think highly of his "interviews," which he admitted to be superficial, but at least his thoughts and his words came easily.

Moreover life was stirring in him again:

There was a time [he wrote in April 1942] when, tortured and harassed by desire, I prayed: May the time soon come

when my conquered flesh will let me give myself wholly to—
But to what? To art? To "pure" thought? To God? What
ignorance! What folly! It was like believing that the flame
will burn better in a lamp whose oil is exhausted. When it
becomes abstract my thinking is extinguished; even today it
is the carnal in me that feeds it, and I now pray: may I
remain carnal and desirous up to death!

And the next day he wrote:

Where did I get that idea that it was all over, that spring
no longer interested me, could no longer take possession of
me? For days now, since the weather has become fine again
and the air is warm, I feel like a migrating bird and think
only of departure.

He engaged passage for Tunis—"Ah, why am I not
there already? The show will have begun and I shall miss
the overture"—and on May 4 he sailed from Marseille.
But even before landing he wrote: "I have had my fill on
earth. One reaches a state of happy equilibrium and comes
to the end of the feast without greatly caring for its prolongation. Others are waiting for my place; it is their turn."

So he continued with his ups and downs, a little curious
to see how the war would end, feeling brief flickers of
desire (he even had some new sexual adventures), reading
and writing a little. He found his thoughts recurring to
the woods around La Rocque and the beech grove of
Cuverville; at night he kept having dreams of Madeleine
and in them all some fantastic barrier kept her from him.
"I don't try very hard to work," he wrote in June of 1942,
"aware as I am that I write nothing of value. Have I still
something to say, some book to write? What am I good for
now? What am I being reserved for?"

He did have in him one more book, the last and one

of the best of his Greek tales. And when Tunis had been
liberated by Allied armies converging from east and west,
and he could move more freely about North Africa, he
set to work. On May 21, 1944, in Algiers, he wrote in his
Journal:

Today . . . I finished *Thésée*. I still have large sections to
rewrite, and especially the beginning, for which at first I
could not find the right tone. But now the canvas is covered.
For a month daily and almost constantly I have worked at it,
in a state of happy fervor I have not had for a long time and
thought never to know again. I seemed to be back at the
time of writing the *Caves*, or my *Prométhée*.

As in *Œdipe*, whose sequel in a way this tale is, Gide is
able to make the traditional materials say what he wants
them to say. He is not to be wholly identified with any
one of the characters, and although he is more often represented by Theseus (and very evidently so at the end)
than the others, he also speaks through Daedalus, Icarus,
and Œdipus; and he makes situations, and even the Cretan
Labyrinth, convey his meaning.

"At the outset," says Theseus to his son (and it might
be Gide talking), "one must well understand who one is.
Then one must become aware of and take in hand one's
heritage. Whether you like it or not, you are, like me,
a king's son. Nothing can be done about it; it is a fact,
and it involves obligations."

His early exploits teach Theseus that "a man's first and
greatest victories must be won against the gods." He learns
also to yield to desire, but to pass beyond it.

On the Cretan adventure Ariadne attaches herself to
him, saying, "You are bound to me and I to you; only by
me and through me can you discover yourself." When he

goes into the Labyrinth there is an argument between them as to who shall hold the ball of twine and who the end, and Theseus wins: Ariadne holds the end of the string which guides Theseus back to safety, but he carries the supply with him, paying it out as he chooses.

It is Daedalus, the constructor of the Labyrinth, who suggests the device of the string (which he calls the "tangible representation of duty") and who, when he talks to Theseus, is like Gide in his old age talking to his younger self: "This string will be your link with the past. Come back to it. Come back to yourself. For nothing starts from nothing and it is on the past that the future finds its purchase." Daedalus' own past is Greek: "Wherever I went or stayed I remained Greek. And it is because I know you and feel you to be a son of Greece that I am interested in you, my cousin." He prefers Theseus to Hercules because of his faculty of joy; Hercules was a rather somber person, distinguished only for heroism. Moreover Theseus has the further advantage of not allowing himself to be impeded by subtleties of thought.

Daedalus constructed the Labyrinth with the idea that no matter how confusing its windings or how high its walls a resolute man would always be able to get out, and that consequently what was needed was to sap his resolution so that he would prefer his prison. In addition to the purely physical difficulties of the maze Daedalus put within it feasts and entertainments and added drugs to the drinks to destroy the will of the victims. But his principal reliance was on vapors released by the burning of certain narcotic plants:

The vapors . . . do not only act upon the will, which they put to sleep; they produce an intoxication full of charm and rich in flattering error, they invite to a vain activity the mind which lets itself be filled with voluptuous illusions; an activity which I call vain because it leads to nothing but the imaginary, to visions and speculations without body, logic or firmness. The effect of these vapors is not the same on each of those who breathe them; each one, in accordance with the confusion which his mind prepares, becomes lost, if I may say so, in his private Labyrinth. For my son Icarus the confusion was metaphysical. . . . But the most astonishing thing is that as soon as one has breathed these perfumes for a time one can no longer get along without them, and that the body and mind acquire a taste for this cunning intoxication, outside of which reality seems unattractive; so that one no longer desires to return, and that also, that especially, keeps one in the Labyrinth.

At this point for the first time in his fiction (but not for the first time in his speculations) Gide explicitly introduces a time problem. The allusion to Icarus in the Labyrinth has been somewhat puzzling to Theseus and becomes still more so when Daedalus offers to show him his son. Had not Icarus, wearing wings of his father's invention, flown too close to the sun and fallen into the sea and drowned? Even so it happened and yet when Daedalus calls, Theseus sees a pale young man enter, talking steadily and seeming not to see the others. His monologue consists of speculations about the existence of God, among which some are familiar:

If I come from God, how shall I reach myself? How shall one reach God starting from man? And yet God is created by man quite as much as God has formed man. It is at the exact crossing of these roads, in the very heart of this cross, that I want to hold my mind, at last at rest. . . . I do not know where God begins and still less where he finishes. I can even express my thought better by saying that he has never finished beginning. Ah, how confused I am with *therefore, because,* and *inasmuch,* with reasoning, with deduction! From the finest syllogism I extract only what I first put in. If I put God in I find him there again. I am tired of wandering on the horizontal plane. I am crawling and I should like to take wing; leave my shadow, my filth; cast off the weight of the past! The blue sky draws me, O poetry! I feel myself drawn from on high. Spirit of man, wherever you rise I mount!

Here we have in parody the history of Gide's own aspirations, although, coming as it does from the confused mind of Icarus, it lacks chronological clarity. There is the early discontent with the "horizontal plane," the urge to direct communion with God; there is the only slightly later involvement with the Symbolists and Mallarmé's passion for *l'azur,* the blue sky of pure poetry; and then there is the credo of 1916, repeated and confirmed only a year before the composition of *Theseus,* of God at the beginning and the end, as starting point and as consummation; and even on this the detached and skeptical Gide of the last years, speaking through Daedalus, casts compassionate aspersions:

Poor dear child [he says]. Since he thought he could no longer escape from the Labyrinth and did not understand that the Labyrinth was within him, at his request I made wings for him with which to take flight. He thought that there was no escape except by the sky, all earthly ways being barred. I knew that he had a mystic predisposition and was not surprised at his wish. An unfulfilled wish, as you have been able to understand from listening to him. In spite of my warnings he tried to fly too high and presumed on his strength. He fell into the sea. He is dead.

In explanation of the apparent impossibility that Icarus can have died and yet still be visibly and audibly present,

Daedalus says that every man who represents some significant idea or attitude does not live merely his one life
on earth:

In time, on the human plane, he develops, makes his gesture,
and dies. But time itself does not exist on another plane, the
true, the eternal plane, where is inscribed every representative gesture, in accordance with its particular meaning. Even
before his birth Icarus was, and he remains after his death, the
image of human unrest, of search, of the flight of poetry,
which during his short life he incarnated.

Here is the idea of the realm of the "Mothers," in
Goethe's second *Faust,* which Gide read in youth; it is also
one of the themes of Shelley's *Prometheus Unbound.*
Moreover it is a reminder of Gide's note of 1921, after
he had read over the Journal of his youth and noticed the
similarity between his recent crisis and that of his early
days: "Everyone always performs the same gesture; or
more exactly there is in everyone's character a propensity
to a particular gesture which determines the conduct
of his whole life." And to reënforce the reminiscence,
Daedalus now adds: "In Hell there is no other punishment
than continually beginning again the gesture uncompleted
during life. That is why Tantalus remains eternally athirst,
why Sisyphus ceaselessly rolls toward an unattainable
summit the rock which ceaselessly falls back."

Protected against the vapors by a mask impregnated
with an antidote, but weaponless, Theseus enters the
Labyrinth. He finds his Greek companions in a banquet
hall and already deeply under the influence of the narcotic
vapors. Beyond, in a garden of flowers, is the Minotaur;
he is a monster, but young, a beautiful harmony of beast
and man, and in his sleep so inoffensive in appearance that

Theseus hesitates to attack him. But when the Minotaur opens an eye totally devoid of intelligence the hero is nerved to the deed. Back in the banquet hall he announces deliverance to the captives. "Deliverance from what?" they say. He has to use force to get them out.

After his return to Athens and his succession to the throne of his father, Theseus realizes that the time for purging the earth of monsters is past and the time for government come. He unifies his kingdom, breaks the power of the hereditarily wealthy nobles, and redistributes possessions. He neither hopes for nor desires a classless society and equality of fortunes; he merely wants a fresh start, a basis on which to build a hierarchy of merit.

I reflected [he says] that man was not free and never would be, and that it was not good that he should be; for then he judges everything by himself and seeks for nothing beyond. But I could not push him ahead without his consent, nor could I obtain it without giving him the illusion of freedom. I wanted to raise him, and refused to let him be content with his lot and keep his head bowed. Humanity, I constantly thought, is capable of more and better things. I remembered the teaching of Daedalus who wanted to enrich man with the spoils of the gods. My great strength was to believe in progress.

His old comrade Pirithous refuses to follow him in these ideas. "Man is not worth so much attention," he objects, but Theseus replies, "What should one pay attention to if not man? He is not yet a shining light, it is true, but he hasn't said his last word."

The book closes on a significant meeting at Colonus between Theseus and Œdipus. The one, having lost wife and son, has poured all his energy into the establishment and government of his state; the other, appalled at the revelation of the crimes on which his happiness was founded, has renounced the world as incurably evil, has put out his own eyes, and is being led by his faithful daughter Antigone. Of his self-blinding, Œdipus says:

No one understood my cry at that time: "O darkness, my light!" and you too, I realize, will understand it no better. People thought I was uttering a complaint; it was a statement of fact. My cry meant that for me the darkness was suddenly lit by a supernatural light, illuminating the world of souls. The cry meant: Darkness, you shall henceforth for me be light. . . . Yes, when the external world was forever veiled from the eyes of flesh, there opened up within me a new vision of the infinite perspectives of the inner world, to which the outer world, previously the only one for me, had made me blind. And this imperceptible world (I mean inapprehensible by our senses) is, I now know, the only true one. All the rest is illusion.

Theseus replies:

I shall not try to deny the importance of this nontemporal world which, thanks to your blindness, you discover; but what I cannot bring myself to understand is why you set it in opposition to the external world in which we live and act.

The answer of Œdipus is that his whole life and that of his family have been soiled and distorted by the acts which he committed when, in his moral blindness, he trusted to the outside world. Nor does he think that his own special case is inapplicable to others, for "some original taint afflicts all humanity, so that even the best are marked, dedicated to evil and perdition, and man cannot escape without divine help to wash him from the first stain and forgive him."

Though he professes respect and admiration for this stand, Theseus recognizes that the way of Œdipus cannot be his: "I remain a child of this earth and believe that man, however tainted you may consider him to be, must play the cards that he has in his hand."

Thirty years before, Gide, returning from Anatolia, saluted the civilization of Greece as his own, his home. But his greatest struggle with Christianity was yet to come and as his ship entered the harbor of Piraeus, instead of looking at the Acropolis, he preferred to read Emily Brontë, that child of the barbarian North. Now, in his seventy-fifth year, his choice is made; it has not perhaps been wholly voluntary, but "man is never free," and he must "play the cards that he has in his hand." He contemplates the Greeks with whom he has associated himself: the hopelessly and helplessly aspiring Icarus, condemned to an eternity in the labyrinth of his own mind; the shrewd and practical Daedalus; the noble mystic Œdipus; and, last and deepest of the identifications, the humanist Theseus. Of them all, and of us, he takes his leave: "I have built my city, and after me my thought will inhabit it forever. It is with full consent that I approach my solitary death. . . . I have accomplished my work. I have lived."

He had said his say, he had bid farewell to life, but for a few more years death would not accept him. He lingered on, reading a little, writing a little, repeating himself, taking cat naps in his armchair, occasionally reviving to take a little interest in his surroundings. The Nobel Prize came, and there were those who thought him puffed up because he was getting more difficult of access. But he was only tired. "Have pity," he wrote in November 1947, "and leave me alone. I need a little silence around me so as to find peace within myself." In the spring of 1948 a projected trip to the United States had to be abandoned because of his heart attacks.

He thought much about death and hoped that it might be painless. "You make your bow and that would be the end. No applause would be enough to draw you back on the stage." But such a simple ending, he feared, was too much to hope for.

With his old distrust of beliefs in which one finds a personal advantage he insisted that he did not believe in survival; for him the idea was "inadmissible, unthinkable, and contrary to reason." And yet, he insisted, he was to "an incredible degree" a believer in spirit. As for the soul—

Of course I believe in it! [he wrote in May 1949]. I believe in it as I believe in the glow of phosphorus. But I cannot imagine this glow without the phosphorus that produces it. . . .

I have written somewhere or other that there is perhaps no saying of the Gospel that I made my own earlier or more completely than "My kingdom is not of this world." So that "this world" which alone, for most people, exists, I don't really believe in. I believe in the spiritual world, and for me the rest is nothing. But I believe that this spiritual world has no existence except through us and in us; that it depends on us, on the support which our bodies give it.

He was unusually tired when he wrote these words, and when the next few days brought only a deeper sinking into lethargy he entered a clinic for examination and treatment. He scarcely expected to come out again alive, but once more he swung back to living, and found himself again in happy quiet among friends in Saint-Paul (in the Alpes-Maritimes). The only sound that night was the pulsing rhythmic chanting of the frogs, breaking out in chorus, stopping, then starting once more, as if to the directions of an invisible conductor.

Between the following October and January of 1950 Gide spoke thirty-four times over the radio, closing the series by reading the closing lines of his *Thésée*. During 1950 he was occupied with making a play out of *Les Caves du Vatican;* a dramatization had been attempted seventeen years before, and there had been performances in a small theatre in Paris and later in Lausanne and Geneva. This time, however, it was the official Théâtre-Français that presented the *Caves,* with a first performance in December of 1950.

The following February his heart condition became worse and he gradually sank into a comatose condition. On Sunday, February 18, he roused a little, and perhaps was aware of old friends around him: Mme Théo, his daughter Catherine and her husband Jean Lambert, Pierre Herbart, Roger Martin du Gard, and Jean Schlumberger, his collaborator on the old *Nouvelle Revue Française*. He seemed a little surprised to be alive and murmured, "Tiens! je suis encore là," before relapsing into unconsciousness. Monday morning he roused again briefly and said to Jean Schlumberger, "If you want to talk to me let me know, so that I will have time to wake up." He said nothing more, and died at half-past ten that night.

15

The Hound of Heaven

ONE CAN MAKE A START TOWARD AN INTERPRETATION OF
Gide's career with common sense and a dash of
psychology.

Temperamentally an introvert, the only child of a
wealthy puritanical mother and of a scholarly father cast
in the unusual role of rich teacher, Gide felt himself from
his earliest years to be different, set apart from the majority. In his autobiography he tells the episode (twice
echoed in the Journal) of how in his schooldays he was
seized one time with convulsive sobbing, which he could
explain to his anxious mother only by "I am not like
others! I am not like others!" In later comment upon the
incident he said, "There is nothing more saddening for
certain people (of whom I am one) than to belong in spite
of oneself to an élite and to be unable to consent to communion with the immense majority of humanity." And
his temperament joined forces with his economic status
to set him apart:

When still quite young I had the feeling of being exceptional when I observed that often I did not react like others,

like most others. After such an experience no matter how much one humbles oneself, depreciates oneself, tries to be like the common people, declines distinction, tries to be absorbed in the masses and be satisfied there—one remains nevertheless a person set apart. This feeling of differentiation can be felt by the child when still very young, sometimes with sorrow, even anguish, and rarely with joy.

A part of his "not reacting like others" is connected with his sexual abnormality, and although decidedly more than a dash of psychology is needed to explain the origin of homosexuality, we can at least note circumstances that may have been contributing factors. A relationship, possibly causal, has often been pointed out between a mother fixation and homosexuality. Gide's fixation, if he had one, is certainly not as obvious as, for example, that of Proust; in his autobiography he speaks of frequent insubordination to his mother and constant argument with her, whereas his father could obtain obedience with the lightest word; and his whole account of her is critical, almost hostile—so much so indeed that he feels obliged to apologize for his attitude and to assure us that she was a very well-meaning person.

More substantial than a tenuous fixation theory is the fact that Gide's mother dominated his childhood and youth and left on him the permanent mark of her religious convictions, her puritanism, her repressive modesty, and her sense of duty. Paul Gide, absorbed in his studies, had relatively little close contact with him and disappeared from the scene before his son's eleventh birthday. It was Gide's mother who sent him to costume parties in the cheapest outfit the department store offered so as not to outshine his less fortunate companions, who considered art as an opportunity for the exercise of the duty of self-improvement, who pronounced the music of Chopin unhealthy, above all who conveyed to him the impression that sex was shameful and that a really good woman submitted to its rites only from a sense of duty to the race. It was she who drove him into revolt and pursued him beyond it with the sense of guilt she had implanted.

Also contributory to his horror of normal sex and consequently to his homosexuality were certain experiences of his childhood and adolescence: being accosted by prostitutes and above all his discovery of the marital infidelity of Madeleine's mother and of the pain it caused his cousin.

As for the habit of masturbation, innocently learned in early childhood and resumed in adolescence with a tremendous sense of guilt, it does not seem likely that in itself it had anything to do with his homosexuality; it is not the act but the accompanying fantasy that is decisive. If we may take him at his word, he never felt any physical curiosity about the opposite sex, only about his own. It is undoubtedly normal for a boy to have a passing curiosity in the genital conformation of other boys and to want to make comparisons, but unless the interest is fixed by pleasurable experiences it soon disappears; it is the other sex, the different conformation, that has the greater attraction. Why Gide, like a minority of others, should have had a strongly established urge toward his own sex long before having any overt homosexual experience (his first occurred when he was twenty-four years old), remains a mystery which the various possibly contributing factors are insufficient to explain. To talk of "arrestation" is to rephrase the problem, not to solve it. Is there in the race a profound psychic androgyny—an "animus" and an "anima" in Jung's terminology—comparable to the physiological traces of a distant hermaphroditism, and is it possible for a discrepancy to occur between the physiological and the psychological preponderances, so that a physiological male may have the psychological urge of a female? Or is there ground for thinking that homosexuality is closely related to narcissism, that it is a convenient projection into the outside world of one's own supremely interesting sex? Such speculations can lead to no decisive result and, however interesting in themselves, they are irrelevant to our immediate problem. What concerns us is that Gide's abnormality accentuated his sense of isolation and gave him, despite all efforts to throw it off, a lasting sense of guilt.

In its sexual aspect the renunciation of 1918 was the abandonment of any further effort to rid himself of his homosexual fantasies and practices and the resolve thenceforth to accept himself as he was. The abandonment proved easier of execution than the resolve, for even in his assurances that he has no regret for something he has done there is still the echo of guilt. Take, for example, this passage written in his seventy-ninth year:

No shame as a result of facile voluptuous pleasure. A sort of vulgar paradise and communion on a low plane. The important thing is not to attribute to it too much importance, not to feel oneself polluted: the mind is not at all involved, any more than the soul, which doesn't pay too much attention. But in the adventure an extraordinary amusement and pleasure accompany the joy of discovery and of novelty.

Gide's sense of isolation, clearly established before adolescence, brought him both pleasure and pain, but both seem to have been preceded by a neutral state. When he was writing his autobiography, what he seemed to dislike most about himself as a child was that for much of the time he was neither bad nor good, neither happy nor unhappy, but just dull, torpid, semiconscious. He needed a stimulus from outside to bestir him, and nature, aided and abetted by Miss Shackleton, performed the service. As a boy in Normandy he began to watch the life that wriggled from beneath stones, or swam in the rivers, or fluttered over the fields; on the Mediterranean shore he hung for hours over the side of a boat, peering through the clear water at the splendor of the submarine flora and watching, after he had been motionless long enough, the rock seem to come to life and fantastic shapes start to move and live. Then there was music—not as practice or as the duty of self-improvement but as an emotional experience, to which he was introduced by his cousin Albert Demarest. Finally and most important of all there was the close relationship, beginning when he was twelve, with Madeleine, a companionship to which nature, music, literature, religious aspiration, and sublimated sexual emotion all contributed.

Once awakened and enriched by the outside world he was able to experience the pleasures of isolation. He liked solitary walks, and acquired the habit, never wholly abandoned, of carrying a book with him wherever he went; in this way he was able to build up an agreeably dissociated state, with his main attention turned inwards and the outside world reduced to the status of a vague scenic backdrop. His walking tour in Brittany, undertaken at the age of eighteen, gave him a good opportunity for indulgence in these pleasures. At appropriately artistic spots he would sit down, brood over a page or two of his book, and contemplate with delight the formation of ideas within him.

Then [we read in his account written at the time], substituting looking for reading, I tasted a hitherto unknown emotion: it seemed to me that the landscape was only a projected emanation of myself—or rather, since I was aware of myself only in it, I felt that I was its center; before my coming it was asleep, inert and potential, and I created it step by step as I perceived its harmonies; I was its consciousness. And I advanced marveling in this garden of my dreams.

For a part of this trip he hired a one-seated carriage, driven by a little old man beside whom he sat, absorbed as usual in a book. Once when he happened to look up the coachman was gone. He had been jolted from his place by a bump, and on leaning over the side Gide could see him about to disappear beneath the wheels. He seized the reins and managed to stop the horse just in time. "I did not feel the slightest emotion," he wrote many years later; "I was merely extraordinarily interested (*amused* would be more exact), very ready moreover to avert an accident, capable of the proper reflexes, etc., but taking part in it all as if at a show *outside of reality*."

The religious training of his childhood was an important contributor to this sense of the unreality of the outside world, and in Gide's view the determining one. "That first Christian education," he wrote in 1929, "detached me irremediably from this world, inculcating in me, not indeed a disgust with this world, but a disbelief in its reality." Yet there is an obvious connection between a disbelief in the reality of the physical world we normally see and the suspicion that in it lurks a true reality which eludes our senses—an idea that Gide developed before adolescence and did not, apparently, invest with religious significance at first. It was more like a secret which he was curious to discover, something that the grownups knew but hid from him because he was only a child. After Paul Gide's death, he tells in his autobiography, he had the idea that his father was not wholly dead but used to come back to see his mother at night. During the day his suspicions remained vague but just before falling asleep at night he felt them become almost a certainty. Looking back on this feeling Gide saw in it a desire to round out life, make it more interesting—a desire which religion would *later* exploit.

But there were also other adventures of the mind, not religious in character as he understood religion, that came to give substance to his childish imaginings. He was deeply impressed by Schopenhauer and by the closely related theory of Symbolist poetry to which he himself gave expression in his *Traité du Narcisse*; both Schopenhauer and the Symbolists claimed that the world as perceived by the ordinary senses was illusory and that the true, the noumenal reality could occasionally be apprehended by the seer in moments of exaltation. And in the ecstatic confusion of adolescent emotions Schopenhauer, Symbolism, Christian aspiration, enthusiasm for poetry and music, an interest—now precise now vaguely poetic— in nature, and the love of Madeleine intermingled without incongruity.

Among these constituents religious aspiration brought him the keenest raptures, the ones that bound him so long to Christianity and that explained the periodic returns to the "divine friend of his youth." But religion as he had been taught it had disadvantages, entailing pains which counterbalanced, and eventually outweighed, its pleasures: it involved faith and morals, both weighted with the sense of duty. In matters of belief and of conduct it is a natural human reaction to rebel against commandment. It is possible to believe something with no sense of obligation but simply because we think it happens to be so; but if we are told that it is right to believe, that we must believe, then a door is immediately opened to doubt. Similarly in morals there is Saint Paul's "I had not known lust, except the law had said, Thou shalt not covet." But in addition to simple human perversity there are, in morals, fundamental human instincts to be considered, which redouble their demands when repressed; and in faith there is honest intellectual doubt, which grows with the cultivation of reason.

The *Cahiers d'André Walter* contains not only a record of these perplexities but an indication of their outcome. There is a clear parting of the ways between religion on the one hand and on the other the assortment of joys of the inward life which can be grouped under the name of art. Religion has been laid aside partly as a result of honest intellectual doubt and partly because of the intolerable suffering caused by failure to live up to its moral injunctions. The language of religion long persists in Gide's writings but it no longer represents a conviction of reality; it appears rather as a relapse due to discouragement or fatigue, or simply as nostalgia for lost joys. He did not ever again really believe in the religious doctrines of his childhood, and if in later times he had succumbed to one of his impulses to conversion to Catholicism it would have been for moral reasons, and in defiance of his reason.

But if he could cast off Protestant doctrines and (at

the price of recurring qualms of guilt) puritan morals, he could not so easily rid himself of a preference for the invisible reality over the physical world which alone most other men felt to be real. Their point of view, had they been consulted and if they could have understood what he was thinking about, would have been that he had merely exchanged one kind of fantasy for another. He was still living in a dream world, still refusing to accept the plain facts of existence.

One need not accept in its entirety the Freudian view (which Freud himself did not continue to find wholly satisfactory) that art is basically a recourse to pleasurable fantasy so as to avoid the pain of confronting reality—in order to see some truth in it for Gide's case. He preferred dreams to action, and he used the outside world as a support to his inner life. As he came increasingly to realize, too much solitude depleted his vitality and dulled his imagination, and contact with the world of nature and humanity reinvigorated him and replenished his mind. But society, unless it was of just the right kind, was more exhausting than refreshing; he enjoyed, particularly in the open, a companionship that could be based upon wordless sympathy—and this, incidentally, was undoubtedly one of the attractions of Madeleine for him; he liked conversation with a small number of intelligent men with whom he could have a stimulating give and take of ideas, but social confusion and random general conversation soon reduced him to a state bordering on prostration.

Through the battles of his early manhood Gide's sense of duty remained undiminished and he relied upon it for support; but as his ideas, aspirations, and emotions began to diverge, his sense of duty (and its obverse, the sense

of guilt) had also to undergo division and separation. The
duty instilled by early training, moral-behavior duty, forbade external sexual contacts; then, to escape from solitary obsession, he drove himself, still in the name of duty,
to experience, after which the obverse of the first duty,
moral guilt, returned to plague him.

Another duty was that of integrity of thinking—refusal
to be satisfied with spurious argument, unmasking of
rationalization, detection of desire behind a belief or an
opinion, honest admission of error. Its chief instrument
was reason, about which he sometimes had doubts; but
from the time when he first became aware of it until the
end of his life, he was unfaltering in his conviction of the
duty of integrity. He sinned against it sometimes, but in
admitting his sin he was again obeying the duty.

Closely related by virtue of being administered by reason was what might be called the duty of psychological
hygiene: understanding himself, his motives, the succession of his moods, the effect upon him of external conditions, and then applying his discoveries in such a way as
to obtain from himself the best return. The duty was nebu-
lously conceived at first and always remained uncertain
in application, but it was one of the chief motives of his
long Journal and contributed much to his other writings.
Self-understanding is beginning when he notes in 1892,
"I feel that in a short time I shall throw myself back into
a frenzied mysticism"; it is still confessedly incomplete
when he says in 1916, "Age comes on without hope of my
understanding my body any better. A happy equilibrium
almost immediately followed my lapse and my distress."

Obeying the duty of psychological hygiene was essentially handling himself in the same spirit as we have used

in dissecting him: with common sense and a dash of psychology. Since self-understanding arises out of experience it is inevitable that it should have been weak at the beginning of his career, and it is reasonable to suppose that its first somewhat tentative victory was the defeat of André Walter, when his creator decided that "on that field the most sensible victory was to let oneself be defeated." Similarly it is at the end of his life, when he is detaching himself from his desires and ambitions and is reviewing the past, that we should expect to find, and do find self-understanding at its peak.

Throughout his life, however, it was decidedly intermittent because, unlike integrity, it was not an ideal in which he could wholeheartedly and at all times believe, and because it so often entered into conflict with other duties. Self-understanding in itself and for itself Gide would at all times have been glad to have, but psychological hygiene was self-understanding for a practical purpose. It was prudent, cautious, the enemy of the ideal; it urged him not to expect miracles, to play the cards he had in his hand, to rely on experience rather than on aspirations. It was his friend and ally in hours of defeat, when God was deaf to his prayers, but the comfort it brought was often a rationalization, bought at the price of a sin against integrity. Its counsels sometimes had a short-range efficacy but in the long run proved more harmful than helpful: this is particularly true as applied to sexual behavior.

Nevertheless, not in a wholly clear way but still in general under the name of psychological hygiene, Gide was led to make some significant discoveries about himself, and the most notable was of his profound need of getting out of himself and into contact with something or someone outside. It is plain enough that his use of nature and of people for the replenishment of his inner life was a counsel of psychological hygiene, but the relation of his art to the problem of isolation is much more obscure. He had a sense of duty, a conscience, about his writing; he worked hard at it, he had high standards for it, and he had a feeling of guilt when he remained too long without writing or when he had difficulty in bringing a work to a successful conclusion. And yet there is his voluble insistence (beginning after his first reading of "The Marriage of Heaven and Hell" in 1914 and extending roughly to 1929) on the diabolic character of art; and we must remember that Gide's Devil was not, like Blake's, a God transposed for the purpose of attacking the ideas of others, but his own Devil, the principle of evil for him. Is there not here another conscience at work, and another sense of guilt? And if so, why and in what sense?

Some light on the question is cast by a sentence in an open letter which Gide wrote in 1927 to Père Poucel, editor of a Catholic review: "I think I am much closer to it [the Church] than you when I say that however much art may strain toward the divine, it always retains something of the diabolic, some echo of *Eritis sicut dii.*" At first glance this suggestion seems too theoretical, too theological even, to have much personal significance. "Ye shall be as gods": in other words the artist is a creator, he sets himself up in rivalry to God, and is consequently of the Devil's party. But if we add to this passage one in his *Dostoevsky*, it takes on a somewhat different aspect: "The work of art is woven on a loom with three pegs, the three concupiscences of which the apostle spoke: 'The

lust of the eyes, the lust of the flesh, and the pride of life.' "
In a letter addressed (but not sent) to François Le Grix
he quoted this sentence and added, "I say that without
sensuality, sexuality, and pride no work of art could
exist."

Pride is the sin of Lucifer, the "lust of the flesh and the
lust of the eyes" are sins of greed, and all three are vices
because they are separative instead of unitive. Moreover,
the Devil in the *Faux-Monnayeurs* represents assertion of
the individual self, just as the angel stands for self-loss.
Is there not here a recognition—only implicit so far as psychological hygiene is concerned—that the way of art increased his isolation and ran counter to the deepest need
of his nature? Similarly, when he dwells on his quality of
"sympathy" with an overinsistence that is suspect, can we
not see it less as a boast than as a counsel of psychological
hygiene? He is trying to argue down his own claim that art
is necessarily diabolic, self-assertive, separative, by recording his earnest desire to make *his* art unitive. Much the
same could be said of his insistence, near the end of his
life, on his need of love:

An extraordinary, an insatiable need of loving and of being
loved: I think that is what has dominated my life and what
urged me to writing; an almost mystical need furthermore, for
I was resigned to its not finding its reward during my lifetime.

He speaks of the "need" of love in such a way as to
make it appear that he has an urge to love, that he has a
loving nature, and he states that this need was what made
him write: a flat contradiction of his own theory of the
diabolic character of art. But if we take "need" literally as
the confession of a lack and as the expression of a desire

to acquire, in spite of the isolating tendency of his art, then the contradiction is explained. A passage of a letter of his to François Mauriac might have been addressed to himself:

> You are glad that God, before recapturing Racine, gave him the time to write his plays, to write them *in spite of* his conversion. In a word, what you are looking for is permission to write *Destins,* permission to be a Christian without having to burn your books; and that is what makes you write them in such a way that, although a Christian, you will not have to disavow them.

If there are grounds for seeing in his guilt about art the obscure recognition of his need to come out of himself, there is even more reason for finding in this need something more than a rule for happy living. Self-loss is involved, a subject of deeper import for Gide than psychological hygiene.

From the point of view of common-sense naturalism (which is that of psychological hygiene) self-loss in a literal sense is an impossibility; it is merely an exaggerated and dramatic way of talking about self-forgetfulness. This experience is always transitory, but it is widely known and its virtues are frequently recommended in such precepts as "Keep busy; it doesn't matter so much what you do so long as you keep busy"; or, "Don't be morbid, don't think so much about yourself; think about someone else for a change." Then there is self-submergence in a cause, there is group feeling engendered by work or play; there is also Dionysianism, which under special circumstances and at particular times may make an appeal to a wide variety of civilized persons, but which, involving as it does the submergence of reason in an uprush of primitive emotion, is likely to have socially dangerous results.

The deliberate self-sacrifice of the devout Christian is an attitude of which Gide was suspicious because he considered it a fertile field for self-deception: laziness, pride, self-pity, and the desire to accumulate merit could all masquerade as self-loss but in essence were its opposite. Nevertheless, Gide tried the Christian way, not only before he had begun to suspect it but after, and in both cases the results were disastrous. He tried meditation, but he was ignorant of techniques and could not get beyond the accentuation of isolation which was its necessary preliminary. He ran the gamut of the substitutes: keeping busy—but his work was writing, little calculated to bring him out of himself; seeing people—but the confusion of social occasions drove him back to solitude; travel—but he could not escape from himself by a mere change of scene; Dionysianism—but it brought disgust; self-submergence in the cause of communism—but he discovered that he was only seeking Christianity in disguise and caught himself feeling self-meritorious at sacrificing his art to the cause.

The trouble with the common-sense attitude toward self-loss—using it as a device to promote his psychological well-being—was that it involved treating himself like a psychic mechanism, and this he was not always prepared to do. He would no doubt have been willing to admit at any time that the psychic mechanism was there, a bundle of reactions that could be thought of as an entity because of belonging to a single physical organism; the past—heredity and the experience of the organism—provided the material and stimuli from without or within made it react, and all in a way strictly determined by laws. The psychic mechanism existed and was worth understanding; his only doubt about it was whether it was identical with the self. The doubt was of a "mystical" character, and the sworn enemy of his reason and common sense; but, like Renan, Gide sometimes felt that reason and common sense were not enough.

What Gide repeatedly attacked after 1918 under the name of mysticism was belief in contradiction of reason. A passage from the Journal for November 8, 1927, is a typical specimen of these attacks:

Under whatever form it presents itself there is no worse enemy than mysticism, as I have good reason to know. And I should like my deep acquaintance with the question, by repeated personal experience and by sympathy (for theoretic or philosophic or historical or scientific acquaintance with the mystic state is not very instructive) to give some weight to my evidence. It is too easy to believe with Souday that any swerve in this direction implies a deficiency in the brain. One should approach the question with sympathy, detachment, self-mistrust, modesty. I claim to be much better qualified to denounce or accuse mysticism than one who has never experienced it.

And what do I mean by "mysticism"?

What presupposes and requires the abdication of reason.

At this period Gide was busily launching invectives against organized religion, in particular Catholicism; belief in defiance of reason was the belief of the Church, or of churches. Obviously such belief does not necessarily imply in the believer a temperament or an experience that would ordinarily be called mystical, that is, related to a direct contact between the individual and suprasensible reality. On the contrary, genuine mystics notoriously have had difficulty in accommodating themselves to organized religion; it is the people without mystical experience of their own who make docile and literal believers. But Gide here also speaks of the "mystical state" as one with which he had had experience; he is lumping together two kinds of mysticism, the one which he defines and the one which he has felt. His attack also is twofold: a part of it is directed against the enemy without, the Church, and a part against the enemy within. As he wrote of his friend Dupouey: "Now that I reread his letters I am struck by the subtle insistence with which he kept bringing our conversation back to the mystic field. My mind, it is true, had the same natural inclination, but I often struggled against what he welcomed."

Gide's own mysticism was natural in two senses of the word: it was a temperamental inclination and it found its sustenance in the world of nature; it was a meeting between a self that was alien to the world of men but sensed in natural scenes a lost paradise in which it was at home. It was intuitional rather than rational, but it was not necessarily irreconcilable with reason. Its ends were not served by formal prayer and meditation but by "living in the third person" in North Africa, by watching the Congo forest as if he were only a disembodied sense of sight, by a glimpse in Paris of a suddenly radiant sky and river, or by working lovingly in his garden at Cuverville and seeing the trunk of a tree "as if transfigured."

Reason could not initiate such experiences but it could perhaps help to order them, make them intellectually assimilable. And so we have in the *Traité du Narcisse* the dream of the Eden of the Ideas, and the division of man into the Idea—the noumenal, the eternal self—and the temporal, the phenomenal self, whose duty it is to subordinate himself to the Idea. In the *Dostoevsky* we have the recognition of the opposing principles of self-assertion and self-loss (the "self" to be lost or asserted being the phenomenal self), we have the assertion of the "secret reason" for living, different from the ostensible one. In *Philoctète* we have fidelity to "that which is above the gods." In *Numquid et tu . . . ?* we have "dying to live," the second birth out of time and into the eternal "Kingdom of God." In the *Symphonie pastorale* we have men's blindness to the omnipresent paradise because of their immersion in self. And through them all run the themes of transfiguration and self-loss.

Here is a system of ideas incompatible with the common-sense naturalism of psychological hygiene. Man is not wholly to be identified with the psychic mechanism; that is his temporal self, but he is more truly his eternal self. The world we see is not the only one, there is another which escapes our ordinary senses. Self-loss is not merely an expedient for improving psychological tone by forgetting oneself, it is a transfer of spiritual allegiance from the temporal to the eternal self.

In Gide's writings there are elements that are demonic in the terms of his own definition. There is the affirmation of sensuality and sexuality, and there is pride—not only the eager desire for personal glory but a subtly pervasive narcissism. There is some truth in Claudel's uncharitable judgment of the Journal:

Gide is fascinated by mirrors. His Journal is only a series of poses before himself. When one looks at oneself one always poses. From this point of view his Journal is a monument of insincerity.

His literary works also are full of himself. Writers of

fiction very commonly use materials out of their own experience, but their achievement—not necessarily as artists
but as novelists—is apt to be measured by the objectivity
with which they handle these materials. Gide seldom
achieved detachment; even when he was not using autobiographic incidents, his characters remained splinters of
himself, and their problems were usually his own. Many
of his tales are works of art of a high order, but they do
not succeed in creating substantial and believable characters. And Gide not only admitted that the creation of
character was the test of a novelist, but insisted that he
met the requirement. In 1931 he told Julian Green that he
had found it impossible to make himself the principal
character of one of his books, much as he would like to do
so; and this, he maintained to Green, proved that he was a
novelist, and that he did *not* put himself into his books.
Yet the *Faux-Monnayeurs*, the first of his books that he
was willing to call a novel, was also the last; he later admitted that he would like to have written another but did
not find it in him.

Gide himself saw two sides to his work, the demonic or
self-assertive side and the self-loss side. With the latter
he associated his letters to Madeleine, of which he wrote:
"It is the best of me which has disappeared and which will
no longer counterbalance the worst. . . . It was in them
above all that I hoped to survive. . . . Hereafter my work
will be a symphony in which the tenderest chord is lacking, a building without the crowning piece." It is impossible to ignore the egotism in his sustained play for Madeleine's sympathy after the loss (day after day of weeping
in the chimney corner, with occasional hopeful glances to
see how she was taking it) and his eager seizing of the op-

portunity to blame somebody else for what was chiefly his fault; but these were aspects of his behavior which he himself later detected. However we may assess the mutilation sustained by Gide's work because of the loss of the letters, we must certainly admit that thereby the dialogue between opposing tendencies on which much of his work had been based was thrown out of balance.

The most opposite tendencies [he wrote in 1919] have never made me feel tormented, only perplexed; for torment accompanies a state from which one would like to escape, and I did not want to escape from what activated all my potentialities; the *state of dialogue,* which for many others is nearly intolerable, was for me necessary . . . it invited me to the work of art and immediately preceded creation.

Gide saw the year 1918 as a sort of hinge on which his career turned, and with certain reservations it is convenient to follow his example. It is clear that the change which then occurred had been for some time in the making and would doubtless have taken place without the burning of the letters; it is impossible to maintain indefinitely a state of

> *. . . being bound to trust*
> *All feelings equally, to hear all sides—*

(as Gide hopefully read in Browning in 1914). Sooner or later one must make a choice; the dispersal of moral continuity is too high a price to pay for literary inspiration. But *Les Caves du Vatican* was already a break from his past and a long step in the direction of the *Faux-Monnayeurs,* and his bitter effort of 1916 to purify himself by prayer and meditation was the death struggle of his declining Christian faith. On the other hand, after 1918 there were many days when, as he admitted, he was tempted to reopen the whole question.

But the decisive factor in accepting 1918 as the turning point of his career is the importance which he himself attached to the date and to the burning of the letters; thereafter he felt different, he conceived himself to be started on a new path. For some fifteen years after the crisis we watch him actively attacking what he previously venerated. He explores the possibilities of the humanism foreshadowed by his salute to the "Greek miracle" in 1914; God, he belligerently asserts (with a reservation about the original creation), is a man-made idea; He never helps man, there is nothing beyond man except what man can make of and for himself. Never has Gide's mind been so active and he pours his teeming ideas into a book which for the first time is consciously and deliberately hostile to all that Madeleine represents. He launches counterattacks against his critics, he insists that he is a born novelist, he is a man who breaks with the past, blazes new trails, points eagerly to the future.

Yet beneath the rush of his new tendency is always the undercurrent of its opposite. *Numquid et tu . . . ?*, the *Symphonie pastorale*, and *Dostoevsky*, all published after 1918, can be considered unfinished business from the past which he thought it a pity to waste; but in the trail-blazing *Faux-Monnayeurs* itself there appear the Devil of self-assertion and the angel of self-loss. There were moments when his now dominant rationalism faltered, and he suspected that perhaps after all there was some truth in his earlier intuitions. He knew the experience described by Browning's Bishop Blougram in a poem which he read and reread:

And now what are we? unbelievers both,
Calm and complete, determinately fixed
Today, tomorrow, and forever, pray?
You'll guarantee me that? Not so, I think!
In no wise! all we've gained is, that belief,
As unbelief before, shakes us by fits,
Confounds us like its predecessor. Where's
The gain? how can we guard our unbelief,
Make it bear fruit to us?—the problem here.
Just when we are safest, there's a sunset touch,
A fancy from a flower-bell, some one's death,
A chorus ending from Euripides,—
And that's enough for fifty hopes and fears
As old and new at once as nature's self,
To rap and knock and enter in our soul,
Take hands and dance there, a fantastic ring,
Round the ancient idol, on its base again,—
The grand Perhaps!

Wrote Gide: "It is much more difficult than one thinks not to believe in God. One would have to have never really looked at nature. The slightest agitation of matter—why should it rise? And toward what?"

As the creative fervor ebbed, as the communist venture proved illusory, as he began to feel tired and discouraged, he turned back to view his life and to attempt to discover its significance. Perhaps he was not after all so much of an innovator as he had thought. He had been, it was true, quickly sensitive to changes of literary climate. He had been one of the first to break with the abstractions of Symbolism and to proclaim the necessity for turning back to the "fruits of the earth." He had recognized that the suavely beautiful style, which charmed the esthetes of the late nineteenth and early twentieth centuries and which found its supreme exemplar in Anatole France, needed reinvigoration, and in *Les Caves du Vatican* he had written a book which a postwar generation could embrace as its own. If, like many others, he had been deluded about communism, he was one of the first to confess his disillusionment. And he had said things about God and man that anticipated the Existentialists.

Still, had he said anything really new? Was he like a man who excitedly points ahead, half-turning to beckon on the laggards, and who discovers that those whom he would encourage are no longer there but out in front? "I feel that I am the product of French culture," he wrote in 1943; "I cling to it with all the strength of my heart and my mind. I can separate myself from this culture only at the cost of losing sight of myself and ceasing to be myself." Lessons of reason, tolerance, integrity of thinking, harmony, balance—these are still only too pertinent and needed, but in giving them one can scarcely lay claim to being an innovator. Gide spent considerable time preparing some remarks on Racine's *Phèdre* and then discovered that someone else had already said, and better than he, what he had had in mind to point out. He prepared an anthology of French poetry; the war interrupted his work on the preface, and when he came back to it his reflections no longer seemed timely, and he concluded it by saying: "This anthology probably represents no more than the outworn breviary of a departing generation. May it at least bring some slight evidence of our state before the return to chaos."

He came to realize that his aspirations toward a spiritual order could not be downed; they were inseparable from him and from his work. It no longer seemed to him that his rationalism had won a righteous victory over his mysticism, but only that it was an inescapable part of his heritage and sometimes a limitation. "I learned to reason with Descartes," he wrote; "if I reason differently from him it seems to me that I am being irrational. . . . Rational and a reasoner I am irremediably, whether I like it or not; no matter how much I try, my mind does not assimilate what has not first passed the inspection of my reason. But the things I want to slip through the inspection (oh, without any cheating) are foreign products that my own country does not naturally produce."

In 1943 he made, through the books of that fervent apostle of the Vedanta, René Guénon, an acquaintance with the Hindu philosophy which he had previously only seen through Schopenhauer's eyes. "What would have happened to me," he speculated, "if I had encountered [these writings] in my youth? . . . Now it is too late. . . . The clearest profit I obtain from my reading is the sharpened conviction of my westernism. . . . I am and I remain on the side of Bacon and Descartes."

Gide's last word on the soul was that it was like the glow of phosphorus: "I cannot imagine this glow without the phosphorus which produces it." This is no new discovery, it is the epiphenomenalism of nineteenth century materialism. He gladly accepted Blake's refusal to distinguish between soul and body, but he disregarded the poet's significant phrasing: Blake did not say that man has no soul apart from the body, but: "Man has no Body distinct from his Soul; for that call'd Body is a portion of Soul discern'd by the five Senses, the chief inlets of Soul in this age." This belief is much like Gide's own "mystical" conviction that man has a higher self to which the lower must subordinate itself; a belief based in part upon an experience he did not wholly trust, a belief on which, in the name of reason, he turned his back.

But the formulations which his reason permitted were not lastingly satisfactory. "Ah, may my mind shed its dead ideas," he wrote at the end, "as the tree sheds its withered leaves. And without too much regret, if possible. The leaves from which the sap has withdrawn."

And at his shoulder was ever the voice of the Other Self, the Observer, the Pursuer, reminding him, "My kingdom is not of this world."

Sources

Since this book is a study of Gide as self-revealed, it would have changed its character and defeated its purpose to have written on what others have said about him. At one time and another I have read a large number of articles and most of the books about Gide (excepting the recent work of Professor Guérard which I have deferred reading until after the completion of this book), and these interpretations have undoubtedly to some extent affected my own. However, with two exceptions to be noted and unless a reference is supplied, I have not written with the works of these critics in mind or at hand, and am unaware of my debts. The exceptions are Jean Hytier's *André Gide* (Algiers, Charlot, 1945) and Irvin Stock's "A View of *Les Faux Monnayeurs*" (in *Yale French Studies* No. 7, 1951). I have quoted neither of these authors, but I am well aware that both have contributed to my interpretation of *Les Faux-Monnayeurs,* and I hereby acknowledge my debt.

The editions to which reference is made in the following pages are:

Œuvres complètes d'André Gide. Paris, Nouvelle Revue Française, 1932-39. 15 v. Contains all of Gide's work through 1929 (with Journal and letters) except *L'École des femmes* and *Un Esprit non prévenu.* I have used it for all works within its scope except for the Journal (which includes *Numquid et tu . . . ?* and *La Marche turque*) and certain letters and "Dictées" included in *Divers.*

Théâtre. 19e éd. Paris, Gallimard, 1947. Used for *Œdipe* and *Perséphone.*

L'École des femmes. Robert. Geneviève. 19e éd. Paris, Gallimard, 1944.

Divers. 11e éd. Paris, Gallimard, 1931. Contains *Caractères, Un Esprit non prévenu, Dictées, Lettres.*

Les Nourritures terrestres et *Les Nouvelles Nourritures.* 137e éd. Paris, Gallimard, 1947. Used for *Les Nouvelles Nourritures.*

Retour de l'U.R.S.S. Paris, Gallimard, 1936.

Retouches à mon Retour de l'U.R.S.S. Paris, Gallimard, 1937.

Interviews imaginaires. N. Y., Pantheon Books, Inc., 1943. Contains also "La Délivrance de Tunis," "Introduction au théâtre de Goethe," "Chardonne 1940."

Anthologie de la poésie française. Paris, Gallimard, 1949.

Feuillets d'automne, précédés de quelques récents écrits. Paris, Mercure de France, 1949.

Littérature engagée, textes réunis et présentés par Yvonne Davet. Paris, Gallimard, 1950. Letters, articles, and speeches by Gide on social questions from 1930 to 1937. Contains also *Robert ou l'Intérêt général.*

Journal, 1889-1939. Paris, Bibliothèque de la Pléiade, 1948.

Journal, 1939-1942. 73e éd. Paris, Gallimard, 1946.

Journal, 1942-1949. 22e éd. Paris, Gallimard, 1950. The translation of the series by Justin O'Brien (N. Y., Knopf, 1948-51, 4 v.) is particularly valuable for notes, indexes, and glossary of persons.

Et nunc manet in te, suivi de Journal intime. 2e éd. Neuchâtel and Paris, Ides et Calendes, 1951.

The most commonly utilized sources for letters (in addition to the *Œuvres complètes, Divers,* and *Littérature engagée,* above) are:

Lettres de Charles Du Bos et réponses d'André Gide. Paris, Corrêa, 1950.

Paul Claudel et Andre Gidé, Correspondance, 1899-1926. Préface et notes par Robert Mallet. 12e éd. Paris, Gallimard, 1949. The introduction and notes of Robert Mallet in this and the succeeding volume are valuable.

Francis Jammes et André Gide, Correspondance, 1893-1938. Préface et notes par Robert Mallet. 8e éd. Paris, Gallimard, 1948.

The following abbreviations are used in reference:

Claudel *Cor.*	for Claudel-Gide *Correspondance*
Du Bos *Cor.*	for *Lettres de Charles Du Bos et réponses d'André Gide*
Et nunc	for *Et nunc manet in te*
F d'a	for *Feuillets d'automne*
Jammes *Cor.*	for Jammes-Gide *Correspondance*
J	for *Journal,* all volumes
Lit. eng.	for *Littérature engagée*
NN	for *Les Nouvelles Nourritures*
Numquid	for *Numquid et tu . . . ?* (in *Journal*)
OC	for *Œuvres complètes*

References

FOREWORD

Page xi. "We each have a reason . . .": *Dostoevsky*, First Lecture, *OC*, XI, 163.

1. PORTRAIT OF A HAUNTED MAN

Page 1. "I suffer absurdly . . .": J, Jan. 1890. Cf. also *OC* I, 545.

Page 2. "that destestable comedy . . .": J, 12 March 1938.

Page 3. "From the artistic and intellectual . . .": interview in *Combat*, 28 March 1947 (Claudel *Cor.*, p. 249).

Valéry's refusal to comment: letter in front of a *Hommage* to Gide, Éditions du Capitole, 1928.

Page 4. Desire to be judged as an artist: J, 25 April 1918, 13 Oct. 1918.

Page 5. "One must dare to be oneself . . .": J. 10 June 1891.
"I felt myself to be . . .": *Œdipe*, end of Act I.
"If you had to sum up . . .": *OC* X, 332.

Page 6. "To create an enduring work . . .": J, 10 April 1943.
"Is it not natural . . .": J, 30 Jan. 1931.

Page 9. Subway incident: J, Wednesday (Sept.) 1916.

Page 11. "In life it is the thought . . .": *Journal des Faux-Monnayeurs*, 15 Nov. 1923 (*OC* XIII, 49).

Barrès incident: Marie D. Molles-Stein, "Conversations with André Gide," *Modern Language Forum*, XXXVI (March-June 1951), 22-23.

Page   12.   "When I hear myself in a conversation . . .":
             J, Thursday (25) Jan. 1912.
             "What happens then . . .": J, 25 March 1927.
Page   13.   "How difficult it is . . .": J, Tuesday (23) Jan. 1912.
Page   14.   "If my Journal is not more . . .": J, 17 Oct. 1932.
Page   15.   "The anguish breathing . . .": J, 28 Aug. 1940.
             "I should like it well enough . . .": OC III, 507-8.
Page   16.   "Why, in the place I'm in . . .": J, 30 Nov. 1929.
             "Never have I been able . . .": J, 14 July 1930.
Page   17.   "I think it comes from the lack . . .": J, 20 Dec.
             1924.
             "I have never succeeded . . .": J, 28 July 1929.
             "I doubt whether any . . .": J, 10 Dec. 1942.
             "Even today I retain . . .": J, 16 June 1931.

2. EMMANUÈLE AND GOD

Page   19.   "born in Paris . . .": OC II, 437.
Page   23.   "I think it might have been said . . .": Si le grain
             ne meurt, OC X, 437-38.
Page   24.   Incident of Littré's dictionary: "Ma Mère," F d'a,
             p. 40.
Page   28.   "I did not much like the name . . .": Et nunc, p. 8.
             Madeleine and Alissa: Jammes Cor., pp. 265, 305,
             306.
Page   29.   "That Alissa Bucolin . . .": La Porte étroite chap. I
             (OC V, 85).
Page   31.   "I think today . . .": OC X, 164.
             "All her life . . .": Et nunc, p. 21.
Page   32.   "Ah, I wish . . .": OC X, 267-68.
Page   33.   "Pure radiance . . .": OC X, 262.
Page   34.   "gifted with the most exquisite . . .": J, 1 July 1931.
             "fundamental inaptitude . . .": OC X, 218.
Page   35.   "You and I are alone . . .": OC I, 41.
Page   36.   "Your mind! . . .": OC I, 77.
             "To lie at your feet . . .": OC I, 108-9.
Page   38.   "Every time I see her again . . .": J, 6 Jan. 1933.
Page   39.   "What would I not give . . .": OC I, 130.
             "At the time when . . .": OC X, 301-2.
Page   40.   "Already I was experiencing . . .": OC X, 298.
             "Yesterday (for during . . .)": OC I, 8.

Page 41. "And we both dream . . .": J, Autumn 1889 (first entry).
Page 43. "The emotions are in a constant . . .": *OC* I, 109.
Page 45. "It soon seemed to me . . .": *OC* I, 203.

3. The Artist and the Saint

Page 49. "I have passionately desired fame . . .": *OC* X, 305.
Page 50. "is it not the characteristic . . .": *F d'a*, p. 149.
Page 53. "Every phenomenon . . .": *OC* I, 215-16, note.
Page 55. For Gide and Wilde, see "Oscar Wilde" (*OC* III, 473-503) and "Le *De Profundis* d'Oscar Wilde" (*OC*, IV, 457-73). Also in *Si le grain ne meurt*, *OC* X, 395-425.
Page 56. "Wilde, I believe . . .": J, 1 Jan. 1892.
Page 59. "I am less and less . . .": this page, written in Munich, was found later and copied into the Journal at Yport, Sept. and Oct. 1893.
           "At La Rocque . . .": *OC* X, 414.
           "I have written no book . . .": J, Aug. 1910.
Page 60. "I can never succeed . . .": J, 10 June 1891.
Page 61. "I have lost the habit . . .": J, 14 July 1893.
Page 62. "I was sad . . .": J, at La Rocque, Aug. or Sept. 1893.
Page 63. "Ah! how I love your poetry . . .": Jammes *Cor.*, pp. 34-35.
           "To be well . . .". J, *Feuillets* following 1893.
           "It is characteristic . . .": J, La Rocque, Aug. or Sept. 1893.
           "I try to discover . . .": J, Friday (Jan.?) 1890.
Page 64. "Sometimes it seemed to me . . .": J, Honfleur (Aug.?) 1893.
           "I always see . . .": J, 12 May 1892.
           "We are a misunderstood . . .": J, 13 Sept. 1893.
Page 65. "Other lives! . . .": J, 3 June 1893.
Page 66. "certain devout and pure pages . . .": J, Honfleur (Aug.?) 1893.
           "O God, let this too narrow . . .": J, Paris, end of April 1893.
           "I now believe . . .": J, *Feuillets* following 1893.

4. EDUCATION FOR FREEDOM

Page 74. "Take me! . . .": X, 378-79.

Page 76. "Desires are natural . . .": J, 13 Oct. 1894.

Page 82. "Was it true, what you said to me? . . .": "Ma mère," *F d'a*, pp. 37-39.

Page 85. "A fatality was leading me . . .": End of *Si le grain ne meurt, OC* X.
"The spiritual strength . . .": *Et nunc*, pp. 27-28.

Page 86. "My friend, that is not a confession . . .": *Et nunc*, p. 27, note.
"indefatigable repose . . .": Jammes *Cor.*, p. 55.

Page 88. "Obsessions of the Orient . . .": J, *Feuilles de route* (1895) 31 Dec.

Page 89. Models in the square at Rome: *Et nunc*, pp. 38-40.
"Rome is still . . .": Jammes *Cor.*, p. 63.

Page 90. "Em. is still languishing . . .": *OC* II, 480.
"Em. tries to hold back . . .": *OC* II, 483.
"So I resolved to set out . . .": J, Nov. 1904.

Page 91. "A few words from Em. . . .": J, 7 Oct. 1916.
"Aren't you irritated . . .": Jammes *Cor.*, p. 62.

Page 92. *bon Dieu portatif:* letter to Bonheur, 8 Sept. 1898 (*Le Retour*, p. 42).

Page 93. "Good faun, thank you . . .": Jammes *Cor.*, p. 66.
"I do not think . . .": *Et nunc*, p. 18.

Page 94. On Gide as mayor at La Rocque, see "Jeunesse," *F d'a*, pp. 19-36.

5. TO AN UNKNOWN GOD

Page 96. For La Rocque in 1898, see Jammes *Cor.*, Introduction, pp. 19-22, and Gide's letter of 2 Sept. 1898, pp. 147-48; also Gide, *Le Retour*, letters of 8 and 20 Sept. 1898 to Raymond Bonheur.

Page 98. "You are too grave . . .": Jammes *Cor.*, p. 71.
"a small boy amusing himself . . .": J, 22 June 1907.
Les Nourritures terrestres in *OC* II.

Page 101. "Never had I dreamed . . .": Jammes *Cor.*, p. 112.
"You have sacrificed . . .": Jammes *Cor.*, p. 124.

Page 102. "It is very hard for me . . .": *OC* II, 481-82.
"As soon as the air . . .": *F d'a*, p. 14.

Page 103.   *Saül* in *OC* II.
Page 105.   *El Hadj* in *OC* III.
Page 106.   *Philoctète* in *OC* III.
Page 108.   *Le Prométhée mal enchaîné* in *OC* III.
Page 113.   "I arrived at a sort of feeling . . .": "Du détermi-
            nisme et de la contrainte," in J, *Feuillets* follow-
            ing 1896.
Page 115.   *Le Roi Candaule* in *OC* III.
Page 117.   *L'Immoraliste* in *OC* IV.
            "Don't try to persuade me . . ." Jammes *Cor.*,
            p. 199.
            "I write it so as to . . .": Jammes *Cor.*, p. 189.
Page 121.   "That there is in me a bud . . .": *OC* IV, 616-17.

6. THE LEAN YEARS

Page 126.   "Since the 25th of October . . .": J, Nov. 1904.
Page 127.   "I was at the age when . . .": *OC* IV, 240.
Page 130.   "Uncertain of the reception . . .": *OC* III, 291-92.
            "Why do I print . . .": J, 8 Jan. 1902.
            "Sometimes it seems to me . . .": Jammes *Cor.*,
            p. 189.
Page 131.   "I hate the crowd . . .": *OC* III, 199-200.
            "Through fatigue I let myself . . .": J, 9 Jan. 1907.
Page 132.   "The artist cannot do without . . .": *OC* IV, 187.
Page 133.   "Why don't you understand . . .": Jammes *Cor.*,
            p. 189.
            "All the demons . . .": Jammes *Cor.*, p. 125.
            "I applied my ingenuity . . .": J, Sunday (Feb.)
            1902.
Page 134.   "My brain is clear . . .": J, Thursday (May) 1905.
Page 135.   "I still have in me . . .": J, 19 July 1905.
Page 137.   "*I thank you,* Claudel . . .": Claudel *Cor.*, p. 51.
Page 138.   "We cannot all become Saints . . .": Claudel *Cor.*,
            p. 53.
            "In his youth . . .": J, 1 Dec. 1905.
Page 139.   "What would you have . . .": Claudel *Cor.*, pp.
            55-56.
            "Since you love souls . . .": Claudel *Cor.*, pp. 58-59.
Page 141.   "For a long time . . .": J, 5 Dec. 1905.
Page 142.   "Religious certainty gives . . .": J, 16 May 1907.
Page 143.   "He lays waste our literature . . .": J, 5 Dec. 1905.

"I have only too much self-reproach . . .": Claudel
 Cor., p. 69.
"resides solely and exclusively . . .": Claudel *Cor.*,
 p. 66.

Page 144. "Impossible to decide . . .": J, Monday (7 Jan.)
 1907.

Page 145. *Le Retour de l'enfant prodigue* in *OC* V.

7. THE STRAIT GATE

Page 149. *La Porte étroite* in 1891: Claudel *Cor.*, p. 89.
 Thinking about it in 1903: Letter of 8 Oct. 1903,
 Jammes *Cor.*, p. 206.

Page 150. "She never quarreled . . .": *OC* X, 128.
 "I am lost in admiration . . .": Jammes *Cor.*, p. 120.
 "She is surrounded . . .": J, Wednesday (16 May)
 1906.

Page 151. "If in *L'Immoraliste* . . .": *Divers*, pp. 56-57.
Page 152. "Alas! I understand it . . .": *OC* V, 224.
Page 157. "of a Protestant soul . . .": Claudel *Cor.*, pp. 103-4.
 "a critique of Protestantism . . .": *OC* VI, 470.
Page 158. "The gross literature . . .": Claudel *Cor.*, pp. 101-2.
Page 159. "She was by the wall . . .": *OC* V, 122-23.
Page 160. "She was extraordinarily changed . . .": *OC* V, 204.
Page 161. "her kindness tempered all this . . .": *Et nunc*, p. 15.
Page 162. "I am *very pleased* . . .": *OC* V, 419.
Page 163. "The invasion of myself . . .": *Divers*, p. 57.
 "It is an anachronism . . .": J, 19 Nov. 1907.
Page 165. Real life epilogue: *Et nunc*, passim.

8. CORYDON

Page 166. The best of himself: Jammes *Cor.*, p. 258.
 "The book now seems to me . . .": J, 7 Nov. 1909.
 "Reread last night . . .": J, first entry of 1913.

Page 167. "If I were to die today . . .": J, 23 May 1910.
 "It is hard for them to admit . . .": J, Cuverville,
 Sept. and Oct. 1909.
 "Of all my books . . .": J, 15 July 1922.

Page 168. "up to the present . . .": Jammes *Cor.*, p. 279.
 "Sometimes I think . . .": J, 26 June 1913. Other
 examples of this sentiment in J, 7 Feb. 1912;

25 Sept. 1913; 11, 13, and 15 June 1914; 6 July 1914.

"You are at perfect liberty . . .": *OC* VI, 18-19.

Page 170.   In a note to the 2nd Dialogue (*OC* IX, 219, note 1) he says that nearly all of it was written in the summer of 1908.

Page 172.   "I call a pederast . . ." and other definitions: J, *Feuillets* following 1918, II, *Corydon*.

Theory of the intermediate sex: cf. Preface to 1924 ed. of *Corydon*, *OC* IX, 178-79, note 1.

Page 175.   "Goethe explained to us . . .": *OC* IX, 281-82.

Page 180.   "I have never had it more strongly . . .":J, 12 July 1910.

Page 181.   *Corydon* the most important: J, 19 Oct. 1942 and 18 Dec. 1946.

"pleasure, art, wit . . .": *OC* IX, 179.

Page 182.   "As soon as desire enters . . .": J, *Feuillets* following 1921.

"It is not what resembles . . .": 15 Nov. 1923, *OC* XIII, 49.

Incuriosity about the opposite sex: *Et nunc*, pp. 30-31; *Si le grain ne meurt*, *OC* X, 245.

Page 183.   "Ceasing to call my desires . . .": J, 10 Oct. 1893.

"It is certain that I am writing it . . .": J, *Feuillets* following 1911, "For Marcel D."

Page 184.   "What first made me undertake it . . .": J, *Feuillets* following 1918, II, *Corydon*.

"I have never been able . . .": J, *Feuillets* following 1923. A note in *Et nunc* (p. 91) tells us that this passage was wrongly placed in the Journal and that it belongs to 1919.

"I find a great danger . . .": J, beginning of *Feuillets* following 1911.

Page 185.   "Have I reached the limit . . .": J, Hotel Bellevue, Neuchâtel, Jan. 1912.

"What shall I say . . .": Claudel *Cor.*, p. 159.

Page 186.   "How many times . . .": Jammes *Cor.*, p. 278.

"I wish I had never known . . .": J, Zurich, Wednesday (Jan.) 1912.

"I do not recognize . . .": J, 30 May 1910.

"Catholicism is inadmissible . . .": J, Saturday mid-
    night (Feb.) 1912.

9. ATTACK ON ROME

Page 188.   "Journal sans dates" (*OC* VI) published 1909-10
    in *NRF*.
    "a semi-playful interlude . . .": *OC* VI, 471.
    "Only one of my books . . .": Charles Du Bos, *Le
    Dialogue avec André Gide*, Paris, Au Sans
    Pareil, 1929, p. 163.
Page 189.   *The Pathetic Illusion: OC* VI, 470.
    "Finished *Les Caves* . . .": J, 24 June 1913.
    Dadaists: Cf. J, 24 June 1924.
Page 190.   *Les Caves* in 1893: J, 25 Sept. 1913.
    Walk on the outer boulevards: J, 20 Jan. 1902.
Page 192.   "Must one therefore be impersonal . . .": *OC* V,
    68-69.
Page 193.   The wen and the wig: J, Wednesday (April) 1905.
        Cf. *Les Caves, OC* VII, 114.
    Lafcadio: J, 3 April 1906.
    "The tone . . ." "last night . . .": J, 24 April and
    20 Oct. 1910.
    "It is probably time . . .": J, 14 Nov. 1910.
Page 194.   Villiers de l'Isle-Adam: cf. *OC* III, 413.
    "The debonair Julius . . .": *OC* VII, 105-6.
    "Soundlessly Véronique . . .": *OC* VII, 107-8.
Page 195.   "thinking *again* of the *Caves*": J, 3 Sept. 1905
        (italics mine).
Page 196.   "Why do I call this book . . .": *OC* VII, 408.
Page 197.   Epigraph from Claudel: Claudel *Cor.*, pp. 224-25
        and note (p. 365) to letter 162.
Page 202.   "Still uncertain . . .": *OC* VII, 138.
Page 208.   Claudel to Rivière: Claudel *Cor.*, p. 233.
    "How should she tell him . . .": *OC* VII, 402-3.

10. THE ROCK OF SISYPHUS

Page 209.   "One day X . . .": J, *Feuillets* following 1921.
    "Were it not for the salutary . . .": J, 28 Oct. 1920.
Page 212.   "In the name of Heaven . . .": Claudel *Cor.*, p. 217.
    Lafcadio's meditations: *OC* VII, 329.
Page 213.   Letters on this issue: Claudel *Cor.*, pp. 217-23.

Page 215. "the prophet Joel": as pointed out by Robert Mallet in a note to this letter (Claudel *Cor.,* p. 365), this is a mistaken allusion by Claudel.

"May I not be forestalled . . .": J, 28 March 1914.

The account of the Turkish journey is given in *La Marche turque* in the Journal, beginning April 1914.

Page 216. "the slow decomposition of France . . .": given retrospectively in J, Sunday (Sept.) 1916.

The account of Gide's behavior in the following pages closely follows that of the Journal, beginning with 11 June 1914.

Page 221. "How often at the Foyer . . .": J, 16 Oct. 1915.

Page 224. "I'm losing all my sauce!": J, 3 May 1904.

Page 225. "A Catholic cured of writing . . .": "Henri Ghéon," in *F d'a,* pp. 116-17.

"From the very beginning . . ." *OC* VIII, 365.

"I was walking . . .": J, 17 Jan. 1916.

Page 233. "I am deliberately using here . . .": J, 16 Feb. 1916.

"No sooner had I supposed . . .": J, *Feuillets* following *Numquid* and 1916.

11. THE RENUNCIATION

Page 245. "I have a horror of indiscretion . . .": *Et nunc,* p. 78 (1 June 1917).

Page 247. Reading memoirs to Madeleine: J, Tuesday (19 Dec.) 1916.

The story of the burning of the letters is given in scattered fashion in *Et nunc,* partly in the introductory essay, partly in the following Journal, and partly in the notes of 1939 accompanying this Journal. The reading of Browning is from the regular Journal.

Page 251. "Every time I plunge back . . .": J, 21 Dec. 1922.

Page 252. "I find that every object . . .": *NN,* p. 220.

Page 253. "There were panics . . .": J, Monday (21 Feb.) 1916.

Page 255. "I shall doubtless feel called upon . . .": J, 30 May 1910.

Title of *Symphonie pastorale:* J, 8 June 1918.

Page 256. "Long after we had left . . .": *La Symphonie pastorale, OC* IX, 32.

Page 257. "Quite as much as a book . . .": J, 22 April 1922.

Page 258. "Dostoevsky is here . . .": *OC* XI, 282-83.

Page 259. "At the origin of every great . . .": *OC* XI, 293.

Page 260. The transfiguration passages are treated by Gide in *OC* XI, 260-62 and 291; in *The Possessed* they occur in Pt. II, ch. 1, and Pt. III, ch. 5.

Page 261. "Every clear-sighted sinner . . .": J, *Feuillets* following 1918, II.

Page 262. "The truth is . . .": J, *Numquid,* 3 Oct. 1916.
"No man lives without . . .": *OC* XI, 162.
"We each have a reason . . .": *OC* XI, 163.

Page 263. "I choose to serve . . .": J, *Feuillets* following 1918, II.

Page 264. "Alas, I realize now . . .": *Et nunc,* p. 84 (25 Nov. 1918).
"I have not regained . . .": J, 28 July 1921.

12. COUNTERFEIT

Page 265. "After that I never again . . .": *Et nunc,* p. 87, note.
"Scarcely a day passes . . .": J, 27 Oct. 1922.

Page 266. "When the road which opens up . . .": J, 12 Jan. 1921.
"It seems to me . . .": J, 11 July 1921.
"What greatly disturbs me . . .": J, 3 Jan. 1922.

Page 267. "I left Cuverville . . .": J, 16 Oct. 1921.
"Arrived last night . . .": J, 1 Nov. 1921.
The journey: J, 26 Nov. 1921.
"What am I to do . . .": *Et nunc,* p. 102.
Since Elisabeth has left him: J, 8 Feb. 1922.
As he learns later: *Et nunc,* pp. 104, 106.

Page 268. "My heart is full . . .": *Et nunc,* pp. 105-7.
"It seems to me that nothing that I do . . .": J, 28 July 1921.

Page 269. "A beautiful life . . .": J, 26 Dec. 1921.
"The most deeply opposed tendencies . . .": J, *Feuillets* after 1923, II. The correct date for this entry is 1919 (*Et nunc,* p. 91, note).
"For a long time . . .": J, *Feuillets* following 1928.

Page 270. "This 'state of security' . . .": Du Bos *Cor.,* p. 90.

13. A HUMANIST IN UTOPIA

Claudel note and letter, Madeleine's reply: Claudel *Cor.*, pp. 242-44.

Page 301. "I had the greatest pleasure . . .": Du Bos *Cor.*, pp. 90-91.

Page 304. "On the 21st of last October . . .": *OC* XIV, 241-44; also 296-97.

Page 308. "Impossible to sleep . . .": *OC* XIII, 189-90.

"the charm of those long days . . .": J, 19 Aug. 1927.

Page 309. "Surely if I remained motionless . . .": *OC* XIII, 354.

Pontigny arrangements: Du Bos *Cor.*, p. 107.

Page 310. "The conversations are becoming . . .": J, 29 Aug. 1926.

Page 312. "The difficulty comes from this . . .": J, 14 June 1926.

"I return to you, Lord Christ . . .": *NN*, p. 221.

Page 313. "Sometimes I diverge from Christ . . .": *Divers*, p. 154 (italics mine).

Page 314. "I have the temerity to assert . . .": *OC* XV, 4.

Page 315. "Skepticism has had its day . . .": J, 11 Nov. 1924.

"When I consider and weigh . . .": *NN*, p. 241.

"This idea of God . . .": J, 6 March 1927.

"Wisdom begins . . .": J, 15 Jan. 1929.

"Humanity cherishes . . .": *NN*, p. 297.

Page 316. "It is much more difficult . . .": *NN*, p. 236.

"seems to me today . . .": *NN*, p. 245.

"Prudence, conscience, goodness . . .": *NN*, pp. 241-42.

Page 317. Angelus Silesius: quoted by Rudolph Steiner, *Mysticism and Modern Thought*, tr. by George Metaxa, Lond., Anthroposophical Publishing Co., 1928, pp. 200-1.

"Some of the 'problems' . . .": *NN*, p. 235.

"The fear of stumbling . . .": *NN*, p. 208.

Page 318. "I have understood at present . . .": *NN*, p. 205.

"If I were not . . .": J, 13 Jan. 1929.

"There can be no question . . .": *F d'a*, pp. 257-59.

Page 320. "It is told that Lot's wife . . .": *NN*, p. 301.

"It is in the negation . . .": J, *Numquid*, 18 Feb. 1916.

"It is the great living hope . . .": J, 19 Oct. 1931.

Page 321.   "No progress of humanity . . .": J, 17 March 1931.
            "You would seek the salvation . . .": *NN*, p. 284.
            "The fear of ridicule . . .": *NN*, p. 272.
Page 322.   "It was total impoverishment . . .": J, *Feuillets*
            following 1923, III.
            "I know that I am close . . .": J, 11 or 12 April
            1929; see also 27 Dec. 1929.
Page 323.   Giving away: J, 6 March 1918.
            "It is not the system . . .": J, *Feuillets* following
            1918, II.
            "What seems to me an error . . .": *NN*, p. 226.
            "Have I for a long time . . .": J, 27 Oct. 1933.
Page 324.   "In my heart . . .": J, 27 Feb. 1932.
            "What draws me to the communists . . .": J, 14
            April 1933.
            "What brings me to communism . . .": J, Vittel,
            June 1933.
            "I am not indifferent . . .": J, 11 or 12 April 1929.
            "determination to destroy . . .": J, 1 July 1931.
            "I should like to cry aloud . . .": J, 27 July 1931.
Page 325.   "I can wish for communism . . .": J, 8 Nov. 1931.
            "It is only with great difficulty . . .": J, Cuverville,
            end of Oct. 1931.
Page 326.   He still hesitated: J, 5 March 1932.
            "To stop simply following . . .": J, 27 Feb. 1932.
            "They are furious . . .": *Lit. eng.*, p. 13.
Page 327.   "Condemned to being . . .": *Lit. eng.*, p. 19.
Page 328.   "Certainly I do not insist . . .": J, 13 June 1932.
            "No, dear comrades . . .": *Lit eng.*, p. 18.
Page 329.   "He who is content to remain . . .": J, 25 July 1934.
            "Letter to the youth of the USSR": *Lit. eng.*, p. 27.
            "I received in November . . .": *Lit. eng.*, p. 65.
Page 330.   "A revolution does not constitute . . .": *Lit. eng.*,
            p. 97.
Page 331.   "There cannot be a Soviet philosophy . . .": *Lit.
            eng.*, p. 75.
            "Communism will be able . . .": *Lit. eng.*, p. 55.
            "Up to now, in all countries . . .": *Lit. eng.*, p. 134.
Page 332.   Russia would eventually triumph . . .: *Retour de
            l'URSS*, p. 17.

"he who is at its head": *Retour de l'URSS*, p. 13.

"allowed himself to be persuaded": J, 30 Oct. 1935.

Page 333. "I tried at first . . .": J, 7 Feb. 1940.

"Dangerous is every mind . . .": "Journal sans dates," *OC* VI, 55.

14. ŒDIPUS AND THESEUS

Page 334. "When social preoccupations . . .": J, 5 Sept. 1936.

"The social question! . . .": J, 30 May 1940.

"Of all my books . . .": J, 31 March 1943.

Page 335. "Sacrifice" of his art: *Lit. eng.*, p. 64.

"If social questions . . .": J, 19 July 1932.

Page 338. "*L'Intérêt général* was . . .": *Lit. eng.*, pp. 221-22.

Page 339. Central conflict of the play: J, 22 Jan. 1932.

Page 342. "For you must know . . .": Act II, *Théâtre*, pp. 283-84.

"No, I shall not . . .": Act III, *Théâtre*, pp. 302-3.

Page 343. "Today, feeling myself . . .": *Et nunc*, pp. 84-85, note.

Page 344. "The approval of a single . . .": J, 13 Feb. 1927.

Page 345. "The slow progress . . .": *Et nunc*, pp. 113-14. The same passage in the Journal is attributed to "X" and Madeleine is not identified.

Page 346. A new harmony: *Et nunc*, pp. 62-63.

Page 347. "I left the lifeless remains . . .": J, 15 May 1949.

The kite: J, 5 Sept. 1938.

Page 348. The bog: J, 21 Aug. 1938.

Bereavement and dejection: J, 26 Aug. 1938.

"What else . . .": J, 7 May 1937.

Page 349. "Everywhere I see . . .": J, 13 May 1937.

Page 350. "Decidedly I shall not speak . . .": J, 30 Oct. 1939.

Page 352. "Is it possible? . . .": J, 24 June 1940.

"It would have been much better . . .": J, 6 April 1941.

"With him every *yes* . . .": "Chardonne 1940," in *Interviews imaginaires*, p. 220.

Page 353. "I am however grateful . . .": J, 30 March 1941.

Page 354. "I don't try very hard . . .": J, 22 June 1942.

Page 356. "The vapors . . . do not only . . .": *Thésée*, pp. 61-62.

Page 357. "If I come from God . . .": *Thésée*, pp. 67-68.

Page 358.   "Poor dear child . . .": *Thésée*, p. 69.
Page 359.   "In time, on the human plane . . .": *Thésée*, p. 70.
"Everyone always performs . . .": J, *Feuillets* following 1921.
Page 360.   "I reflected that man . . .": *Thésée*, pp. 110-11.
Page 361.   "No one understood . . .": *Thésée*, pp. 118-19.
Page 362.   "Have pity and leave me alone . . .": F *d'a*, p. 269.
Page 363.   "You make your bow . . .": J, 15 May 1949.
"inadmissible, unthinkable . . .": dated May 1948; F *d'a*, p. 279.
A believer in spirit: J, 15 May 1949.
"Of course I believe in it! . . .": J, 15 May 1949.
In Saint-Paul: J, 31 May 1949.
Page 364:   Details of death: in *Figaro littéraire*, 24 Feb. 1951.

15. THE HOUND OF HEAVEN

Page 365.   "When still quite young . . .": J, 27 June 1937.
Page 368.   "No shame as a result . . .": J, 24 Jan. 1948.
Page 370.   "Then, substituting . . .": "Notes d'un voyage en Bretagne," *OC* I, 9.
"I did not feel the slightest emotion . . .": J, 20 Dec. 1924.
"That first Christian education . . .": J, 28 July 1929.
Page 371.   Idea about father: *OC* X, 52-53.
Page 374.   "I feel that in a short time . . .": J, Easter Sunday 1892.
"Age comes on . . .": J, 17 Oct. 1916.
Page 375.   "on that field the most sensible victory . . .": *OC* I, 203.
Page 376.   "I think I am much closer . . .": *Divers*, p. 165.
"The work of art is woven . . .": *OC* XI, 284.
Page 377.   "I say that without sensuality . . .": letter in front of René Lalou, *André Gide*, Strasbourg, Joseph Heissler, 1928.
"An extraordinary, an insatiable . . .": J, 3 Sept. 1948.
Page 378.   "You are glad that God . . .": *Divers*, pp. 175-76.
Page 381.   "Now that I reread . . .": *OC* VIII, 356.
Tree "as if transfigured": J, 2 April 1916.
Page 382.   "Gide is fascinated . . .": Interview in *Combat*, 28 March 1947 (Claudel *Cor.*, p. 250).

Page 383. Conversation with Green: Julian Green, *Personal Record, 1928-1939,* tr. by Jocelyn Godefroi, N. Y., Harper & Brothers, 1939, p. 40.

"It is the best of me . . .": *Et nunc,* pp. 79, 91.

Page 384. "The most opposite tendencies . . .": J, *Feuillets* following 1923 (real date 1919, as stated in *Et nunc,* p. 91, note).

Page 386. "It is much more difficult . . .": *NN,* p. 236.

Page 387. "I feel that I am the product . . .": J, 13 Feb. 1943.

On *Lettres à Catherine,* J, 2 Sept. 1941.

Page 388. "I learned to reason . . .": J, *Feuillets* following 1937, I.

"What would have happened to me . . .": J, Fès, Oct. 1943.

"I cannot imagine this glow . . .": J, 15 May 1949.

Page 389. "Ah, may my mind . . .": *F d'a,* p. 271.

Chronology of Works

(Translations not included. Place of publication is Paris unless otherwise stated)

1891   *Les Cahiers d'André Walter. Œuvre posthume.* (Anon.)
        Le Traité du Narcisse (Théorie du Symbole).
           Private edition. 1st public edition 1892.

1892   *Les Poésies d'André Walter. Œuvre posthume.*

1893   *Le Voyage d'Urien.*
        La Tentative amoureuse.

1895   *Paludes.*

1897   *Les Nourritures terrestres.*
        Réflexions sur quelques points de littérature et de morale.

1899   *Philoctète. Le Traité du Narcisse. La Tentative amoureuse.*
        Feuilles de route 1895-1896. Bruxelles.
        Le Prométhée mal enchaîné.
        El Hadj.

1900   *Lettres à Angèle (1898-1899).*
        De l'influence en littérature.

1901   *Le Roi Candaule.*
        Les Limites de l'art.

1902   *L'Immoraliste.*

1903   *Saül.*
        De l'importance du public.
        Prétextes.

1906   *Amyntas.*
        (Contains *Mopsus, Feuilles de route, De Biskra à Touggourt, Le Renoncement au voyage.*)
1907   *Le Retour de l'enfant prodigue.*
1908   *Dostoïevsky d'après sa correspondance.*
1909   *La Porte étroite.*
1910   *Oscar Wilde. In memoriam (Souvenirs). Le "De Profundis."*
1911   *Nouveaux Prétextes.*
        Charles-Louis Philippe.
        C.R.D.N. Bruges. (*Corydon.* Anon.)
        Isabelle.
1912   *Bethsabé.*
1913   *Souvenirs de la Cour d'Assises.*
1914   *Les Caves du Vatican.*
1919   *La Symphonie pastorale.*
1920   *Si le grain ne meurt.* Bruges. (1st volume, anon., 12 copies.)
        Corydon. Bruges. (Anon.)
1921   *Si le grain ne meurt. Deuxième volume.* Bruges. (Anon., 13 copies.)
        Morceaux choisis.
1922   *Numquid et tu . . . ?* Bruges. (Anon.)
1923   *Dostoïevsky.*
1924   *Corydon.* (1st public ed. with name of author.)
        Incidences.
        Si le grain ne meurt. (1st public edition with name of author. Not put on sale until 1926.)
1925   *Caractères.*
        Les Faux-Monnayeurs.
1926   *Le Journal des Faux-Monnayeurs.*
1927   *Dindiki.* Liège.
        Voyage au Congo.
1927-28 *Faits Divers.*
1928   *Le Retour du Tchad.*
        Feuillets.
1928-29 *Lettres.*
1929   *L'École des femmes.*
        Pages retrouvées.
        Suivant Montaigne.
        Essai sur Montaigne.

Un Esprit non prévenu.
Dictées.
1930 *Lettres.* Liège.
L'Affaire Redureau, suivie de *Faits Divers.* Documents réunis par André Gide.
La Séquestrée de Poitiers. Documents réunis par André Gide.
Deux Préfaces.
Robert.
1931 *Divers.*
(Contains *Caractères, Un Esprit non prévenu, Dictées, Lettres.*)
Œdipe.
1932 *Jacques Rivière.*
Goethe.
1932-39 *Œuvres complètes.* 15 v.
1934 *Perséphone.*
Pages de Journal (1929-1932).
1935 *Les Nouvelles Nourritures.*
Le Treizième Arbre, plaisanterie en un acte.
1936 *Nouvelles Pages de Journal (1932-1935).*
Geneviève.
Retour de l'U.R.S.S.
1937 *Retouches à mon Retour de l'U.R.S.S.*
1939 *Journal (1889-1939).*
1943 *Interviews imaginaires.* N. Y.
(Contains also "La Délivrance de Tunis—Pages de Journal mai 1943," "Introduction au théâtre de Goethe," "Chardonne 1940").
Attendu que . . . Alger.
(Most of the material in this collection is reprinted elsewhere, but there is additional material in the *Interviews imaginaires* and it contains "Conseils à une jeune actrice—Phèdre").
1944 *Pages de Journal (1939-1942).* N. Y. (*Journal 1939-1942).* Paris, 1946.
1944-45 *Robert, ou l'Intérêt général.* Alger.
1945 *L'Enseignement de Poussin.*
Jeunesse. Neuchâtel.
1946 *Thésée.* N. Y.
Le Retour. Neuchâtel and Paris.

(One act of projected libretto for composer Raymond Bonheur. Contains also letters of Gide to Bonheur.)

1947 *Et nunc manet in te.* Neuchâtel and Paris. (Private ed. of 13 copies. 1st public ed. 1951.)

1948 *Rencontres.* Neuchâtel and Paris.
(All but four of these twelve short pieces reprinted in *Feuillets d'automne.*)
Éloges. Neuchâtel and Paris.
(All but two of the fourteen pieces either appeared in *F d'a* or had already appeared elsewhere.)
Poétique. Neuchâtel and Paris.
(The preface to *Anthologie de la poésie française.*)
Préfaces. Neuchâtel and Paris.

1949 *Anthologie de la poésie française.*
Feuillets d'automne.

1950 *Littérature engagée.*
Journal (1942-1949).
Les Caves du Vatican, farce en trois actes et dix-neuf tableaux tirée de la sotie du même auteur.

Index

415